Romanticizing masculinity in Baathist Syria

Manchester University Press

Series editors: Simon Mabon, Edward Wastnidge and May Darwich

After the Arab Uprisings and the ensuing fragmentation of regime-society relations across the Middle East, identities and geopolitics have become increasingly contested, with serious implications for the ordering of political life at domestic, regional and international levels, best seen in conflicts in Syria and Yemen. The Middle East is the most militarised region in the world where geopolitical factors remain predominant factors in shaping political dynamics. Another common feature of the regional landscape is the continued degeneration of communal relations as societal actors retreat into sub-state identities, while difference becomes increasingly violent, spilling out beyond state borders. The power of religion – and trans-state nature of religious views and linkages – thus provides the means for regional actors (such as Saudi Arabia and Iran) to exert influence over a number of groups across the region and beyond. This series provides space for the engagement with these ideas and the broader political, legal and theological factors to create space for an intellectual re-imagining of socio-political life in the Middle East.

Originating from the SEPAD project (www.sepad.org.uk), this series facilitates the re-imagining of political ideas, identities and organisation across the Middle East, moving beyond the exclusionary and binary forms of identity to reveal the contingent factors that shape and order life across the region.

To buy or to find out more about the books currently available in this series, please go to: https://manchesteruniversitypress.co.uk/series/identities-and-geopolitics-in-the-middle-east/

# Romanticizing masculinity in Baathist Syria

## Gender, identity, and ideology

Rahaf Aldoughli

MANCHESTER UNIVERSITY PRESS

Copyright © Rahaf Aldoughli 2024

The right of Rahaf Aldoughli to be identified as the author of this work has been asserted in accordance with the Copyright, Designs and Patents Act 1988.

This book will be made open access within three years of publication thanks to Path to Open, a program developed in partnership between JSTOR, the American Council of Learned Societies (ACLS), University of Michigan Press, and The University of North Carolina Press to bring about equitable access and impact for the entire scholarly community, including authors, researchers, libraries, and university presses around the world. Learn more at https://about.jstor.org/path-to-open/

Published by Manchester University Press
Oxford Road, Manchester, M13 9PL

www.manchesteruniversitypress.co.uk

British Library Cataloguing-in-Publication Data
A catalogue record for this book is available from the British Library

ISBN 978 1 5261 4762 2 hardback

First published 2024

The publisher has no responsibility for the persistence or accuracy of URLs for any external or third-party internet websites referred to in this book, and does not guarantee that any content on such websites is, or will remain, accurate or appropriate.

Typeset by Newgen Publishing UK

*To Hamza and Sam*

# Contents

| | |
|---|---|
| *Acknowledgments* | *page* viii |
| Introduction: The "woman question" and the Syrian state | 1 |
| 1 Romantic borrowings in early Syrian nationalism: The writings of Sati al-Husri, Michel Aflaq, and Zaki al-Arsuzi | 30 |
| 2 The centrality of gender constructs in early Syrian nationalist narratives | 60 |
| 3 Implementing masculinism under Baathist hegemony | 90 |
| 4 Constructing the muscular nation in song and performance | 123 |
| 5 War and muscular revival after 2011 | 151 |
| Conclusion: Citizen activism and prospects for reform in postwar Syria | 169 |
| *Bibliography* | 186 |
| *Index* | 202 |

# Acknowledgments

This book has its origins in my doctoral dissertation at Lancaster University. I am grateful to the Department of Politics, Philosophy, and Religion at Lancaster for the financial and intellectual support that I received during the early years of the project. When I started my Ph.D. in 2013, I was supported by funding from the Syrian Ministry of Higher Education; however, this scholarship was cut because of the Syrian war. If it were not for the subsequent joint-funding grant that I received from Lancaster University and the Council for At-Risk Academics (CARA), the research and writing of this book would not have been possible. To Professor Amalendu Misra, under whose guidance I began this project, I offer my sincerest gratitude for his encouragement and for his personal example as a model of intellectual inquiry. His magnanimous support and critical advice over the years have helped to sustain my faith in the work. I also extend my thanks to Robert Byron, my editor at Manchester University Press, for his continuous support and constructive comments on the early drafts of the manuscript.

My journey while writing this book has included many major life events, starting with enforced exile from my country of origin, and continuing through the experiences of giving birth, getting divorced, and other new beginnings. The developing manuscript travelled with me across various countries and continents. A particularly significant landmark in this journey was the fellowship I received from Women in International Security (WIIS) in Washington, DC, which provided a tremendous opportunity to engage with other diverse feminist academics regarding my developing ideas on masculinity and militarism. The key themes in this book have also benefited from conversations about shared experiences with friends who are personally familiar with Syria, who contributed to my thinking about national and cultural belonging. I shall remain ever thankful for close friends including Haian Dukhan, Samer Bakkour, Rua Al-Taweel, Ghina al-Soumari, Noor al-Huda Murad, Muhammed Ateek, Mohammed Hamchi, Hamza al-Mustafa, and Eylaf Bader Eddin, among others, with whom I shared my excitement and energetic talk about my research ideas.

The project was also sustained in great measure by the reassuring presence and constancy of family support. My two children, Hamza and Sam, have encouraged me and inspired the love and ambition to complete this book. My older son, Hamza, taught me how to challenge traditional constructions of motherhood and pushed me to sustain my resilience and professional goals. My youngest, Sam, showed me that a contagious smile can solve the biggest problems. I will always remember that I finished the first draft of this manuscript in the emergency room at the hospital just one hour before giving birth to Sam, showing me that family and intellectual creation are in no way conflicting passions. Despite my theoretical grounding in women's rights and the legal protections afforded to me as a British citizen, my personal struggle in court for the custody of my children was a stark reminder of the challenges women face. This experience underscored the gap between legal rights and the societal expectations and stereotypes that often define our roles as mothers, emotional partners, and successful individuals. This book is dedicated to Hamza and Sam, for whom I fought tirelessly. It is a testament to the enduring spirit of women navigating complex personal and legal battles, often compounded by deeply ingrained cultural norms.

To my own parents, I owe more than I can ever acknowledge. My father and mother taught me early how to dream and to go after my dreams. From them I also learned both a healthy skepticism and the value of supporting a just cause. My brothers (Hussam and Moe) and sister (Dana) have shown me immense support and respect to my personal choices in life. Thank you to my dear friend, Jackie Williams, whose support and kindness for the last decade have shown me that exile and familial bonds are not subject to blood relations.

Finally, my deepest gratitude goes to Homam, whose unwavering emotional support and companionship have been the bedrock upon which this project's final stages were completed. His enduring presence, imbued with kindness and patience, helped navigate the storms that this endeavor brought into our lives. Homam's ability to bring light and humor into even the most challenging moments has been nothing short of a blessing. His love and steadfast support have been my sanctuary, providing strength and inspiration at every turn. This journey, with its highs and lows, has been deeply intertwined with the love and understanding he has generously given.

# Introduction: The "woman question" and the Syrian state

As you walk the streets of Syria, it's impossible to miss the dominance of Assad statues occupying every intersection, government building, and educational edifice. The inevitable representation of Hafez al-Assad as a strong and muscular founder of the nation in these imposing monuments tells the story of relentless authoritarianism. It also particularly complicates women's sense of belonging to the nation. During my time at Damascus University, the huge statue of Hafez al-Assad overlooking the entrance of the school used to give me a sense of suffocation on an everyday basis. The demand for citizens to participate in spectacles of adoration for this patriarchal figure, the required marches to hail the leader with slogans and songs saturated with romantic claptrap, and the constant stirrings of the nationalistic soul in the state media all can have a particularly unsettling resonance for those of the female gender.

In the early days of the Syrian uprisings, one of the most remarkable chants widely heard among protestors was: "We don't love you; we don't love you! … Go away with your party!" It might be surprising to outside observers why so many Syrians chose to express their opposition to the regime in these terms. The answer can be found in the way that Syrian national identity and regime loyalty have been saturated with emotional appeals based on gendered and familial rhetoric of "love" and "blood." I have studied these political and cultural narratives extensively, particularly as they are expressed in speeches and songs, and have noticed the remarkable persistence and universality of images of blood ties—family, brothers, sisters, husbands, mothers, forefathers, homeland—as they are leveraged to create the emotional foundations of inclusion and exclusion in the rhetoric of the Baathist state.

The Assad regime has used such language from the beginning, drawing rhetorical power from the writings of Syrian state ideologues such as Sati al-Husri, Michel Aflaq, and Zaki al-Arsuzi, who in the early Baathist era endorsed a philosophically Romantic view of national belonging. These theorists drew a direct line between unconditional love for one's family and loyalty to the nation, emphasizing affective ties that bind the individual to obligations of submission, sacrifice, and a heroic readiness to die for the community. While it is not unusual for national identity to be associated with the commemoration of kinship, warfare, and masculine struggle on behalf of the state,[1] the Assad regime has gone to extreme lengths to institutionalize such "virtues" and present them as a required form of emotional attachment for all legitimate citizens.

In reality, the people of Syria are heterogeneous, grounded in a multitude of separate ethnic and religious identities, and there is no "blood relation" that defines the nation as a whole. But regime ideologues have theorized ties of affection and kinship as a rhetorical tool to define and promote an image of a unified nation, to the extent that children of my generation were forced in elementary school to memorize and repeat the slogan: "With blood and soul, we sacrifice ourselves for you, Hafez!" Thus, to whatever extent this emotional national affinity does exist, it is grounded not in actual organic ties of familial affection but in top-down, enforced ideologies. The regime's forceful invocations of national kinship and attachment have circulated continuously in Syrian society, exerting a magnetic pull that is far removed from voluntary, thoughtful civic participation. Rather than a free choice to support beneficial institutions, belonging in the state was presented as an involuntary Romantic compulsion, heedless of thought or reason.

In the early days of the regime, these nationalist appeals foregrounded the Syrian state institution, somewhat more than Hafez al-Assad himself, as the locus of affection. However, during the 1980s and 1990s the emotional appeals morphed from a broad concept of Syrian national identity and protection of the homeland advocated by idealists like al-Husri, Aflaq, and al-Arsuzi to become increasingly identified with personal loyalty to the Assads. The rhetoric digressed even further after Bashar al-Assad succeeded his father as the leader of the Syrian Baath Party in the year 2000. Some observers believed that the relatively Westernized and youthful Assad would move Syria toward a more democratic style of governance. These optimistic views proved to be unfounded, as Bashar in fact oversaw an adaptation in which the Romanticism and masculinization of the Assad personality cult actually increased—from the stern-yet-affectionate father image projected by Hafez al-Assad during his later years, to a more passionate and forceful presentation of the nationalist attachment heralded by Bashar. Mostly eschewing the established Baathist solidarity rhetoric of "brothers and sisters," Bashar al-Assad gravitated toward more demanding concepts of "love" and "faithfulness" as emotional bonds between the Syrian people and the person of the president. Women in this rhetoric were no longer even symbols of the land to be protected, but rather subjects whose submissive compliance to the regime was required. As protest movements began to spread during the lead-up to the current Syrian war, the dynamics of the regime's emotional appeal became ever more intense, with opposition movements regularly characterized in Bashar's speeches as being "unloving" or "unfaithful."[2]

This "love and blood" rhetoric, saturated with references to heroism, physical strength, and manhood, continues to exert a hold over a significant number of Syrians. When Assad ran for reelection in 2021, there were videos that circulated online in Syria of loyalists literally piercing their fingers in the polling stations to vote "yes" in blood. It's hard to say if such affective gestures are entirely authentic, if they are apocryphal, if they emerged from a calculated intent on the part of the performers to obtain the material benefits of loyalty, if they are a product of fear and need, or if they are simply staged. What is clear is that the co-option of emotional ties and a particular form of masculine identity to promote relationships of hierarchy and subjugation is a political strategy with a long and sordid history in Assad's Syria. Today, this strategy continues to serve a tragic role as an ideological component in the ongoing civil war.

Drawing on my own experience as a culturally Sunni woman who has lived most of my life in Syria, I address in this book how Romantic masculinism has unfolded in this national context and how it has shaped our struggles over belonging and identity. I am particularly interested in how masculinism itself is often rendered "invisible," or at least subterranean, in appeals to love and loyalty, and how this phenomenon distorts and problematizes women's sense of national belonging. This book is not a catalogue of all the diverse forms that masculinity may take in Syrian society; nor is it an attempt to reduce the entirety of masculinism to a product of nationalist ideology. Instead, it examines how certain preexisting models of masculinity have been adopted and promulgated by the Baathist regime in an effort to forge a link between patriarchal family structures and political affiliations. Throughout the book, I look in detail at the history of this construct in its symbolic and pragmatic dimensions, before ultimately turning to the role of gender in the current Syrian war and discussing the ways in which civic activism is increasingly challenging the gendered meanings of Syrian national identity.

## Belonging to the manly nation

At the time of this writing, Bashar al-Assad is being sworn in for a fourth presidential term, having reportedly received 95 percent of the vote in the 2021 elections. His acceptance speech is marked by a notable military presence, which is unsurprising due to the current war. However, I cannot help but consider the symbolic aspect of this military imagery for the Assads, who seized control of the Syrian Baathist Party in a 1970 coup in which troops personally loyal to Hafiz al-Assad took control of the Congress and other government buildings. In the acceptance speech, on July 17, 2021,[3] Bashar repeatedly refers to the military and its activities as emblematic of Syrian identity, for example by stating that "the heroic deeds of the Army are the only manifestation and the true meaning of nationalism!"[4] Similar rhetoric was reflected in more detail in a celebratory speech from just a few weeks earlier (May 28, 2021),[5] in which Assad thanked his loyalist voters:

> You have offered your own definition of nationalism ... It was a smashing of their arrogance and false pride [here, Assad is referring to opposition groups] ... This is the highest expression of sincere loyalty to the homeland ... It is a slap to those who draw plans for their own success at the expense of our money, our blood, our honor, and our dignity! There is no place for partners except for brothers and friends!

In addition to rejecting civic partnerships and rights that extend beyond affective bonds, these speeches are full of overtly masculinized language, such as exclusive references to "brothers" (*'ikhwa*) and men's "honor" (*sharaf*), which effectively removes women and our experiences from Assad's nationalist discourse. Men, in this rhetoric, are called upon to vigorously protect the nation and its/their honor, while women essentially disappear, except perhaps as objects to be claimed.

Such rhetoric is certainly not new in the Syrian context. For example, in another landmark speech given to local leaders and parliamentarians on July 26, 2015,[6] Bashar al-Assad stated: "The fatherland [*watan*] is not for those who just live in it or hold its passport, but for those who defend and protect it!" The context of this statement was a broader exhortation for listeners to join and/or support the Syrian Army, but it is notable for the extent to which Assad invokes gendered language ("fatherland") and excludes "those who just live here" from his vision of national belonging. Assad's definition of who deserves to be considered a true and valuable Syrian is part of a long-standing ideological trajectory, and as I will argue in detail, it leverages a traditionalist view of masculine virtues and patrimony to exclude both political opponents and women in general from equal civic participation. Underlying the notions of sacrificial heroism, overtly male "brotherhood," and readiness to fight and die for the cause as the foundation of national identity is an outlook that elevates the image and power of an active martial man. This rhetoric of Romantic masculine nationalism has always been present in the Baathist regime, and it has become more broadly manifested and entrenched during the seemingly endless war (as I will discuss in more detail in Chapter 5), sending reverberations into the domestic sphere and throughout society.

I was initially introduced to the subject of Syrian nationalism in a compulsory fashion—by my state-mandated conscription into two Baathist youth organizations: the Syrian National Organization for Childhood (*talā'e' al-Baath*) and the Syrian Revolutionary Youth Union (*shabībat al-thawra*). These two organizations were formed to mobilize children and introduce them to paramilitary concepts, and their activities were highly gendered: while all of us had to participate in weekly sessions dedicated to learning about nationalist ideals, combat, and physical fitness, the men were sent to training camps focused specifically on weapons and soldierly teamwork, while women students attended classroom sessions that taught us about the glorious past of the Syrian nation and the heroic deeds of men, as well as practical skills such as cooking and sewing. The nationalist songs and slogans that we had to learn and perform were focused almost exclusively on men's accomplishments of strength, bravery, and military might, giving the impression that the success of society is based purely on such endeavors. As a woman, I was taught that it was my job to recognize and admire such martial accomplishments, and to view my own assigned sphere of contributions as a lesser merit.

To elucidate the experience of belonging to a manly nation, and how such a social context impacts women in particular, I analyze in this book the history of the Syrian nationalist ideal and its expression in culture and rhetoric. I also examine the identity conflicts that women encounter in such an environment, and how it affects our self-image as we seek to construct our lives. The book argues, first and foremost, that gender constructs—stringently normative outlooks on masculine and feminine roles—are central to the Syrian national ideal and are intricately intertwined with long-standing concepts of the "good Syrian citizen." Of course, this does not make Syria unique, as concepts of gender have been closely linked to the idea of the nation in many parts of the world and throughout most of modern history.[7] The case of Syria is interesting, however, in that it is a relatively recent postcolonial nation, and one that was overtly founded on the principle of rejecting European imperialist rule and supposedly forging a new path of self-determination. It is also a regime that tends to pride itself on being modern and "progressive," at least in relation to traditional local cultures and religious authorities. As I will show in the following chapters, Syrian nationalists have nonetheless eagerly embraced patriarchal constructs as a means of imagining the nation into being, thereby persistently negating the civil rights and autonomy of women (as well as, sometimes, nonconforming men).

The arguments in this book add to the growing literature on gendered nationalism in the postcolonial context in several important ways. First, while recently published work has admirably expanded the discussion of gender and nationalism beyond the field's European- and Anglocentric origins,[8] there is not, to my knowledge, any prior book-length study on gender constructs and the Syrian Baathist state. Thus, the book fills a specific content gap by looking at the forms that gendered nationalism has taken in the Syrian context. Second, in my analysis I foreground the historical trajectory of the specific gendered constructs invoked by Syrian nationalists. I demonstrate that these gender constructs were derived primarily not from local forms of patriarchy in the Middle East but rather from European Romanticism, a "foreign" intellectual trend that was strongly and overtly influential in the writings of Syrian ideologues in the early twentieth century. I show how these European-derived perceptions of gender and the state affected the imaginative construction of men and women in the cultural and legislative spheres in the emerging Syrian nation, and the impact that Baathist nationalism had on women's everyday lives during this period. The extent and impact of these historical borrowings, which establish a link between the framing and trajectory of the Syrian state and earlier European nationalist ideologies, have to the best of my knowledge not been previously clarified in the literature on Syrian politics. A final and related contribution of my analysis is that it provides a critique of the widespread view that the subordination of women in Syria is purely a result of local tribalism, sectarianism, and authoritarianism emerging from Middle Eastern cultures.[9] In response, my work shows that the supposedly unifying, secular, and modernizing national ideology of the Baathist regime has also persistently endorsed harmful masculinist rhetoric and constructed women as inferior.

To make these arguments, I begin in the initial chapters of the book with a discussion of the historical context in which the Baathist state arose in Syria, and particularly the imperative that the regime confronted in finding common ground to link together diverse preexisting social power structures. The formation of modern national identities in the region was a somewhat haphazard and inorganic development, as colonial authorities carved new nations out of the Ottoman Empire with little respect for preexisting ethnic or sectarian loyalties.[10] Thus, the regime faced an existential imperative to locate a unifying ideal that would legitimize its rule and generate a state-centered national consciousness. The Baath Party approached this task in Syria by declaring a modernizing and secular vision, which was intended in part to reduce the power of religious and tribal elites.[11]

Officially, modernizing the social status of women was one of the regime's goals. Women's right to vote, for example, was supported by the Baathists, and the franchise was first established in Syria in 1949, much earlier than in other parts of the world (women in Switzerland, for example, did not achieve the right to vote until 1971). For most Syrian women, however, these rights remained purely symbolic and never expanded into substantive civic participation or real inclusion in the political leadership culture, in large part due to pervasive assumptions about the nature of women's subjectivity and social roles. Instead, patriarchal concepts were enshrined as a pervasive theme in Baathist rhetoric. I will argue that these gender concepts actually served as a major part of the ideological glue holding the nationalist coalition together—a situation that, as I show in the later chapters of the book, continues up to the current day. While rhetorically, and perhaps as seen from an external perspective, the Baathists were exemplars of progressive modernization, in reality they achieved few substantive advances in how women were portrayed, treated, and enculturated. The result was that the so-called "modernizing" Baathist Syria came to rank close to last globally in terms of women's education, health, political empowerment, and economic participation.[12]

## Considering my identity as a Syrian academic

There is a growing recognition in scholarly circles that the social position of the researcher matters, and that it often has an impact on access to data, selected modes of analysis, and the overall life experiences that an author brings to the text. Morten Valbjørn and Waleed Hazbun have written extensively about the importance of scholarly identities in shaping the direction of Middle East research, and they recently organized a workshop at Aarhus University in Denmark to address these topics.[13] These scholars have noted the impact of researchers' religious, ethnic, and national background; and in the context of the current book, I must also add the tremendous importance of gender background in shaping the focus of researchers' attention and the types of experiences to which we have access. These features of social positioning and background, as complex and multilayered as they may be, unavoidably affect the extent to which we can understand and accurately analyze the experiences of others.

    I have long felt that there were important omissions in my chosen field of study. When examining the literature on Arab nationalism and the Baathist ideology, I was very concerned to discuss the patriarchal aspects of these worldviews, and I wondered why previous scholars had not done the same, given the almost unavoidable prominence of strongly gendered concepts in Syrian nationalist discourses and texts.[14] I soon realized that my attentiveness to these issues was built on the foundation of living as a woman in Baathist Syria for twenty-five years, an experience that none of the scholars whom I was reading had shared, rendering them apparently oblivious to certain aspects of the empirical data. Instead, scholars often blithely accepted or replicated the Assad regime's own assertion that it was "progressive" on gender and was liberating women from the shackles of tradition.[15] In contrast, in my own personal background of coming of age in Syria, I gradually came to understand that the regime had put me through an intense, intentional, top-down process of homogenizing my identity and my subjectivity as a woman. I started to see how my everyday life, as well as the lives of other women and indeed of everyone in Syrian society, was shaped by the process of Baathist nationalist rhetoric and gendered "education" imposed by the regime.

For me, religious tradition never appeared to be the main problem that subordinated women in Syria, in large part because the authoritarian state was officially nonreligious, and it strongly limited the scope of acceptable public religious expression.[16] Instead, the memory that I most associate with authoritarian gender straightjackets was the enforced nationalism class (*qawmiyya*) that I had to participate in at every educational level, and the associated exams that we were required to complete. This "education" included reading and memorizing the words of the early Syrian nationalist thinkers and their concepts of national belonging that are discussed later in this book (indeed, some of the schools that I attended in my youth were named after these figures), as well as the sayings of the Assads and various heroic slogans and songs glorifying the love of the nation and of the regime. Not only were some of these class activities segregated by gender—as young men underwent paramilitary training while young women were slated into sewing and cooking classes—but also the contents of the overall lessons were highly gendered in their emphasis on the active roles of men and the language of valor, honor, and martial heroism. Since all of the active heroes and founding thinkers that we were expected to love and support were men, the sense of "brotherhood" and camaraderie that suffused these nationalist tales was not a circle that was amiable or welcoming to women participants, and the historical or current contributions of women in building society seemed to matter not at all.

As I grew older, for a time traditional religious dress codes became for me a flash point and a way to challenge this imposed secular nationalist ideology. I began to adopt and act on the view that the hijab, and other symbols of religious belief, could serve as a tool of resistance against the secular authoritarian regime, particularly in schools where women had been mandated to remove their head coverings upon entering. At the same time, perhaps contradictorily, I was steadfast in my opposition to private religious authoritarianism that demanded women must wear the hijab. I began to realize that the context of these symbols mattered, and a major part of my early political awakening was grounded in the understanding that individual choice of whether and when to participate in social performances was a defining feature of coercive control as well as opposition to that control.

This is why I found it somewhat depressing that, after the uprising against the regime in 2011 and the outbreak of the civil war, the glorification of blind Romantic attachment to one's faction, along with the familiar, women-excluding language of heroism, physical sacrifice, masculine swagger, and militarism, became even louder and suffused across all sides of the conflict. I knew that these discourses were not a newly emerging feature of the current war but rather something that had long been celebrated under Baathist rule, as has been the case across many societies and nations worldwide. In Syria it was an intrinsic part of the secular nationalist culture and an indoctrination imposed upon generations of children. It seems that we have not yet overcome it.

Another concern that profoundly motivated me while conducting this research and writing the book is the issue of academic abstraction, which can sometimes minimize the personal impact and lived experience of the phenomena that we are discussing. While striving for greater "objectivity" is a worthy goal, it should not come at the expense of removing the depth of experience and felt meaning from the work, or ignoring the reality of differing social positions. As noted above, these personal experiences do inevitably affect the shape of our intellectual attention, and it is an unfortunate truth that claims to objectivity often entail ignoring the limits of one's viewpoint, analyses, and data, rather than trying to expand those limits.[17] One of the ways in which this concern emerged during my writing was in regard to the transcription of important Arabic terms. It is most common in academic works to use standardized Romanization systems with extensive diacritics. However, I have found these presentations to contribute to the sense of "alienness" with which many English speakers approach these terms. The standard Romanizations also fail to reflect my native Damascene dialect, rendering the Arabic words into pronunciations that seemed foreign even to me. Thus, as part of embracing the inherent specificity of academic research, I have elected to take a more informal approach to the Romanization of Arabic terms in this book, omitting nearly all diacritical marks and striving to represent the sound of the language as it is commonly spoken in Syria.

I also want to emphasize that I do not claim to speak for all Syrian women in this book, much less for all women globally. What I do try to provide is a nuanced discussion that refrains from reducing women or men to passive reflections of various sectarian, ethnic, or political factions.[18] I draw from my extensive background of growing up and living in Syria to address some of the more intimate aspects of how its citizens have experienced complex, situational, and overlapping identities in the context of the Baathist regime.[19] My approach is commensurate with Charlotte Hooper's "postpositivist" outlook, in the sense that I focus on the micro-politics and complexity of power in the local context and try to steer away from excessive abstraction or universalization (which Hooper associates with masculine perspectives).[20] It is not my intention to forge universal conclusions about nationalism as a general form of human organization or to analyze its global impacts—other scholars have conducted such comparative work, but it is beyond my expertise, and I regard it with some suspicion, as the broad scope of comparison tends to inevitably elide the nuances of specific regional histories.[21]

A variety of previous feminist scholars have made similar observations about the situatedness of knowledge and the need to avoid overgeneralization, notably including Donna Haraway, Jon Anderson, Peter Hopkins, Sanjukta Mukherjee, and Nira Yuval-Davis.[22] Most of these theorists have also considered reductive academic discourses as intrinsically connected to colonialism. I would add, however, that anti-colonial discourses, such as those adopted by the Syrian regime, can present the same rigid abstractions. One way in which the discourses surrounding national ideology have tended to evade gender is by positing a fundamental and persistent colonial legacy that trivializes any other analytical lenses. In such discussions the "positional superiority" (to borrow Edward Said's term) of the participating speakers vis-à-vis gender is usually assumed; in other words, they give voice to a male-gendered experience by default.[23] As I will show in great detail in the following chapters, this rhetoric preserves relations of dominance by first limiting the outlooks that are expressed, and then second presenting the expressed outlooks as gender-neutral, universal, or "objective" and failing to discuss certain aspects of the speakers' positions. Thus, even when they grasp toward modernization or improving "women's status" as a legitimization framework, power relationships among men continue to take center stage as the default political and discursive focus.

Contesting this discursive production of knowledge that renders the play of national identities as "genderless" (which simply means normatively masculine) raises the question of whether or not there is an alternative category of subaltern woman-centered knowledge about nationalism or national belonging in Syria waiting to emerge. The current book will make some gestures in such a direction, as part of the effort to "decolonize the epistemic landscape."[24] This involves showing how the hegemonic discourses of Syrian nationalism have incorporated specific concepts of gender, and then reconstructing the discussion of the postcolonial state in an alternative fashion. Toward the end of this book, I will give a variety of specific examples of how perceptions of national identities and belonging in Syria could be revised and strengthened by integrating women's perspectives and empowering a wider array of gender expressions.

## The complex interactions of gender, nationalism, and postcolonialism

My analysis of the Syrian context has benefited from the general insights of many prior scholars of nationalism. One of these central thinkers was Benedict Anderson, who in the 1980s famously defined the nation as an "imagined community," in which features of shared identity and the boundaries separating the nation from other peoples are constructed through ideological discourse, media, and performance.[25] I find Anderson's outlook on social boundary formation to be particularly useful in thinking about how "legitimate" gender identities were framed and conveyed in the Syrian national imagining, and how these ideals were distributed through books, songs, and public performances. While Anderson did not overtly discuss the issue of gender, his basic approach of considering discursive identity formation and boundary-setting through the dissemination of texts is an essential touchstone for the manner in which I, and most other scholars, now approach the study of nationalist ideologies. My decision to focus on textual analysis in the current book (rather than interviews, ethnography, etc.) owes much to Anderson's approach.

Another prominent thinker in this area is Homi K. Bhabha, who similarly emphasized the discursive nature of national identities. Bhabha's work is strongly interested in the way that nations tend to hide their artificial nature or historical contingency, for example by falsely projecting the national concept back into the primordial past.[26] Bhabha also emphasized that nationalist discourses are not a simple byproduct or "function" of state power, but are rather broad identity formations that resonate in many aspects of life and serve as a constant scene of ideological and interpersonal negotiation.[27] This outlook is reflected in my analysis of Syrian national identity as an entirely artificial construct that has always, ineffectively, been in search of a primordial foundation. The social depth and complexity of the Syrian nationalist ideal can also be seen in my focus on how that identity was linked to the micro-politics of gender in a conflicted and, ultimately, contested manner. Understanding the nation as a narrative (or in Anderson's terms, an imagined community) can help draw our attention to how various individuals' life stories are presented in that narrative. In the case of Syrian nationalism, I will show it is a narrative in which women are highly regarded as symbols but virtually absent as human agents, and in which men are engaged in a heroic physical struggle to protect, build, and fight for the cause. The reductive gendered aspect of the nationalist discourse in Syria has led many individuals to feel that they cannot see themselves in those stories, or that their lives are regarded as of lesser value. I also find it hopeful, however, to consider that if the nation rests on a bedrock of narratives, then those narratives are intrinsically contestable and changeable.[28]

In a related body of scholarship, the gendered aspects of nationalism have been extensively discussed by feminist scholars who sought to reclaim women's role in nation formation, or to question women's exclusion from nationalist narratives. The patriarchal aspects of nationalism have often been seen by these critics as intrinsic—for example, Jan Jindy Pettman argued that nationalism inevitably entails "reconsolidating centralized control of authority ... including gender privilege."[29] Anne McClintock similarly concluded that "all nationalisms are gendered, all are invented, and all are dangerous."[30] Wendy Bracewell discussed "a straightforward equation between male interests, masculinity, and nationalism",[31] while Cynthia Enloe indicated that nationalism has "typically sprung from masculinized memory, masculinized humiliation, and masculinized hope."[32] Nira Yuval-Davis identified a list of ways in which gender intersects with nationalism, including perceptions of women as the "biological producers" of the nation, as symbols of national boundaries (by refusing marriage from outside the community), as transmitters of national values in roles as mothers and teachers, and, occasionally, as active participants in nationalist movements.[33] While the above formulations are mostly grounded in Eurocentric scholarship, and are perhaps a bit too reductive in curtailing the true diversity and complexity of nationalist movements worldwide, I similarly argue in this book that the Baathist strain of nationalism in Syria has privileged the concerns and activities of men and relegated women to disempowered roles. My emphasis, however, is on the specific historical trajectories and features of these gender constructs, and the curious complexity of how eighteenth- and nineteenth-century European Romantic ideologies came to be implemented in the Syrian context.

In postcolonial states such as Syria, the relationship between gender and nationalism becomes more complex, in part due to the commitment of many such regimes to pursuing a "liberatory" or "progressive" agenda in opposition to imperialist control. Often, newly formed states in previously colonized regions, including the Middle East, have presented the emancipation of women as part and parcel of their nationalist projects and used this goal as an aspect of their legitimizing frameworks.[34] Deniz Kandiyoti has argued that nationalist projects in postcolonial societies often "manipulate" women by pushing them into the role of signifiers or symbols of progress, while simultaneously failing to promote women's self-determination or material status in any significant way.[35] Women's emancipation in such contexts can become a top-down affair, with regimes unwilling to tolerate civic dissent or the emergence of authentic grassroots women's organizations outside of the Party control.[36] Nonetheless, this tendency of the regimes to adopt a liberatory discourse complicates the discussion of gender and nationalism, in comparison to the European and Anglocentric contexts that have

Introduction 13

preoccupied much of the feminist scholarship on this topic. Scholars such as Suad Joseph have shown that postcolonial states often exhibit a bewildering and exhausting complexity in their rhetoric on gender, as women are simultaneously held up as symbols of modernity and liberation from traditionalism while also being severely constrained and subordinated in their civic participation and freedom of expression.[37]

One of the particularly incongruous overlaps that scholars have noted emerging in some postcolonial contexts is the leveraging of male "protection" rhetoric simultaneous to discourses of women's liberation. In such views women's newfound "emancipation" from traditionalism continues to be predicated on the protection of male fighters and benefactors, and women's roles are also persistently still associated with imagery of motherhood, national reproduction, and feminine vulnerability in the service of their supposed benefactors.[38] The current book is very much interested in these overlaps and contradictions. I will show in detail how the Baathists were able to pursue a "liberatory" discourse on women as a legitimizing framework and a counter to traditional religious authority, while simultaneously imposing their own severe vision of Romanticized gender roles and formal and informal constraints on women's autonomy. For the most part, this was done simply by subsuming or appending feminist aspirations to the nationalist project in a rhetorical fashion, as can be seen, for example, in Hafez al-Assad's succinct explanation: "women's struggle for more rights is part of their national struggle."[39] After Bashar al-Assad came to power, he similarly made numerous promises and pronouncements about the importance of securing women's rights, mostly in the context of modernizing the country and constraining the influence of religion.[40] However, such statements remained profoundly vague in the details of how he intended to implement gender equality. Instead, they were focused on leveraging support by making women feel afraid of what would happen to them without the regime's paternalistic and authoritarian protection. I will show in detail in the following chapters that these contradictions and ambiguities in regard to women's rights have been a continuous theme throughout the Party's history.

To more fully understand this context, it is worth briefly noting some of the ways in which Syrian women have been controlled in the interest of demarcating and preserving the Baathist nationalist project. It may seem striking, in the context of a regime that has been rhetorically invested in secularism and liberating women from religious tradition, to discover that the Baathists failed to give women the right to choose their own romantic partners across religious lines, and instead (as I discuss in more detail in Chapter 3) persistently heightened the influence and binary nature of ethnic and religious identity in the country's personal and penal laws. The supposed commitment to "modernizing" women's rights seemingly did not make any difference when acting to reinforce patriarchal family structures could serve as a means of garnering political support. As I will discuss, Baathist legislation also severely restricted women's bodily autonomy and reproductive rights, absolved rapists if they were willing to marry their victims, and failed to regard "honor killings" as serious crimes—all while emphasizing the "progress" that the regime had achieved for women.

Furthermore, the regime has been adamant about prohibiting the emergence of any grassroots feminist organizations functioning independently of the state, often labeling such organizations as "subversive" and a product of foreign/imperialist influences. The overarching impact of such actions, I would argue, is to instrumentalize women's concerns and render them as an insincerely held adjunct to authoritarianism—with the reinforcement of the regime's power always being the real underlying concern. While doing so, the regime also foregrounded its own version of broadly enforced, patriarchal gender dichotomies, which rendered men and women hostages to a particular form of national imagining.

## What is masculinism?

This book invokes a variety of concepts that are familiar in common discussion but that need precise definition and theorization for scholarly purposes. Among the most fundamental are the concepts of *masculinity* and *femininity*. I view these gender concepts as social ideologies and as forms of expressive behavior, produced by virtue of constant cultural repetition and experimentation. Often, social performances of masculinity and femininity come to seem "natural" for those who participate in them, despite the fact that they vary widely across different communities and contexts, even sometimes in different areas of life for the same individual.[41] These gender constructs do not originate with the state, but they are frequently leveraged for political effect by various actors, either intentionally or because those actors have themselves fully internalized the associated habits and ideologies. Gender expression has a complicated relationship to biological sex (which itself is not a mono-dimensional dichotomy), and women may be identified and treated in particular ways based on nuanced combinations of both physical and behavioral factors.[42]

As noted in the previous section, many theorists have argued that nationalism is always highly gendered, and that it is so to the detriment of women. I feel that it is important to leave open the prospect that the nation—as well as gender—may mean different things to different people, and that it could be possible to pursue a nationalist project that does not entail the marginalization of women, or in which masculine and feminine roles are not so rigidly defined. As such, there is a need to be more specific in our terminology about the type of nationalist ideology that foregrounds reductive and hierarchical ideas about gender. Some scholars have pursued such nuance by talking about a specific type of "gendered nationalism," which V. Spike Peterson and Anne Sisson Runyan, for example, defined as "the construction of a national identity and solidarity based on masculinist notions of self-determination and autonomy, which is at the expense of women's self-definitions and solidarity."[43] However, this definition only somewhat defers the issue by raising the question of what we mean by *masculinism*. This concept, also, is a bit problematic in that it quietly selects, emphasizes, and universalizes a particular type of masculinity and reinscribes its essentialist framing.

Due to the wide variety of masculinities that actually exist and their variance in relation to class, race, and geographic setting, among other factors, it is important to be clear about what specific types of identities and behavioral expectations we are referring to when discussing masculinism.[44] The term generally describes a strong and overt ideology of privileged gender roles and behaviors that benefit men at the expense of women,[45] but the exact form that these ideologies take needs to be clearly contextualized. In the current book I occasionally use the term "masculinism" in the Syrian nationalist context; when doing so I am describing a specific social construct that emphasizes a manly image of passionate loyalty to the regime, physical heroism, and Romanticized martial valor. This type of masculism places a premium on a man's willingness and ability to engage in acts of physical violence and control, including self-sacrifice or suffering for that purpose, and it elevates such activities as the supposed foundation of society. In addition to associating such martial roles with men and presenting diverging concepts of women's less empowered contributions, the construct also emphasizes competition and hierarchical power relations among men themselves, and foregrounds boundaries between superior and inferior men based on their participation in these masculinist roles.

Sikata Banerjee has recently introduced what I think is an ever better term for such social constructs. Banerjee discussed a phenomenon that she called "muscular nationalism" in the context of India and Ireland—defined by a specific type of national identity that leverages imagery of men's physical power and passionate action:

> Examples of muscular nationalism center an adult male body poised to sacrifice and kill for the nation. Usually, this view of masculinity is juxtaposed with a chaste female body that both symbolizes national honor and provides a moral code for the lives of women in the nation.[46]

I have found this concept of muscular nationalism to be strongly applicable in the Syrian context as well—and I would argue that it is not coincidental that the contexts of these nationalist movements (in India, Ireland, and, as I will show, in Syria) all have strong associations with intellectual roots in the European Romantic tradition. Banerjee similarly traced the ideological origins of the movements she studies to nineteenth-century European nationalism, and she argued that these political ideologies continue to play a role in many modern conflicts and civil wars.[47]

I discuss the impact of the Romantic nationalist ideal in Syria in relation to two conceptual images—first, the Baathist warrior figure, describing the man who is ready to passionately fight and sacrifice himself for the modern nation, and is perceived as superior to other men who are not ready to do this. Second, the patriarchal father and husband figure, who serves as a passionate domestic protector and as such exerts control and supervision over women. Ultimately, the two images come together in the figure of the ruler, who is both the idealized military leader and the "father of the nation," allegorizing the controlling relationship between men and women in the private sphere. I will discuss how these models shaped the boundaries of citizenship in Baathist Syria, as expressed intellectually, legislatively, and in popular discourse. Notably, my analysis focuses strongly on the ideological, rather than purely material, impact of muscular nationalism in Syria. It is undoubtable that these trends have a material component, for example in the institutionalized role of the military in political and public life, and in the regime's use of the Army's force in consolidating dominance and control.[48] Focusing purely on such material power relations, however, only takes us further into the trap of assuming that martial action is the true foundation of society. In contrast, I examine how muscular nationalism played a role in shaping ideologies of consent, political legitimacy, and the overall shape of civic society in Syria. As I will discuss in the following chapters, the Baathists did not cherish militarism simply for its material impact but also for its emotive, commemorative, interpersonal, and intellectual aspects. Under the regime, militarism was viewed as an essential part of the educational process and as a means of fostering identity and loyalty.

## Women under the microscope

When I first embarked on this research project in 2013, scholarship on Syrian society was scattered and scant due to the years of dictatorship that had locked down the country, as well as a general lack of interest among intellectuals. It was especially difficult at the time to find well-developed studies either in Arabic or in other languages that analyzed the situation of women in Syria. The Baathist state intelligence agencies (*mukhābarāt*) engage in severe monitoring and restriction on research that makes it nearly impossible to conduct reliable surveys or ethnographic studies.[49] Various minor works published in Arabic under Baathist supervision had discussed women's conditions in a critical light, but these analyses were limited by the political necessity of avoiding any criticism of the regime—they tended to portray the Baathists and Syrian nationalism in a uniformly flattering perspective and, predictably, to attribute any obstacles that women encountered to lingering religious traditionalism.[50]

Starting in the late 1990s, a few studies began to emerge that took a more nuanced view of Syrian women's experiences, and that did not automatically genuflect to the Baathists. Fiona Hill, for example, examined Syrian women's progress in both the national and religious spheres, and was critical of the lack of progress made by the regime. While still highly skeptical of Islamic tradition, which she saw as a locus of patriarchal norms, and viewing Westernization as synonymous with liberation, Hill also observed the ways in which the Baathist state had contributed to women's oppression.[51] The Syrian feminist scholar and activist Mia al-Rahbi also during this time began to regularly address the experiences of women in the region, without the usual pro-Baathist slant.[52] Additionally, two major studies of nationalism in the Middle East were written during this period, one by Fatema Muge Gocek and another by Beverly Milton-Edwards, that emphasized the role of gender in state discourses, though they treated Syria as only a peripheral example.

Milton-Edwards, in particular, described Baathist nationalism as an "expression of patriarchy" and argued that:

> The history of the women's struggle during this period [the postcolonial era], then, may be reflected through the lens of nationalism, be it Egyptian, Iraqi, Syrian, or Palestinian. As such, the independence, development, progress, setbacks, concrete gains, and perceived losses of the movement for women's rights can only be understood by understanding the political climate of the time, which dictated the role that such individuals and movements would have.[53]

This is an important work in that it specifically pointed out how a tendency to focus on narrow and perhaps culturally prejudicial markers of women's empowerment—such as removing headscarves and limiting the role of religion in the state—can create significant blind spots in regard to analyzing the continuing operation of patriarchy in secular nationalist contexts.[54] A similar argument was developed by Elham Manea, who linked the subordination of women in Yemen, Kuwait, and Syria to the authoritarian nature of state political power in these nations.[55] In the current book I develop this thesis even more strongly, by showing how Baathist nationalism has functioned as the primary locus of women's disempowerment in recent Syrian history, and discussing the ways in which harmful gender ideologies were "baked in" to the nationalist project from its very beginning.

In the broader context of Western feminist scholarship, there is a long tradition of conceptually linking together the themes of masculinism, militarism, and nationalism.[56] Thus, it is a bit surprising that in the Syrian context, the impact of modern nationalism on women has largely been elided, in favor of attributing all harms to the influence of religious institutions. Indeed, numerous scholars have encouraged Middle Eastern women to view nationalist regimes as the exclusive vehicle for their emancipation, despite the abject failure of those regimes to deliver the promised autonomy and equal citizenship.[57] In response to this tendency, I focus directly on the patriarchal aspects of the Baathist nationalist project in Syria, and how this state masculinism has filtered down throughout society to harm women. This is not to deny the complexity of women's and men's diverse experiences in Syria—certainly, there have been women involved in the Baathist project who may have experienced it as liberating, and there are women who have been harmed under religious institutions. However, I aim to show through a detailed analysis of the cultural impact of Baathism that this form of authoritarian secular nationalism should not be held up as emancipatory for women in general.

In recent years the civic uprisings from 2011 onward have revitalized questions of identity and belonging for Syrians, as the fracturing of the Baathist state hegemony has been accompanied by an impulse to question, redefine, reconfigure, and reimagine one's communal affiliations. Like many civil conflicts worldwide, the Syrian war has brought to the forefront the hidden struggles of everyday people, and has led to the establishment of diverse movements and organizations, including feminist organizations. These civic-oriented groups should be considered the cornerstone for any prospect of a future independent Syrian state that encompasses pluralist and democratic principles.[58] Currently, however, there remain significant tensions among Syrian civic groups that are often affiliated with different religious, ethnic, or ideological outlooks. Women's groups, in particular, are engaged in ongoing conversations about how to identify common ground without negating intersectional concerns around religious and ethnic identity.[59] Focusing on the often-overlooked continuation of masculinism under the secular regime, as I do in this book, can be a means of emphasizing that common ground.

Methodologically speaking, the book relies primarily on textual analysis, in the broad sense of "texts" as essays, songs, speeches, manifestos, articles of legislation, blogs, and so forth. I did not include ethnographic or interview/survey methods in this research—this is in part due to my historical focus but also for pragmatic reasons, as the current situation in Syria is not safe for social researchers and participants in such work. My main focus was to examine the records of culture that can be found in, for example, the influential writings of Baathist ideologues, legislative documents, and the songs that Syrian children were required to memorize in school, as a means of documenting gendered realities and sources of gender indoctrination that have often been downplayed or denied in previous scholarship on the regime. The book follows the trajectory of muscular nationalism in Syria from the founding and rise of the Baathist Party in the early twentieth century up to the height of its hegemony and the outbreak of the current war. In general, the material is organized chronologically, demonstrating an arc of masculinist secular nationalism in Syria and its outcomes.

This book adopts the concept of muscular nationalism by Banerjee,[60] yet extends it to comprise what appears to be in the Syrian context romanticizing masculinity. The term "romantic masculinity" centers on idolizing the male body as an entity ready to sacrifice and kill for the nation and its leader. As such, the analysis of this term focuses on how the shaping of the body politic has been around perpetuating an ethos of militarized masculinism, which results in constructing national belonging as existentially attached to willingness to die for the nation. Romantic-based nationalism draws its origins from the early ideological borrowings from European nationalist thinkers that were adopted by Syrian ideologues. The romanticized language used in the cultural, legislative, and nationalist spheres associates between violence/aggression and love/belonging in the national community. This formulation creates a persistent link between maleness, military action, and romantic sentiment. This is evidenced as Baathist power became institutionalized in Syria where the regime sought to impose its viewpoints by reshaping the cultural outlooks of what it means to belong to the nation. As this book will show, this endeavor included the creation and dissemination of patriotic symbols that constitute using mass consumption such as popularizing public statues, spectacles, and songs. At the same time, the perpetuation of romantic masculinity is instilled by Baathist rule in a manner that these concepts override the Constitutional right-based order that facilitated a cultural shift in Syria in which women, on a daily basis, have to confront aggression and direct misogyny in the private and public spheres. Given the complexity of the geopolitical context surrounding the Syrian case, this book aims to answer an important question as to what romantic masculinity is and how Baathism has perpetuated masculinism. Thus, this book presents an opportunity to explore how dominant national ideology endorses masculinist values, on the one hand, and offers a sustained and deeper exploration of the multifaceted and multilayered conceptualization of militarism and masculinism in modern Syria. Although I started researching this book before the Syrian war, this investigation tackles the saliency of martial values that can be provide understanding to how construction of hierarchal gendered identity instigates violence and perpetuates national exclusion.

It is important to emphasize the specific scope of this study, because there are important aspects of Syrian women's experiences and Syrian masculinism that will not be covered in the current book. In particular, contemporary Islamist political narratives, although certainly related to women's subordination, fall outside the scope of the work. The rise of Islamism and its gendered dimensions have been thoroughly analyzed elsewhere, and indeed such scholarship comprises the bulk of the prior analysis of the "woman question" in Syria.[61] The topic of religion in general in Syria is much too vast to be addressed here, and while I occasionally touch on the interactions of the Baathists with religious leaders, I have endeavored to keep the focus clearly on the rhetoric and cultural influence of the secular regime.[62] Furthermore, in accordance with my historical focus, the book gives only limited attention to discussing future prospects for Syria or the broad range of exciting and necessary work that is currently being carried out by women's organizations and other civic groups in the country. This topic is addressed briefly in Chapter 5, but overall, the current book is intended to help understand "how we got here," which is a fundamental basis for the ongoing work of deciding how to move forward. A fully nuanced analysis of current women's work and resistance in Syria would merit an entire additional volume.

Space limitations also require me to be selective about the texts that I analyze in detail. For example, in Chapters 2 and 3 I closely examine the writings of three "founding fathers" of the Baathist Party (al-Husri, Aflaq, and al-Arsuzi). These individuals were profoundly influential in the formation of the Party, and their works are venerated by the Assad regime, widely published through official channels, and used pervasively in educational contexts in Syria. (As I noted above, Syrian students are often required to memorize and recite portions of their writings.) However, I do not mean to suggest that these are the *only* theorists of Syrian nationalism; other writers, such as Qustantine Zurayk and Salah al-Bitar, also exerted a more limited influence. When I set out to examine and to document gender ideologies in the Baathist Party, the writings of these three primary "founders" seemed an obvious place to begin, both because of their profound historical influence in shaping the Party's doctrine and culture, and because of their continuing use in national educational contexts today.

This approach to the topic of gender and nationalism in Syria is indebted to the work of the political theorist Susan Moller Okin, who argued that investigating the representations of women and gender in foundational political texts can show the ideological origins of gender-related outcomes in subsequent states and societies.[63] However, my conclusions about the Syrian context differ significantly from Okin's analysis of works by Aristotle, Plato, Mill, and Rousseau. Okin found that these classical Western theorists tended to restrict women to the private/familial sphere, and she argued that this differentiation of public vs. private roles was the origin of gender inequality in the societies that venerated their writings. This was not the case in Baathist Syria, as the Party and most of its founding thinkers were if anything more encouraging of women's public participation compared to other societies of the era. Instead, I show that a pervasive muscular nationalism grounded in Romantic, heroic, and martial ideals served to establish gender hierarchies and discount cultural activities and social contributions associated with women and femininity. These nationalist concepts carried an implicit bias in that the ideal imagined citizen was a man (similar to the classical Western theorists), but they were grounded in a very different ideological climate that emphasized emotional, Romantic solidarity, and loyalism as a basis for the privileged masculine identity. These constructs relegated women to roles that were considered supporting and secondary, albeit not necessarily private.

After completing a careful analysis of the views on gender expressed by the primary Syrian "founding fathers," I then wanted to examine the extent to which these views were formalized or put into practice in the emerging Syrian nation. This led me to an examination of central state documents, including the Syrian Constitution and early legislation, along with other archival study. This research revealed the novelty of the specific concepts of gender that were spreading in Syria at that time of the Baathists' rise, and the profound impact that the new national legal and institutional structures had on women's lives. Finally, I turned to a consideration of popular Baathist cultural symbols at the height of the regime's power, to examine how the specific gender concepts found in the nationalist rhetoric were broadly adopted and disseminated by loyalists. In this analysis I found that I was again required to make a selection of some of the most common and representative texts. I chose to focus mostly on popular nationalist songs, due to their pervasiveness in Syrian culture and their clarity as textual sources. If my research time had allowed, I would have liked to review in detail other sites such as national holiday commemorations and the iconography of public statues, to discuss their profound representations of normative gender. Such evidence quickly becomes redundant, however, and I have elected instead to include a broader swath of historical material in the book so as to document the trajectory of Baathist masculinism from the beginnings up to the present. Throughout the analysis, I foreground the following questions: What specific views of gender have shaped Baathist thought and practice? What are the historical and cultural origins of these gender constructs? How broadly were these views of gender disbursed and reflected among Party loyalists? What impact did these ideas about gender have on the lives of Syrian men and women?

## Chapter roadmap

In Chapter 1 I will begin the historical journey by examining intellectual influences that preoccupied the Baathist "founding fathers." An important argument in this chapter is that Baathism's intellectual origins are grounded more in the identity concerns of eighteenth- and nineteenth-century European nationalists than in the philosophies and conversations of their pan-Arabist contemporaries. This discussion highlights the limitations of previous analyses of Baathist ideology and explains why the Party needs to be regarded as its own unique political genre. Most of the works that I examine in this section were written in Arabic and, surprisingly, have not been previously translated into other languages, despite their profound influence and continuing extensive circulation in Baathist Syria. This language barrier, I suggest, may have contributed to an insufficient awareness or attentiveness in the broader scholarly community about the foundations of Baathism and its deeply rooted modes of thought that continue to impact the lives of Syrians today. Examining these texts and their intellectual preoccupations helps to clarify that, in the specific context of Baathist Syria, European Romantic ideologies of national belonging and identity were intrinsic to the emerging state formation.

Chapter 2 turns to the Baathist founders' views on gender and their portrayals of women and the national community. The chapter will show how each of these thinkers pursued an analogy that represented the national community as an extension of a traditional patriarchal family, with assigned roles and relationships for women and men in public life. I explore how the frequent use of gendered terms in these texts to describe the national community and active Party members, such as "brothers" (*'ikhwa*), "men" (*rijāl*), and "young men" (*shabāb*), served to constrain the role of women by omission and render them into a passive position. Finally, I will show that the "muscular" concept in these foundational writings, which emphasized passionate martial action as the highest national ideal and the strongest bond of solidarity, was exclusionary toward women's participation and placed women's contributions (along with those of men who were unable or unwilling to embrace the "muscular" construct) into a position of reduced agency and worth in the nationalist imagination.

In Chapter 3 I zoom out from the founder's conceptual writings to address the practical impact of these ideas and the associated culture of muscular nationalism on the Party's early leadership. I show how this martial worldview was eventually reflected in foundational documents such as the Syrian Constitution of 1973, and I discuss how the emergence of the new Syrian nation affected the gendered identities and lives of the country's women and men. I argue that the importance of the military in the Baathists' rise to power served to further entrench a particular type of masculinity defined by values such as passionate loyalty, physical strength, martial prowess, and tactical teamwork as definitive elements in the national imagination. These values were reflected in foundational national documents and legislation, which consecrated the importance of masculine valor for secure citizenship while relegating women as well as anyone involved with the more "mundane" tasks of society to supporting and precarious roles.

Chapter 4 moves further forward in time to analyze the cultural narratives that became hegemonic in Syria during the height of Baathist power in the 1990s and early 2000s. Focusing primarily on nationalist songs that were pervasive in educational contexts and in state celebrations, I demonstrate the direct line of continuation from the Party founders' nationalism and militarism to these later cultural expressions. I examine how women are portrayed in these songs, and I discuss their use of gendered language to elevate an idealized masculine citizen while pushing other members of society to the periphery. Taking these songs as representative of the Baathists' vision of ideal citizenship and social relations, I show how central the concepts of hierarchy and gender roles were under the secular regime. I also discuss the impact of this cultural framework on women in both the public and domestic spheres, as it filtered down into everyday life and relationships. As with most of the texts discussed in this book, these nationalist songs are in Arabic and have not been previously translated.

Chapter 5 brings us to the current Syrian civil war. I analyze how the muscular identity concept previously instilled by the Baathists has served to buttress the regime during this time of conflict. While other scholars have evaluated factors such as sectarianism, securitization, and material patronage as a way of explaining the regime's staying power, I focus on the ideological aspects of loyalist support and the ways in which gendered identity constructs linked to the regime have served to create passionate emotional attachments. Looking again at loyalist songs and associated performances, I note that the top-down, enforced production that marked the era of Baathist hegemony has given way to more bottom-up, populist productions during the conflict. Ordinary loyalist citizens came to increasingly embrace this form of cultural production, taking it upon themselves to create and distribute the muscular propaganda that was previously organized by the Party. I argue that these loyalists have come to identify the survival of the regime with the survival of their privileged gendered identities, and that this phenomenon demonstrates the profound impact of the Romantic masculinist concept on the lives of ordinary citizens.

Finally, the book's Conclusion will address the ways in which Syrians today are challenging these identities and explore how citizen activism can reconstruct Syrian national identity. The chapter ends with offering prospects for reform in postwar Syria.

## Notes

1 See Anthony D. Smith. *Nationalism: Theory, Ideology, History*. Cambridge: Polity, 2001.
2 Rahaf Aldoughli. "Securitization as a Tool of Regime Survival: The Deployment of Religious Rhetoric in Bashar al-Asad's Speeches." *Middle East Journal* 75, no. 1 (2021a): 9–32. https://doi.org/10.3751/75.1.11; Rahaf Aldoughli. "Romancing the Nation." *Middle East Journal of Culture and Communication* 15, no. 4 (2022): 427–39.
3 Bashar al-Assad. "The Constitutional Oath Ceremony and the Speech of President Bashar al-Assad." YouTube video, posted by "Syrian Presidency," July 17, 2021b. www.youtube.com/watch?v=ATC54C4eiPo.
4 There are currently no official repositories or transcriptions for most of the political speeches discussed in this book; however, videos are widely available online on YouTube. All translations of these speeches are my own.
5 Bashar al-Assad. "Al-Assad's Speech on the Occasion of His Winning in the Presidential Elections." YouTube video, posted by "Syrian Presidency," May 28, 2021a. www.youtube.com/watch?v=AYuOolis8iM.
6 Bashar al-Assad. "President Bashar al-Assad's Speech during His Meeting with Members of Trade Unions, and Chambers of Industry, Commerce, Agriculture, and Tourism in Damascus." Syrian Arab News Agency (SANA), July 26, 2015. www.sana.sy/?p=245771.
7 Vera Tolz and Stephenie Booth. *Nation and Gender in Contemporary Europe*. Manchester: Manchester University Press, 2005; Nicola Montagana, Erin Sanders McDonagh, and Jon Mulholland. *Gendering Nationalism Intersections of Nation, Gender and Sexuality*. London: Palgrave Macmillan, 2018.
8 For example, Fatema Muge Gocek (ed.). *Social Constructions of Nationalism in the Middle East*. Albany, NY: State University of New York Press, 2002; Susan Slyomovics and Suad Joseph. *Women and Power in the Middle East*. Philadelphia, PA: University of Pennsylvania Press, 2011.
9 This reductive view is common even in scholarly analyses. See, for example, Esther Van Eijk. *Family Law in Syria: Patriarchy, Pluralism and Personal Status Codes*. London and New York: I.B. Tauris, 2016; Elham Manea. *The Arab State and Women's Rights: The Trap of Authoritarian Governance*. London and New York: Routledge, 2011; and Beth Baron. *Egypt as a Woman: Nationalism, Gender, and Politics*. Berkeley, CA: University of California Press, 2005.

10 See Lisa Wedeen. *Authoritarian Apprehensions: Ideology, Judgment, and Mourning in Syria*. Chicago, IL: University of Chicago Press, 2019.
11 Rahaf Aldoughli. "Departing 'Secularism': Boundary Appropriation and Extension of the Syrian State in the Religious Domain since 2011." *British Journal of Middle Eastern Studies* 49, no. 2 (2020): 360–85.
12 Ricardo Hausmann, Laura D. Tyson, and Saadia Zahidi. *The Global Gender Gap Report 2011*. Geneva: World Economic Forum, 2011, p. 149. www3.weforum.org/docs/WEF_GenderGap_Report_2011.pdf. Accessed April 13, 2015.
13 See Morten Valbjørn and Waleed Hazbun. "Scholarly Identities and the Making of Middle East IR." *APSA-MENA Newsletter* 3 (2017): 3–6. For broader views emphasizing the importance of positionality in social science research, see Cecilie Basberg Neumann and Iver B. Neumann. *Power, Culture and Situated Research Methodology Autobiography, Field, Text*. Cham: Springer International Publishing, 2018; Wendy Rowe. "Positionality in Action Research." Edited by David Coghlan and Mary Brydon Miller. *SAGE Encyclopedia of Action Research* 1 (2014): 628. https://doi.org/10.4135/9781446294406.n277; Beverley Mullings. "Insider or Outsider, Both or Neither: Some Dilemmas of Interviewing in a Cross-Cultural Setting." *Geoforum* 30, no. 4 (1999): 337–50. https://doi.org/10.1016/s0016-7185(99)00025-1; Alan Bryman. *Social Research Methods*. Fifth edition. Oxford: Oxford University Press, 2016; Kirsti Malterud. "Qualitative Research: Standards, Challenges, and Guidelines." *The Lancet* 358, no. 9280 (2001): 483–88. https://doi.org/10.1016/s0140-6736(01)05627-6; and Maggi Savin-Baden and Claire Howell Major. *Qualitative Research: The Essential Guide to Theory and Practice*. London: Routledge, 2013, p. 71.
14 See Rahaf Aldoughli. "Interrogating the Construction of Gendered Identity in the Syrian Nationalist Narrative: Al-Husri, Aflaq, and al-Arsuzi." *Syria Studies* 9, no. 1 (2017): 65–120; Rahaf Aldoughli. "Interrogating the Construction of Masculinist Protection and Militarism in the Syrian Constitution of 1973." *Journal of Middle East Women Studies* 15, no. 1 (2019a): 48–74.
15 See, for example, Bouthaina Shaaban. "The Status of Women in Syria." In *Arab Women: Between Defiance and Restraint*, edited by Suha Sabbagh, pp. 54–61. New York: Olive Branch Press, 2003.
16 The constraints that the Baathist regime placed on religious expression are discussed in more detail in Thomas Pierret. *Religion and State in Syria: The Sunni Ulema under the Ba'th*. New York: Cambridge University Press, 2013.
17 See Donna Haraway. "Situated Knowledges: The Science Question in Feminism and the Privilege of Partial Perspective." *Feminist Studies* 14, no. 3 (1988): 575–99. https://doi.org/10.2307/3178066.
18 See Sadiki Larbi and Rima Majed. "The Theoretical and Methodological Traps in Studying Sectarianism in the Middle East." In *Routledge Handbook of Middle East Politics*, pp. 540–53. New York: Routledge, 2020, p. 541.
19 For more on situational identities, see Karina V. Korostelina. "Readiness to Fight in Crimea: How It Interrelates with National and Ethnic Identities." *Identity Matters: Ethnic and Sectarian Conflict*, 2007, pp. 49–72. https://doi.org/10.1515/9780857456892-007; William E. Cross. *Shades of Black: Diversity*

*in African-American Identity*. Philadelphia, PA: Temple University Press, 1991; Marilynn B. Brewer. "The Many Faces of Social Identity: Implications for Political Psychology." *Political Psychology* 22, no. 1 (2001): 115–26. https://doi.org/10.1111/0162-895x.00229; and Fanar Haddad. "Sectarian Relations in Arab Iraq: Contextualising the Civil War of 2006–2007." *British Journal of Middle Eastern Studies* 40, no. 2 (2013): 115–38. https://doi.org/10.1080/13530194.2013.790289.

20 Charlotte Hooper. *Manly States: Masculinities, International Relations, and Gender Politics*. New York: Columbia University Press, 2001.

21 For examples of effective comparative scholarship on nationalism in the regional and global contexts, see Beverley Milton-Edwards. *Contemporary Politics in the Middle East*. Cambridge: Polity Press, 2006; Visakha Kumari Jayawardena. *Feminism and Nationalism in the Third World*. London: Zed Books, 1986; Suad Joseph. "Working-Class Women's Networks in a Sectarian State: A Political Paradox." *American Ethnologist* 10, no. 1 (1983): 1–22. https://doi.org/10.1525/ae.1983.10.1.02a00010.

22 Haraway 1988; Benedict Anderson. *Imagined Communities: Reflections on the Origin and Spread of Nationalism*. New York and London: Verso, 2006, p. 61; Peter E. Hopkins. "Women, Men, Positionalities and Emotion: Doing Feminist Geographies of Religion." *ACME: An International Journal for Critical Geographies* 8, no. 1 (2009): 1–17. https://doi.org/10.1080/13530194.2020.1805299; Sanjukta Mukherjee. "Troubling Positionality: Politics of 'Studying Up' in Transnational Contexts." *The Professional Geographer* 69, no. 2 (2017): 291–98. https://doi.org/10.1080/00330124.2016.1208509; Marcel Stoetzler and Nira Yuval-Davis. "Standpoint Theory, Situated Knowledge and the Situated Imagination." *Feminist Theory* 3, no. 3 (2002): 315–33. https://doi.org/10.1177/146470002762492024.

23 For "positional superiority," see Edward W. Said. *Orientalism*. New York: Vintage Books, 1979, p. 7.

24 Amy K. Donahue and Rohan Kalyan. "Introduction: On the Imperative, Challenges, and Prospects of Decolonizing Comparative Methodologies." *Comparative and Continental Philosophy* 7, no. 2 (2015): 128. https://doi.org/10.1179/1757063815z.00000000058.

25 Anderson 2006, p. 26.

26 Homi K. Bhabha (ed.). *Nation and Narration*. London: Routledge, 1990, p. 1.

27 Ibid., pp. 6–7.

28 See: Anders Ahlbäck. *Manhood and the Making of the Military: Conscription, Military Service and Masculinity in Finland 1917–39*. London and New York: Routledge, 2016, p. 20; and Sheila Rowbotham. *Hidden from History: 300 Years of Women's Oppression and the Fight against It*. London: Pluto Press, 1973, p. 32.

29 Jan Jindy Pettman. *Worlding Women: A Feminist International Politics*. London: Routledge, 1996, p. 138.

30 Anne McClintock. "'No Longer in a Future Heaven': Women and Nationalism in South Africa." *Transition* 51 (1991): 104–23, pp. 104–05.

31 Wendy Bracewell. "Rape in Kosovo: Masculinity and Serbian Nationalism." *Nations and Nationalism* 6, no. 4 (2000): 563–90, p. 566.
32 Cynthia Enloe. *Bananas, Beaches, and Bases: Making Feminist Sense of International Politics*. Berkeley, CA: University of California Press, 1990, p. 45. Some additional examples of these kinds of broad claims can be found in Claudia Koonz. *Mothers in the Fatherland*. London: Methuen, 1988, p. 21; Victoria De Grazia. *How Fascism Ruled Women: Italy, 1922–1945*. London: University of California Press, 1992, pp. 2–6; Tamar Mayer. *Women and the Israeli Occupation: The Politics of Change*. London and New York: Routledge, 1994, pp. 1–15; R. Radhakrishnan. "Nationalism, Gender, and the Narrative of Identity." In *Nationalisms and Sexualities*, edited by Andrew Parker, Mary Russo, Doris Sommer, and Patricia Yaeger, pp. 77–95. London and New York: Routledge, 1992, p. 78; V. Spike Peterson and Anne Sisson Runyan. *Global Gender Issues*. Oxford: Westview, 1993, p. 190; and Jennifer Heuer. "Gender and Nationalism." In *Nations and Nationalism: A Global Historical Overview 1770–1880*, pp. 43–58. California: ABC-CLIO, 2008, pp. 43–47.
33 Nira Yuval-Davis. *Gender and Nation*. London: SAGE, 1997, pp. 21–25.
34 Lila Abu-Lughod. *Remaking Women: Feminism and Modernity in the Middle East*. Princeton, NJ: Princeton University Press, 1998; Charlotte Weber. "Between Nationalism and Feminism: The Eastern Women's Congresses of 1930 and 1932." *Middle East Women's Studies* 4, no. 1 (2008): 83–106. https://doi.org/doi.org/10.2979/mew.2008.4.1.83.
35 Deniz Kandiyoti. "Bargaining with Patriarchy." *Gender & Society* 2, no. 3 (1998): 273–90, p. 273. https://doi.org/10.4324/9781315680675-24.
36 Deniz Kandiyoti. "Women, Islam and the State." *Middle East Report* 173 (1991): 9–14. https://doi.org/10.2307/3012623.
37 Suad Joseph. "Working-Class Women's Networks in a Sectarian State: A Political Paradox." *American Ethnologist* 10, no. 1 (1983): 1–22, pp. 5–6. https://doi.org/10.1525/ae.1983.10.1.02a00010.
38 See Baron 2005, pp. 5–10.
39 Hafez al-Assad. *The Issue of Women in the Thought of the Leader Hafez al-Assad*. Damascus: Women's General Union, 1994.
40 See Aldoughli 2021a.
41 See Todd W. Reeser. *Masculinities in Theory: An Introduction*. Chichester: Wiley-Blackwell, 2009, p. 18.
42 See Toril Moi. *Sexual/Textual Politics*, London and New York: Routledge, 2002, p. 180.
43 Peterson and Sisson Runyan 1993, p. 190. See also Ida Blom, Karen Hagemann, and Catherine Hall (eds). *Gendered Nations: Nationalism and Gender Order in the Long Nineteenth Century*. Oxford: Oxford International Publishers, 2000; Enloe 1990; Cynthia H. Enloe. *Manoeuvres: The International Politics of Militarizing Women's Lives*. Berkeley, CA: University of California Press, 2000; Kumari Jayawardena 1986; McClintock 1991; Anne McClintock. "Family Feuds: Gender, Nationalism and the Family." *Feminist Review* 44

(Summer 1993): 61–80; Tamar Mayer. "Gender Ironies of Nationalism: Setting the Stage." In *Gender Ironies of Nationalism: Sexing the Nation*, edited by Tamar Mayer, pp. 1–22. London and New York: Routledge, 2000; and Yuval-Davis 1997.

44 On different types of masculinities, see Gail Bederman. *Manliness and Civilization: A Cultural History of Gender and Race in the United States, 1880–1917*. Chicago, IL: University of Chicago Press, 1995; R. W. Connell. *Masculinities*. Berkeley, CA: University of California Press, 1995; and Ronald F. Levant. "The Masculinity Crisis." *Journal of Men's Studies* 5, no. 3 (February 1997): 221–31.

45 Charlotte Hooper. *Manly States: Masculinities, International Relations, and Gender Politics*. New York: Columbia University Press, 2001, p. 33.

46 Sikata Banerjee. *Gender, Nation and Popular Film in India: Globalizing Muscular Nationalism*. New York: Routledge, 2016, p. 2.

47 Ibid., pp. 6–9.

48 For more on the pragmatic role of the military in consolidating Baathist rule, see Adeed Dawisha. *Arab Nationalism in the Twentieth Century: From Triumph to Despair*. Princeton, NJ: Princeton University Press, 2003. There are also numerous excellent studies on the institutional influence of the military in Middle Eastern politics more broadly, for example Yezid Sayigh. "Militaries, Civilians and the Crisis of the Arab state." *The Washington Post*, December 8, 2014. www.washingtonpost.com/news/monkey-cage/wp/2014/12/08/militaries-civilians-and-the-crisis-of-the-arab-state/?utm_term=.912536e221d8. Accessed May 10, 2016; Adham Saouli. *The Arab State: Dilemmas of Late Formation*. New York: Routledge, 2012; and Nazih Ayubi. *Over-Stating the Arab State: Politics and Society in the Middle East*. London: I.B. Tauris, 2009.

49 See Raymond A. Hinnebusch. "Modern Syrian Politics." *History Compass* 6, no. 1 (January 2008): 263–85; and Lisa Wedeen. *Ambiguities of Domination: Politics, Rhetoric, and Symbols in Contemporary Syria*. Chicago, IL, and London: University of Chicago Press, 1999.

50 Some examples of these early pro-Baathist studies include Muhammad Safuh Akhras. *Tarkīb al-'ā'ila al-'arabiyya wa wazā'ifuhā*. Damascus: Ministry of Culture Press, 1976, which examined the roles of women in traditional Syrian families; Nabil Sulayman. *An-Nisawiyya fī'l-Kitāb s-Sūrī l-Madrasī 1967–1976*. Damascus: Ministry of Culture, 1978, which discussed the persistence of gender stereotypes in Syrian textbooks; George Tarabishi. *Al-Mar'a l-'arabiyya s-sūriyya fī 'ahd al-mar'a d-dawlī 1975–1985*. Damascus: Ministry of Culture, 1985, which catalogued women's supposed advances under the Baathist regime; and Bouthaina Shaaban. *Both Right and Left-Handed: Arab Women Talk about Their Lives*. Bloomington, IN: Indiana University Press, 1991, which criticized the influence of patriarchal religion in Syria.

51 Fiona Hill. "Syrian Women and Feminist Agenda." In Paul J. White and William S. Logan (eds). *Remaking the Middle East*, pp. 129–151. New York and Oxford: Berg Publishers, 1997.

52 Mia al-Rahbi. *Feminism: Concepts and Issues*. Damascus: Al Rahba Publishing House, 2014.

53 Milton-Edwards 2006, p. 191.
54 Ibid., pp. 200–03.
55 Manea 2011.
56 For example, Jean Bethke Elshtain. *Public Man, Private Women: Women in Social and Political Thought*. Princeton, NJ: Princeton University Press, 1981; Jean Bethke Elshtain. "Reflections on War and Political Discourse." *Political Theory* 13, no. 1 (1985): 39–57; Enloe 1990; McClintock 1991; McClintock 1993; Joane Nagel. "Masculinity and Nationalism: Gender and Sexuality in the Making of Nations." *Ethnic and Racial Studies* 21, no. 2 (March 1998): 243–69; Sylvia Walby. *Theorising Patriarchy*. Oxford: Blackwell, 1990.
57 Examples of scholarship that portray nationalism as emancipatory for women in the Middle East include Margot Badran. *Feminism, Islam, and Nation: Gender and the Making of Modern Egypt*. Princeton, NJ: Princeton University Press, 1995; Kumari Jayawardena 1986; Milton-Edwards 2006, p. 193; Chandra T. Mohanty. Cartographies of Struggle: Third World Women and the Politics of Feminism." In *Third World Women and the Politics of Feminism*, edited by Chandra T. Mohanty, Ann Russo, and Lourdes Torres, pp. 1–47. Bloomington, IN: Indiana University Press, 1991; and Nira Yuval-Davis and Pnina Werbner (eds). *Women, Citizenship and Difference*. London: Zed Books, 1999.
58 See Ellis M. West. "A Proposed Neutral Definition of Civil Religion." *Journal of Church and State* 22, no. 1 (1980): 23–40 on the importance of voluntary civic organizations in democracies.
59 This issue of Middle Eastern women seeking common ground across sectarian and ethnic lines is not new, and today's women's groups have some strong models to draw from. Suad Joseph. "Working-Class Women's Networks in a Sectarian State: A Political Paradox." *American Ethnologist* 10, no. 1 (1983): 1–22. https://doi.org/10.1525/ae.1983.10.1.02a00010, for example, documented how working-class women in Lebanon, during that country's protracted civil war, challenged sectarian politics and formed cross-sectarian support networks.
60 Banerjee 2016.
61 Particularly nuanced analyses of Islamism and gender in the Syrian context have been conducted by Omar Imady. "Organisationally Secular: Damascene Islamist Movements and the Syrian Uprising." *Syria Studies* 8, no. 1 (2016): 66–91; and Shaaban 2003.
62 See Aldoughli 2020 and 2021a.
63 Susan Moller Okin. *Women in Western Political Thought*. London: Virago, 1980.

# 1

# Romantic borrowings in early Syrian nationalism: The writings of Sati al-Husri, Michel Aflaq, and Zaki al-Arsuzi

In analyzing the nature of Baathist ideology, it is useful to consider its historical origins—what is this strand of Syrian nationalism, and where did it come from? What ideas and philosophies were central in the development of the nation and the Party? It is common in Middle Eastern contexts to perceive local nationalist movements as running counter to European influences as well as to foreign control. I will show in this chapter, however, that Baathist thought has a direct intellectual debt and continuity with political outlooks that emerged in Europe during the eighteenth and nineteenth centuries. To do so, I focus on the writings of three central early theorists of the Syrian nation: Sati al-Husri, Michel Aflaq, and Zaki al-Arsuzi. As I mentioned in the previous chapter, these thinkers were considered foundational by the Baathists, and their works have been widely and continuously taught in the Syrian educational system. However, they have been relatively understudied outside of the country. A few previous scholars have noted the importance of these three thinkers in Baathism, and some have even considered that their outlooks may have paved the way for dictatorship, violence, and racism in the subsequent Syrian state.[1] However, the full writings of these three ideologues have not been translated into other languages outside of their native Arabic (unless otherwise noted, all translations in this book are my own), and the details of their philosophies are not widely known outside of Syria. In looking at these "founding fathers" of Baathism, I emphasize the surprising extent to which their nationalist views were consciously borrowed from a previous generation of European philosophers such as Johann Gottfried Herder, Johann Gottlieb Fichte, and Ernest Renan. Tracing these intellectual influences will help to establish the conceptual trajectory of Syrian nationalist thought, and will lay the groundwork for better understanding the Party's specific perspectives on gender in the following chapters.

## Theoretical overview: visions of nationalism

In the realm of theoretical discourse, the exploration of what precisely constitutes "nations" and "nationalism" unveils the inherent complexity in forging a uniform definition of these ideologically laden concepts.[2] Despite this intricacy, there is a consensus among scholars that the eighteenth century heralded the birth of these concepts in their politicized form. This era witnessed the crystallization of nationalism as a distinctively Western intellectual construct,[3] a revolutionary ideation that gradually found resonance across diverse global landscapes.[4] Central to the modernist English school of nationalism are the pivotal contributions of theorists such as Anthony Smith, Benedict Anderson, Ernest Gellner, and John Breuilly, whose works profoundly shaped contemporary understanding of these phenomena.[5]

The theoretical underpinnings of nationalism, as propounded by these scholars, underscore the essential "subjective" and "emotional" characters intrinsic to the concept of the nation. Their elucidation of nationalism accentuates the primacy of shared language, culture, racial purity, educational heritage, historical narrative, and a deep-seated attachment to one's native soil. This interpretation posits national belonging as an inherent, nonvoluntary attribute, portraying the nation fundamentally as an extension of familial bonds. German Romanticism's influence, particularly during the late eighteenth and early nineteenth centuries, was instrumental in sculpting the contours of nationalist thought. This period, marked by the aftermath of the Napoleonic Wars, saw the emergence of German nationalism as a movement advocating the cultural unification of Germany. Foremost in this intellectual vanguard were Johann Gottfried Herder and Johann Gottlieb Fichte, despite their divergent philosophical trajectories.[6]

Herder, fervently dedicated to the rejuvenation of German culture and language, adopted a "constitutive approach to language," positing it as the quintessential expression of collective thought and interaction.[7] For Herder, language was not merely a communicative tool but a fundamental marker of national identity. While he acknowledged the role of blood ties in the conception of the German nation, he eschewed notions of racial superiority, advocating instead for a recognition of the distinct linguistic, racial, and cultural characteristics that define each nation, thereby celebrating a tapestry of global diversity.[8] Fichte, in alignment with Herder's emphasis on linguistic identity, introduced additional dimensions to his conceptualization of nationalism. His reaction to Prussia's defeat at Jena in 1806 catalyzed a more politically charged vision of German nationalism, diverging from Herder's more culturally oriented ideology. Fichte's nationalism, while grounded in linguistic and cultural identity, advocated for the establishment of a German state, thus marrying cultural unity with political aspirations. This bifurcation of nationalism into cultural and political phases—the former represented by Herder's view of the nation as a cultural entity and the latter by Fichte's vision of cultural identity as a precursor to political sovereignty—delineates a complex evolution of nationalist thought.[9] Fichte's thesis thus extends beyond the preservation of cultural identity to encompass the actualization of political autonomy, positioning the nation's journey as one that must navigate both the preservation of its unique cultural character and the realization of its political sovereignty.[10]

Fichte, in his discourse on nationalism, advanced the notion that the essence of a nation is encapsulated not only in its language and culture but also necessitates the establishment of a sovereign state.[11] This conceptualization of nationalism, deeply rooted in primordialist thought, unfolds in two distinct yet interconnected phases—the cultural and the political. Within this framework, Herder is seen as the progenitor of the cultural dimension, positing the nation as a cultural mosaic, defined by unique linguistic groups, each distinct in its own right.

The second phase, as articulated by Fichte, builds upon this cultural foundation, postulating that once a nation has achieved a unified cultural identity—a synthesis of language and historical experience—it must then embark on the journey toward statehood.[12] This progression marks a critical juncture in the evolution of nationalist thought, where the nation, having cultivated its cultural singularity, must now assert its political sovereignty. In this regard, Fichte's perspective delineates a more expansive trajectory for the nation, one that extends beyond the preservation of cultural identity to encompass the realization of political autonomy.[13] This duality of nationalism, as theorized by Fichte, underscores a continual struggle: the preservation of a nation's cultural essence and the simultaneous pursuit of its political sovereignty. In this intellectual schema, the nation invariably predates the state. The actualization of a political state, according to this view, is contingent upon the prior establishment of a cohesive cultural identity. Fichte's exposition, therefore, extends the discourse beyond Herder's cultural nationalism, introducing a dynamic where the notion of nationhood is not static but evolves toward the ultimate goal of statehood.

## Civic/modernist perception

In the waning years of the eighteenth century, an intellectual ferment emerged within the cauldron of French thought, fostering nascent nationalist sentiments that sought to counter the organic conception of nationhood espoused by German Romantics. The French intellectual counterpoint distinctly posited that national affiliation was not an inborn or natural state but rather a voluntary act of association. The Enlightenment, with its emphasis on rationality and the liberties of the individual, envisioned the nation as a collective sovereign, thereby sowing the earliest seeds of the concept of "civil" nations.

Ernest Renan, a luminary in the firmament of French nationalism, whose ideological stance was galvanized by the ignominious French defeat in the Franco–Prussian War (1871), emerged as a preeminent proponent of this ideology. In his seminal treatise "What Is a Nation?,"[14] Renan mounted a formidable challenge against the tripartite Romantic assertions that language, race, and geographical determinism constituted the bedrock of national identity. Renan's thesis robustly refuted the notion of an unadulterated "pure race," positing instead that the genesis of a nation rests upon the collective volition and resolve of its populace. He contended that shared experiences of adversity, the collective struggle, and a common destiny are the crucibles within which national consciousness is forged. Renan advocated for the strategic curation of historical memory, suggesting that the act of "forgetting" particular historical episodes is instrumental in the cultivation of a national ethos. His conceptualization of the nation was predicated on a communal aspiration to share a multitude of commonalities, disavowing the claims of racial, linguistic, and cultural purity as untenable, given the historical intermingling resultant from wars, matrimonial alliances, and treaties.[15]

Diametrically opposed to the Germanic doctrine, Renan advanced the proposition that the essence of nationhood is not a byproduct of ethnolinguistic homogeneity but rather a political construction affirmed through the consent of the governed. Renan articulated, "There is something in man which is superior to language, namely, the will."[16] This assertion underscored his perspective that human volition transcends linguistic affinities. Furthermore, Renan, in stark contrast to Fichte and Herder, adjudged the state not as an organic outgrowth of the nation but as a political entity in its own right, with the nation subservient to the state. This inversion underscores Renan's depiction of the nation as a "legitimate" political authority, not as an ethno-cultural inevitability demarcated by linguistic and cultural identity.[17]

## Pan-Syrianism, pan-Arabism, or Syrian nationalism?

It is common in scholarly and journalistic literature to use the term "Syrian nationalism" when discussing the Baathist state or current conflicts in the region, a convention that I have adopted in the current book. However, in many cases the term is used without a nuanced differentiation among various regional political philosophies and their tenets. One particular error is the frequent conflation of Baathist "Syrian nationalism" (*al-wataniyya al-Sūriyya*) with the concept of "pan-Syrianism." The latter term refers to a twentieth-century political movement toward an integrated cultural homeland in the greater Levant (which includes present-day Syria, Lebanon, Iraq, Jordan, Palestine, and sometimes even broader territories).[18] This concept of pan-Syrianism does not generally overlap with nationalist loyalty toward the Baathist state, and therefore using "Syrian nationalism" to refer to both ideas can be misleading. At times, Syrian nationalism is also conceptualized as a subset or product of Arab nationalism—a region-wide ethnic and linguistic construct, which again does not entail any specific loyalty to the Baathist regime or its political outlooks.[19] I argue that it is vital to separate out a distinct concept of Syrian state nationalism, defined as an identity attachment to the existing Syrian government, its Baathist ruling Party, and the political doctrines of that Party, as distinct from the broader philosophies of pan-Syrianism and Arab nationalism. Doing so allows us to more accurately pinpoint the contours of this state-oriented Syrian nationalism and its ideological perspectives.

Due to its origin in the rather arbitrary partitioning of the Ottoman Empire after World War I, the state of Syria has never had a strong territorial identity or a unified culture.[20] Syria is a mosaic of ethnicities, religions, sects, and national backgrounds, including significant minorities who have little identification with the current Baathist state and instead consider themselves Armenians, Assyrians, Druze, Palestinians, Kurds, Yazidi, Mhallami, Arab Christians, Mandaeans, Turkmens, or Greeks, among others. When the Baath Party rose to power in independent Syria in the 1960s, it did so in part by promoting a new type of national identity that sought to merge the mosaic of Syrian society into a more cohesive and stable structure. I will show that Syrian state nationalism, which continues into the present day, centers around a project of homogenizing these diverse Syrian subjects into a novel imagined cultural identity. Since there was little preexisting ethnic, geographic, or historical continuity to form the basis of this national community, Baathist thinkers have tended to foreground the Party itself, which was lent a primordial and emotive character through rhetoric emphasizing bonds of "love," "brotherhood," and "loyalty" between the country's people and the Party leadership. Such personality cults are not uncommon in the Middle East, and many of the new states that emerged in the region during the twentieth century foregrounded authoritarian leaders (for example, Saddam Hussein in Iraq, Muamar Ghadhafi in Libya, and Jamal Ab al-Nasser in Egypt). However, I argue that the Syrian case is unusual in that the regime did not rely primarily on the tenets of pan-Arabism as a legitimizing framework but rather embraced a particular set of European-derived Romantic nationalist ideas to forge a novel ideology and identity that could tie together the country's diverse ethnic groups.

It is important to emphasize that, as Suliman Salameh has discussed in detail, Syrian national identity did not exist prior to the twentieth century, not "in literature, historiography, or even popular expression."[21] Furthermore, while many Syrians are of Arab decent, this ethnicity has rarely been seen as taking precedence over other forms of identity or political outlooks in Syria, as Yahya Sadowski succinctly explained:

> The 90 percent of the Syrian population who can claim Arab ancestry (basically everyone except the Kurds, the Armenians, and the shrinking Jewish community) have not stopped thinking of themselves as Arabs—indeed, they continue to take great pride in that identity. But they are Arabs today in much the sense that the French are Europeans: the cultural identification is solid, but how much political collaboration that entails depends on changing circumstances.[22]

This absence of political attachment to "Arabness" in Syria, and the foregrounding of other ethnic and religious identities over Arabness, corresponds to my own experiences through many decades of living in the country. It is part of the reason why I question scholars and journalists who reflexively view Baathist nationalism through the lens of broader regional pan-Arabist movements. Doing so is a fairly widespread tendency; for example, Raymond Hinnebusch went so far as to argue that there is no Syrian national identity apart from pan-Arabist ideology: "Syrian identity wholly distinct from Arabism has not emerged, with the content of Syrian identity remaining Arab, and the regime continuing to see its legitimacy as contingent on being seen to represent Arab causes."[23] In a similar vein, Christopher Phillips has argued that Arabism overrides state nationalism in Syria and that competing claims to Arab identity are the basis of the current conflict.[24] My argument in this chapter is directly counter to such perspectives, as I contend that Baathist ideology, and the outlines of Syrian politics in general, have very little sincere relationship at all to Arabism. While some of the early Baathist thinkers that I discuss here regularly referred to the "Arab" character of the nation, I contend that this was little more than a nod toward broader regional trends—the ethnic construct did not comprise a substantive aspect of their politics, and over time it gradually fell out of use. Much of the scholarship that focuses on pan-Arabism as an interpretive framework for the Baathist regime fails to account for the actual intellectual origins of the Party's ideology, as well as its current dimensions, rhetoric, and expressed identities.

Similarly, the tendency to link the Baathists to the political movement of pan-Syrianism is profoundly misplaced. This ideology, which foregrounds the long-standing dream of a united broader Fertile Crescent region (*al-hilāl al-khasīb*), is associated with a political movement founded in 1932 by Antun Sa'adeh. Today, this movement has evolved into the Syrian Social Nationalist Party, which is notably distinct from the Baathist regime. Several studies have highlighted the concept of pan-Syrianism as an explanatory factor for current political conflicts; for example, some decades ago Thomas Collelo suggested that many Syrians were skeptical of the Baathist Party because they did not view the Assads as reflecting the broader vision of a unified Fertile Crescent.[25] These views may be somewhat outdated, as pan-Syrianism today is a mostly defunct political movement and has not played a central role in the current uprisings and war. More important is that despite the strong ideological and institutional distinctions between Baathism and pan-Syrianism, many commentators fail to fully differentiate between them.

It is common to see work suggesting that the Baathist state emerged from pan-Syrianism and has never really strayed far from its tenets. Eyal Zisser, for example, argued that: "Syrian state identity … has not yet supplanted the initial Arabist or the Syrian identities, but coexists with them somewhat uncertainly."[26] Adel Beshara, while discussing various strands of thought that contributed to the emergence of "Syrian nationalism," foregrounded the philosophies of pan-Syrianist thinkers such as Butrus al-Bustani, Jurji Zaydan, Khalil al-Khuri, and Rashid Rida—while failing to note that these individuals were not admired by the Baathists and exerted no influence whatsoever on the formation of the Party and the subsequent, actually existing Syrian state.[27] Other scholars and journalists, perhaps under the influence of the aforementioned literature, can sometimes be ambivalent in their terminology, substituting "Syrianism" for Baathism and vice versa. In the current book I want to be clear that I am using the term Syrian nationalism to refer specifically to the social identities and political engagements associated with the Baathist regime. I will retain the terms pan-Syrianism and Arab nationalism (or Arabism) to refer to those separate and highly distinct political movements.

Since the start of the uprisings in 2011, there has been a great deal of partisan-oriented discussion of Syrian nationalism and identity. Opponents of the regime have tended to argue that a shared Syrian national identity is a complete fantasy in the imagination and rhetoric of the Assads, with very little uptake or reality among the country's population.[28] Such commentaries generally focus on the need to build a new civil state (*dawla madaniyya*) oriented toward pluralism and rights-based citizenship rather than the belief in a unifying national culture. In contrast, regime-sponsored literature has argued, rather unconvincingly, that the recent violence has fractured the historical unity of the "traditional Syrian people" and led to the rise of novel sub-state identities.[29] This polarized political situation has further contributed to the difficulty of clarifying the actual ideological foundations, scope, and impact of Syrian Baathist nationalism. Both opponents and proponents of the regime tend to regard "nationalism" as a singular concept within the horizons of political possibility, which effaces the precise ideological trajectory of Syrian nationalism under the Baathists and its specific intellectual heritage. My investigation in this chapter is intended to clarify that ideological lineage, so that we do not lose sight of what specific forms of thought shaped the regime.

I do not mean to suggest that Arabism or pan-Syrian identity is entirely lost to the region, but rather that such ideological trends are emphatically distinct from the muscular Baathist identity cult and its political ideologies. The nationalist claims of the Baathists were perhaps most accurately observed by Yahya Sadowski, who wrote that in the regime's view, "[people should not be seen as] Arabs, Muslims, or socialists, but as Syrians—citizens of a state called Syria, a country distinct from Lebanon and Iraq, who as a result share common interests and a common culture."[30] As such, Baathist ideologues only ever gave at most lip service to the broader pan-Syrian and pan-Arab ideologies of their contemporaries. With the understanding that a specific Arab ethnic concept, or a broader regional identity, was *not* the core concept of the Baathist state, rather Arabism was instrumentalized by the Baaathist regime for survival and legitimacy purposes. As such, the use of Arabism in official discourse cannot but be perceived as part of the social constructs employed by the regime to bring together Syria's diverse population into a cohesive national identity. This ideological and cultural discourse, as I will describe in the following sections, was grounded in the eighteenth- and nineteenth-century European Romantic view of national affiliation as the foundational demarcation of a "people." These philosophies carried with them important assumptions about privileged identities and behaviors, including the importance of passionate, muscular masculinity in the shaping and preservation of the national community.

## The Syrian "founding fathers" and the forging of the nation

Al-Husri, Aflaq, and al-Arsuzi have for many years been celebrated by the Baathist Party as the primary founders of Syrian secular nationalism. These thinkers hailed from widely different ethnic and religious communities—al-Husri was born into a wealthy Ottoman Muslim family and was the son of a prominent government official; Aflaq was from a middle-class, Orthodox Christian background and from an early age was active in communist politics; and al-Arsuzi was from an Alawite family with a well-established tradition of resistance against Ottoman rule. Perhaps the most central thread tying together the biographies of these diverse theorists is that they each studied in French schools during their youth and were exposed to the French nationalist ideology. At the time (around 1890–1930), education in Syria was profoundly influenced by colonial powers, and attending European universities was considered the peak of social accomplishment by a certain segment of Middle Eastern intellectuals. Both Aflaq and al-Arsuzi lived in Paris for several years and studied at the Sorbonne, while al-Husri was educated in French and Turkish in Constantinople.[31] These formative educational experiences are presumably part of the reason why they each demonstrated such a sustained and profound interest in nineteenth-century European thinkers throughout their later writings.

A few previous scholars have noted the surprising extent of European influences in the work of these Syrian nationalist thinkers. Paul Salem, for example, concluded in a general manner that the early Baathists had "a devotion to the emanation of the spirit of modern Western nationalism."[32] Writing in 1971, William Cleveland likewise approvingly stated that al-Husri's nationalist concepts were "drawn mainly from nineteenth century European thinkers … [al-Husri] himself was largely a man of French culture and outlook."[33] However, this observation has been ignored or downplayed by the majority of commentators on the Baathist regime, who as discussed in the previous section tend to lump the Party together with Arabist thought and/or pan-Syrian movements. The early Baathist writers themselves (especially Aflaq) were sometimes less than forthcoming about their influences—it would not have been seemly in the postcolonial moment to openly present their theories as representing nineteenth-century European viewpoints.

The concept of a unified national culture that al-Husri, Aflaq, and al-Arsuzi discovered in French and German thinkers was especially pertinent to their ambition to forge a sense of pragmatic and emotional solidarity among Syria's diverse population. As other scholars have noted, this particular European Romantic concept of the national community as a "people" or a "family" was a novel invention of the eighteenth and nineteenth centuries, and was distinct from other concepts of the polity that can be found in previous eras and other geographic contexts.[34] For the Baathist founders, the idea that the modern nation itself could be the locus of passionate identity seemed compelling as a salve or a replacement for Syria's internal ethnic and sectarian tensions. The Syrian thinkers struggled, however, with some of the Europeans' views of the nation as a biological or primordial group into which one is born, a view that was particularly prominent in Herder and Fichte. This "organic" concept of the nation emphasized the centrality of language, race, long-standing cultural traditions, and historical attachment to the "soil" or land, most of which was viewed as being an involuntary heritage.[35] The desired Syrian nation had few such commonalities, other than a widely shared familiarity with the Arabic language, to which the Syrian nationalists gave much attention. For the most part, these Syrian thinkers veered away from racialized concepts of the nation and instead gravitated toward the thinking of the French political philosopher Renan, who argued for a form of Romantic nationalism in which one's passionate attachment to the community is voluntarily chosen or "willed" into being.

Renan's view, which was predominant in post-revolutionary France, overtly rejected the notion of historical language, race, or culture as the basis for belonging to the nation, and instead argued that individuals had sovereign choices and agency about what polity they wanted to join. However, Renan concurred with other European Romantic thinkers in emphasizing that bonds of affection and the passionate struggle to forge a shared community was the central basis of governance. In this outlook the nation was viewed more like a "chosen family" rather than a "birth family," and Renan even emphasized that it might be necessary for individuals to reject or forget aspects of their past in order to join the nation and cultivate solidarity.[36] Essentially, where Herder and Fichte viewed the nation as organically preceding the state and finding its realization through the state, Renan argued that the nation, as a common identity, was not brought into being until after the state was formed. As such, the nation was derivative of the political state and dependent upon it—individuals came together to voluntarily forge a state, and through that vigorous effort they eventually developed a shared national culture and identity.

Tensions between the primordial and voluntary views of the Romanticized nation were a central preoccupation of the Syrian "founding fathers," and as I will show in later chapters, these ideological conflicts were never really resolved in Baathist discourse, continuing up to the current day. While nominally Renan's view of the chosen or voluntary nation informed the philosophical conclusions of the Syrian founders, the felt imperative to establish and then preserve the nation against dissent and alternative authorities meant that the Baathists were continuously seeking to add more primordialism, essentialism, or necessity into their national discourse. This, I will argue, is one of the reasons why reductive, Romanticized concepts of gender became so prominent under the regime. While the diverse ethnic and religious landscape of Syria offered substantial resistance against imagining a homogeneous national identity, the concept of muscular national masculinity was not directly threatening to preexisting power structures and could therefore serve as a shared foundation for national affiliation. Al-Husri's infatuation and struggle with the concepts of primordialism and volunteerism in European national thought was the starting point of this trajectory in Syria. His writings then later influenced Aflaq and al-Arsuzi, and through them the later direction of the Baath Party and its governing institutions.

## The emergence of Syrian secular nationalism: Sati al-Husri

The influence of al-Husri's outlooks on Syrian society can be traced back to his prominent role in the newly established Syrian state after the fall of the Ottoman Empire. After working for King Faisal I during that monarch's brief, British-sponsored reign in Syria in 1920, al-Husri went on to become a dean of the Faculty of Law at the University of Baghdad. During the 1940s, near the end of the French Mandate, he returned to serve as the Syrian Minister of Education where he oversaw the development of a new curriculum oriented toward instilling a sense of national identity.[37] Al-Husri placed a strong emphasis throughout his career on the role of historical knowledge as a means of promoting national consciousness, publishing more than twenty books on the subject. He considered educational institutions to be a primary path of spreading his nationalist ideology, and took a strong interest in the way history was taught in Syrian schools.[38] In his writings he vigorously analyzed and debated the foundations of national identity, and nearly all of his intellectual references for this topic were European philosophers in the German and French schools of thought. Al-Husri's primary rhetorical approach was to adopt a question-and-answer format to frame his conceptual screeds, asking, for example: "What is a nation?" "What are the main characteristics that distinguish nations from each other?" "What are the main factors that make certain groups of people feel that they are one nation?"[39] Al-Husri then answered these questions with his own unique perspective, which combined primordialist and volunteerist outlooks in interesting ways.

Al-Husri's central concept was that the nation is formed in two stages—the first is a gradual evolutionary process through which a shared language and history emerges, and the second is a "conscious" stage in which these shared social features are recognized, embraced, and institutionalized via the will and determination of individuals who have selected their historical affiliations. In one passage, for example, he writes: "What a beautiful nation, that has achieved national unity, and completed its political identity, and that has managed to make its political borders the same as its national ones."[40] In much of his writing, al-Husri reflected the "organic" view of the nation promoted by Herder and Fichte, focusing strongly on the significance of a common language:

> The foundations for creating the nation and nationalism are the unity of language and history. This is because unity in these two factors paves the way for unity of feelings and inclinations, unity of sufferings and hopes, unity of culture and traditions—thus making the people feel that they are the sons of one nation, distinguished from other nations.[41]

In numerous such passages, al-Husri overtly adopted Herder's argument that the internalization of language affects one's manner of thinking and one's way of being in the world. In his influential 1928 lecture on the "Elements of Nationalism" (*'Awāmel al-Qawmiyya*), he stated that "This section is taken from Herder and … it is very influential to what we believe," before going on to directly translate phrases such as "the tribal core" that Herder had used to characterize a linguistic national community.[42] In another passage from the same lecture, al-Husri argued that:

> Language is the most influential spiritual tie which binds mankind together.
>
> First, it is the means of mutual understanding among individuals. In addition, it is the instrument of thought … Finally, language is the means for transmission from ideas and acquired knowledge from fathers to sons, from ancestors to descendants. The language with which man grows up melds his thought in a special manner just as it deeply influences his sentiments as the language which the individual listens to since childhood is the language of the mother, it is these childhood lyrics that influence his sentimental identity. Therefore, it is found that unity of language establishes a kind of unity of thought and feelings which binds individuals with a long and interconnected series of intellectual and sentimental ties. Within this context, we can say that language is the strongest tie that binds individuals with groups.[43]

This excerpt foregrounds al-Husri's essentialist view of language transmission, rooted in familial rearing, echoing Herder's conception of language's pivotal role in preserving national distinctiveness amid conflict, subjugation, and oppression.

Al-Husri's dialogues with Herder further manifest in the concept of a unique national character, sculpted through the recreation of history, positing each individual as a "folk-character"—a mirror of "national culture." It becomes incumbent, therefore, to conserve and perpetuate this national character across generations. Herder articulates this notion, asserting:

> As a mineral water derives its component parts, its operative powers, and its flavor from the soil through which it flows, so the ancient character of peoples arose from the family features, the climate, the way of life and education, the early actions and employments that were peculiar to them. The manners of the fathers took deep root and became the internal prototype of the race.[44]

Herder's words illuminate the intrinsic, often involuntary, affinity to the nation, affirming that the singularities of national identity are engendered by the immutable attributes of each nation, perpetuated and intensified through racial and environmental lineage. Nonetheless, while al-Husri assimilated Fichte's and Herder's linguistic and cultural underpinnings of national identity, he eschewed the premise that racial purity or environmental factors are prerequisites for nation formation. In this vein, al-Husri refutes Herder's postulation, aligning instead with Renan's counter-argument against the feasibility of forging a uniform national identity predicated on race and environment.[45]

The implicit gendering in al-Husri's narrative is noteworthy—associating the "transmission of ideas" and "knowledge" with paternal communication, juxtaposed with the "sentiments" attributed to maternal influence. The nuances and origins of such gender constructs within early Syrian intellectual thought will be further explored in subsequent chapters.

It is imperative to underscore the degree to which al-Husri's conception of the nation is steeped in Romanticism, reflecting a profound appropriation of the perspectives and lexicon from European Romantic thinkers of the eighteenth and nineteenth centuries. One of the points that I want to make emphatically here is the extent to which al-Husri adopted a Romantic concept of the nation, in the sense of directly borrowing views and terminology from the eighteenth- and nineteenth-century European Romantic thinkers. From a Middle Eastern perspective, what is novel in this language (e.g., the "tribal core" of the nation, or its "unity of sufferings and hopes," as cited in the above paragraphs) is how it foregrounded affective, emotional ties to the modern state and conflated the nation with one's family or community—a sense of direct emotional and personal attachment that was not present, for example, in the Ottoman Empire. In some passages al-Husri went so far as to anthropomorphize the nation, describing it as "a living being, with life and feeling: life through its language and feeling through its history."[46] Such rhetoric elevates the nation into something beyond a mere social institution or political power structure, aligning it with the most intimate aspects of felt human experience and personal relationships.

It is not a coincidence that al-Husri gravitated toward the concept of language—rather than race, ethnicity, or religion—as a main part of the primordial glue holding this Romantic sense of the nation together. Whereas German thinkers such as Herder moved fluidly among these various primordialist concepts, it would have been difficult in Syria to argue for a shared ethnic or religious continuity, and doing so would have raised the question of why the new nation did not follow in the contours of preexisting tribal or religious authorities. Thus, shared language became al-Husri's focus of attention. He rejected the concept of race and argued that nations were held together by "psychological and spiritual kinship" rather than "blood relations."[47] The centrality of shared language as the origins of national kinship was repeated insistently throughout his numerous works:

> Every Arab-speaking people is an Arab people. Every individual belonging to one of these Arabic-speaking peoples is an Arab. And if he does not recognize this, and if he is not proud of his Arabism, then we must look for the reasons

that have made him take this stand … Under no circumstances should we say: "If he does not wish to be an Arab, and is disdainful of his Arabness, then he is not an Arab." He is an Arab regardless of his own wishes. Whether ignorant, indifferent, undutiful, or disloyal, he is an Arab.[48]

The persistent echo of Herder's intellectual legacy in al-Husri's writings is not a mere scholarly oversight; rather, it is a deliberate and conscious act of intellectual engagement. A meticulous examination of al-Husri's oeuvre affirms the recurrence of Herderian ideas.[49] Al-Husri, fully aware of this intellectual lineage, nonetheless laid claim to these conceptualizations as originally his own—an act of intellectual audacity that Tibi has incisively critiqued, observing that al-Husri "gives a number of quotations from Herder's writings and comes to the conclusion that he was a pioneer of the idea of the nation adopted by al-Husri himself."[50]

In his treatment of history, al-Husri's delineation of a unified historical consciousness mirrors Herder's formulation of cultural identity.[51] According to al-Husri, the fabric of the nation is woven from the threads of collective memory. He elucidates, "Unity of history gives rise to shared feelings … It leads to common memories of bygone exploits and past misfortunes, and to mutual faith in the awakening and to mutually shared hopes for the future … Every nation feels its self-consciousness and creates its personality by means of its special history."[52]

Here, the importance of history is articulated through its uniqueness, and while al-Husri's constructivist approach resonates with Herder's vision of history as a "chain of traditions,"[53] and Fichte's notion of constructing a particular national identity through historical narrative,[54] it also reflects Renan's emphasis on the necessity of "forgetting" certain historical aspects to craft a national identity.[55] Al-Husri's selective historical lens underscores an ideological alignment with Renan.[56] More particularly, al-Husri clarifies what he means of history as not the one "recorded in books and buried between the pages of manuscripts" but, rather, the history "which lives in the minds and which possesses traditions."[57] This conception bears a striking similarity to Benedict Anderson's portrayal of the nation as an "imagined community."[58] Al-Husri advocates for a selective historical narrative that crafts a constructed memory, one that is discursively imagined and invented, fostering belief in the nation through the veneration of "our glorious past."[59] While such a notion of a heroic past is not solely the purview of Herder or Fichte,[60] and even Renan acknowledged it, al-Husri's focus on selective memory and the process of forgetting particular historical elements underscores his ideological borrowings from Renan, thus aligning with Renan's constructivist perspective of the nation as a collective bound by a "common destiny."[61]

Al-Husri's ruminations on language and history as conduits for "cultural survival continuity" extend into discussions on nurturing national consciousness and instilling an ethos of unyielding sacrifice for the nation.[62] Here, the ideological lineage traces back to Fichte, whose radical nationalist sentiment al-Husri openly admires, proclaiming, "Fichte is an extreme enthusiastic nationalist thinker ... [and] the following quotes is what I want to include in my theorization."[63] Fichte envisions education as a "moral agent" that ingrains in individuals the requisite will "to act in accordance with the unconditional duties that have both as moral agents and as members of the German nation."[64] Fichte posits a bifurcated model of national education, marked by an initial phase of strict discipline, which evolves into a developed sense of communal responsibility; in his words education encompasses two stages, the first "of which was characterized by disciplinarian submission and the second by the development of a sense of autonomous responsibility for the community."[65]

In the initial phase of educational development, the emphasis is placed on fostering a "love for order that intensifies to an ideal," achieved through the strategic implementation of a disciplinary framework.[66] This foundational stage is not an end in itself but a precursor to cultivating a disposition of obedience to societal norms. Such early internalization of structure and discipline is instrumental in equipping individuals for the subsequent phase of their educational journey, which is marked by a cultivated willingness to make the ultimate sacrifice for the nation. This transition reflects a pedagogical strategy where the formative imposition of order serves as the groundwork for instilling a profound sense of national duty and allegiance.[67]

In his intellectual trajectory, al-Husri's appropriation of Fichte's philosophy is evident in his approach to education, which he views as a conduit for inculcating a sense of obedience and collective order. Drawing from Fichte's insights, al-Husri advocates a transformative reformation of national education aimed at extirpating selfish tendencies and instead fostering a readiness for selfless sacrifice through military service. Al-Husri identifies excessive self-regard as the most pernicious threat to the nation, contrasting it with the virtues of "altruism" and "sacrifice."[68] In "Speeches and Reflections upon Arab Nationalism," al-Husri articulates the role of education as a mechanism for reinforcing a cohesive national identity and inculcating societal morality.[69]

Al-Husri delineates a bipartite structure for national education, positing the formative years in school as the first critical phase, followed by military service as the second, pragmatic stage. Within the scholastic environment, described in "Speeches on Education and Society,"[70] al-Husri envisages the school as a microcosmic "big society" where the foundational elements of "morality" and "order" are imparted to the child, thereby shaping their character.[71] Delving further into pedagogical strategies in "Views and

Discussions upon Pedagogy and Education," he emphasizes the cultivation of "sociability" as a pivotal trait in forging national identity.[72] Embracing Fichte's dichotomy of theoretical and practical stages of education, al-Husri posits the school as the crucible for embedding principles of order and idealism. This period of intellectual and moral formation sets the groundwork for the subsequent phase of practical application, where, after internalizing a profound devotion to the nation, individuals stand prepared to engage in the ultimate act of sacrifice for their country as epitomized by military conscription. In this schema the school's role is paramount, instilling not just knowledge but shaping the ethos of the child, thereby ensuring that the ensuing call to national service is answered with unwavering commitment and patriotism.[73]

The emphasis on "Arabness" in passages such as this locates al-Husri alongside other pan-Arabist thinkers of his time (more so than Aflaq, al-Arsuzi, or the later Baathists, as discussed below). However, whereas other Arabists such as Nasser centered the pragmatic project of transnational political unification across the Middle East, the topic that most concerned al-Husri was the formation of a conscious, Romanticized identity that could supersede attachments to tribe or religion. Al-Husri's persistent focus on the Romantic or personal aspects of Arabness made his views more amiable to later Baathist thinkers who split with Nasser and advocated for a specific Syrian national, rather than regional, identity.

Despite his efforts to locate a shared primordial identity in Arabic language and history, al-Husri also regularly returned to the view that the nation would dissipate, or fail to achieve its political consciousness, without the continuous determination of its people to choose their national affiliation over competing interests. Volunteerism and political choice, he argued, are key components of the second, "conscious" stage of nation-building, in which a specific polity embraces its shared heritage and decides to implement and maintain political institutions and borders.[74] In this sense, al-Husri's thought shows more of the influence of Renan, as he openly recognized that the history and contours of the nation were selectively constructed as an act of imagination and discourse, requiring the "forgetting" of some aspects of history and identity and the active embrace of others. The failure to affirm such kinship and achieve national consciousness was, in al-Husri's view, entirely possible, and as such the "national character" needed to be constantly inculcated and reinforced. He argued that belief in the nation's history and common destiny (*al-maseer al-mushtarak*) should be one of the goals of education, as it was not inherently known by the people. (The term "common destiny," which al-Husri used often in his descriptions of national consciousness, is itself most likely borrowed from the writings of Renan.)[75]

Al-Husri's view that Syrians had a shared primordial identity, but that they might fail to consciously recognize or institutionalize it without "assistance," led to some troubling practical implications. Not only did he tend to view education as a process of indoctrination—what we might call the "forced forgetting" of contrary identities—but he also consistently advocated militarism and universal male conscription as an integral part of this educational process. Al-Husri expressed admiration for the German thinker Fichte on this account, citing Fichte's discussion of militarism as the subordination of personal aspiration to the national need and the merging of individual and national consciousness. Accordingly, al-Husri called for education in Syria to emphasize selflessness, martial sacrifice, and love for the nation, and he argued that young men should be able to move smoothly from the schoolhouse to the military barracks.[76]

In this manner, the volunteerism or chosen/"willed" aspects of the nation that al-Husri took from Renan sit very uneasily with his regular turns toward inescapable or involuntary identity. The French revolutionary tradition that linked the application of "will and determination" to democratic governance and the explicit consent or choice of the governed was not entirely agreeable to al-Husri, as he believed that without top–down influences, Syrians would likely fail to achieve his desired national consciousness and would instead gravitate toward tribal and sectarian identities. This tension between voluntary and involuntary belonging in the nation was further troubled by the fact that, despite his emphasis on education and national service, al-Husri remained rather hazy about the exact features of his desired political state, its institutions, or its geographical scope. As I will show in the following sections, this left an opening for later theorists whose ideas were much more politically concrete to leverage al-Husri's influence and cultural preoccupations to suit their own ambitions.

## Michel Aflaq's political passion

The second primary "founding father" of Baathist thought is Michel Aflaq, whose prominence in Syrian politics began to take shape about twenty years after al-Husri's. Born into a middle-class Christian family in Damascus, Aflaq studied at the Sorbonne, where he was exposed to the still-influential philosophies of the Germanic and French nationalist traditions. He returned to Syria in 1932 equipped with strong political ideas about the future of the region. Aflaq was one of the founders of the Baath Party and was elected as the Party leader during its first congress in 1947.[77] His Syrian nationalist writings drew persistently from the work of al-Husri, while evincing a much more pragmatic focus on the active consolidation of political power.

In effect, Alfaq served as a bridge between al-Husri's philosophical concept of the unified Romantic Arab nation and the political realization of the Baathist Party apparatus and state institutions in Syria.

Given the anti-colonial political context in which Aflaq formulated his ideology, it is perhaps unsurprising to find that his voice was rather strident and that he consistently emphasized the need for an impassioned military struggle against imperialism. While al-Husri was relatively open about his European influences, Aflaq disavowed any attraction to Western philosophy and theory, preferring to represent his views as indigenous. At the same time, however, Aflaq more fully consummated the Romantic strain in al-Husri's writings, by almost entirely rejecting rational analysis and political moderation. In his view such analytical and transactional approaches "strip things of their flesh and blood, and rob them of color and taste."[78] Aflaq emphasized that to him, nationalism was a form of "faith" and "love," experienced primarily in the heart or the emotions, and in true Romantic fashion, he declared that such feelings of national sentiment precede all knowledge and reason. Compared to al-Husri's didactic writings, Aflaq's outlooks were conveyed in a profoundly different tone, and they foregrounded an approach to nation-building that was based more in action rather than rational discourse.

Accordingly, Aflaq's words are often flowery and passionate, and even at the height of his influence, they were regularly criticized as lacking in substance.[79] In pursuit of the ideal of Baathism (which can be translated as "awakening" or "resurrection"), Aflaq called on his generation to renounce the drudgery of everyday life. He stated that the tension between aspiration and reality must be resolved, "Either by deadening the urge for the mission and the genuine aims, by acquiescing to facile reality and surrendering to it—or by moving the forces that respond to the aspiration of the nation to realize the genuineness of its existence!"[80] Fundamentally, these words convey the ideas of enthusiasm and force for regenerating society through the Baathist message of rebirth and action. Later in the same passage, Aflaq described the need to move out from "the realm of sentimental and inactive wistfulness" and into "a combative interaction with the will, forces, and vital interests" of the historical moment.[81]

Aflaq's mystical way of approaching nationalism tends to obscure his intellectual sources; nonetheless, his grounding in the Romantic rhetorical tradition is highly discernable. The most prominent influence is likely Fichte, with whom Aflaq shared a preoccupation toward a renewed "heroic" era of passionate conflict. In this discourse, the nation is viewed as an entity that has fallen from a glorious past and is in need of rousing itself from its current indignity. In an article titled "The Age of Heroism," Aflaq described this recovery from a fallen state: "Now we close a page of weakness from our history and open a new one ... A page full of patriotism and heroic action!"[82] Similarly, in a speech delivered in 1943, Aflaq stressed the necessity of renewing the glorious past: "We should remove the barriers of inertia and decadence and restore our inherited glorious blood. We should purify our land and sky to elicit the souls of our heroic ancestors."[83] These phrases are almost identical to Fichte's discussions of the need to "restore" the heroic German spirit, which he diagnosed as having become lost from its national identity and independence, and therefore "sunk into an existence of a lower order."[84]

The Germanic message of national loss and renewal was highly salient in Syria during Aflaq's rise to political prominence in the 1940s and 1950s, particularly after the humiliating defeat of Syrian forces during the 1948 Arab–Israeli War. Aflaq argued that Syrians must form a more unified and militarily powerful state or they would always remain a diminished people:

> Brethren, at times when waves of pessimism and defeatism increase as do calamities and disasters, the true Arabs feel that the day of salvation is approaching, for the road has been opened at last for our psyche to be shaken, to be deeply moved so that we remember ourselves and our task, and rise with alacrity, vitality, and faith![85]

Again mirroring Fichte, Aflaq wrote that the nation's leader—by which he meant himself, in his role as the head of the incipient Baathist Party—should not pander to the masses or make compromises, but instead forge and implement a persuasive nationalist vision: "The leader, in times of weakness of the 'idea' and its constriction, is not one to appeal to the majority or to a consensus, but rather seeks opposition and enmity ... He is not an ingatherer, but a unifier. In other words, he is the master of the singular idea."[86]

In all of these passages, the specific concept of the modern state or party is suffused with a sense of personal identity and purpose, even to the extent of providing "the day of salvation." A Romantic attachment to "the idea" is regarded as taking precedence over ordinary political concerns, negotiations, or policies.

In contrast to al-Husri's complex discussion of volunteerism and the need to achieve national consciousness, Aflaq simply assumes that the national identity is already known and internalized, and that it only needs to be acted upon. In this sense, he takes a strongly primordial view, even bringing back concepts such as "blood" and "purity" that al-Husri had overtly rejected.[87] For example, in his early essay "Nationalism Is Love Before Anything Else" (*al-qawmiyya hub qabl kul shay'*), Aflaq described the involuntary attachment to the nation as a form of Romantic passion and as the "highest" expression of human life. As was the case with

Herder and especially Fichte, his primordialist language was suffused with concepts of sacrifice and heroism:

> Nationalism is like every love ... And love is associated with sacrifice, and thus with nationalism. The sacrifice for nationalism leads to heroism, for the one who sacrifices for his nation and its glorious past and for the happiness of its future, is perfecting life in its highest image ... He who loves does not ask for reasons.[88]

In the same essay, Aflaq continues on to explain that love of the nation is transmitted genetically from parents to children, a process that he compares to the inheritance of physical features.[89] This intrinsic bond of affection, grounded vaguely in the presumed historical essence or "spirit" of the nation (a concept that was also borrowed from the German thinkers) is presented as a driving metaphysical force strengthening the will to achieve unity.

Aflaq's emotive rhetorical style and primordialist outlook continued to be a driving influence throughout the early Baathist era as the Party took control of the Syrian state and established its hegemony. For example, in a 1966 speech he stated:

> The doctrinal movement cannot grow if it ceases to have a bond with its heritage and its past. This does not mean that we should stand still with regard to the past, but that we should have a living and conscious link with it in a way that realizes the unity of the party, its trajectory, and the soundness of its orientation.[90]

This argument, which was presented as a rebuttal to other Party members whom Aflaq viewed as overemphasizing socialist theory at the expense Romantic nationalism, highlights the extent to which the primordialist view continued to motivate Aflaq's political outlooks in his leadership role. Throughout his career, he persistently returned to mythopoetic imagery of the nation's journey from a fallen state to resurrection, inevitably to be achieved through shared experiences of conflict and adversity. In one speech titled "Arabism and Suffering" (al-'urūba wa al-'alam), he went so far as to state that nationhood can *only* be experienced through "struggle and pain."[91] In this outlook the active physical struggle basically came to stand in for the role of education and "consciousness" in al-Husri's works—that is, the primordial national spirit achieves its fulfillment and expression not merely through greater historical awareness and choice but through action and combat:

> We should not forget that Arab culture in the past was not possible and could not have been realized had it not been for that period of struggle that lasted for a few decades. But it was the spiritual yeast, the psychological and moral treasure that permitted the Arabs to expand.[92]

The more pragmatic direction of Aflaq's thought compared to al-Husri's was part and parcel of his position as the leader of a revolutionary Party, and Aflaq's references to Arabism were persistently linked to how that concept could be applied toward legitimizing and supporting the Party's activities. While Aflaq was the most primordialist of the thinkers discussed here, he was also the most concerned with obtaining and applying institutionalized political power.

### The modernist vision of Zaki al-Arsuzi

The political philosopher Zaki al-Arsuzi was born into an Alawite family—a religious minority that was marginalized under the Ottoman Empire, but that would prove to be highly influential within the Baathist regime. Al-Arsuzi's father was for a while imprisoned for political activism against the Ottomans, and this family experience was a primary factor that shaped the younger al-Arsuzi's nationalist passion and ideologies.[93] Like the other Baathist founders, however, al-Arsuzi also lived in France for several years and studied at the Sorbonne, where he was exposed to the Romantic nationalist currents that were prevalent in European intellectual circles. He returned to Syria in 1930, almost precisely contemporary to Aflaq, and took a teaching position in which he incited the ire of the French Mandate authorities due to his anti-colonial pedagogies. Al-Arsuzi is less broadly known than al-Husri and Aflaq—perhaps because his work displayed neither the authoritative pedagogical strength of al-Husri's writings nor Aflaq's ardent and flowery rhetoric. However, despite his more pragmatic outlook, al-Arsuzi was very influential within the ideological circles of early Syrian nationalism, and is sometimes credited with coining the term "Baath" as the Party name.[94]

Over the course of his life and writings, al-Arsuzi introduced into the Baathist worldview a relatively greater emphasis on democracy and participatory politics. Of the three Syrian thinkers discussed here, he was the most profoundly influenced by Renan's volunteeristic view of the nation. This emphasis on civics and democracy led to him being relatively marginalized in the Party after it came under the control of Hafez al-Assad in the 1960s. However, al-Arsuzi was never fully out of favor, and his work has continued to exert an influence on the shape of the Baathist ideology up to the present time.[95] Al-Arsuzi's outlooks demonstrate an interesting trajectory in which his youthful interest in the primordial nation was quickly tempered by more civic-oriented perspectives as the actual Baathist state came into existence—an intellectual transition that many of his contemporaries, including Aflaq and Assad, did not make.

In the earliest phase of his writing, al-Arsuzi's approach to the concept of the nation was similar to al-Husri's, showing a strong emphasis on the primordial ideal of shared language and viewing the nation in essentialist terms, almost as a metaphysical being. Al-Arsuzi also adopted a similar discursive tone to al-Husri's, presenting the nationalist passion in a didactic style. For example, during his early period al-Arsuzi wrote that:

> The terms nation ['*umma*] and mother ['*umm*] derive from the same root, and the mother is the living image of the nation. And like the subjects of society, is the mother with her sons; and above all, the nation is the fountainhead of customs and public institutions. And by public institutions we mean language, literature, art, and other things that represent public life.[96]

In early texts such as this, al-Arsuzi clearly defined the experience of belonging to the nation as involuntary, and he occasionally veered into the racialized concepts that al-Husri abjured. For example, in one passage he conflated the world's linguistic groupings with racialized identities, and argued for the "genetic greatness" of Arabs in comparison to other groups—concepts that appear to be lifted directly from Fichte and translated into the Syrian context.[97] In line with such beliefs, al-Arsuzi was very much against racial intermarriage, and he contributed to the Baathist prohibition on Syrian women transmitting their citizenship to children they had with non-Syrians.[98]

To his credit, al-Arsuzi reconsidered many of these views in his later work. Following the rash of military coups and political discord that plagued Syria and other Middle Eastern states during the postcolonial era, he came to believe that a homogeneous cultural identity was not the ideal basis for national unity. He came to overtly reject this concept and made it plain that a primordial national identity was simply a myth, adopting instead Renan's view that the nation's existence is based on people's collective will and their determination to live together. For example, in this later period he argued that: "Because the state represents the identity of a mature society ... The task of the state is to take care of its citizens and raise their national consciousness to the level of freedom; this awareness will lead the citizens to participate voluntarily in public affairs."[99] The terminology used by al-Arsuzi in these later writings is notable—unlike al-Husri or Aflaq, he came to regularly use the term "citizen" (*muwāten*) as a political concept. Furthermore, while his work shows a persistent, al-Husri-influenced emphasis on education as a tool to instill national pride and transmit values, al-Arsuzi did not associate this education with militarism or passion but rather with the cultivation of rational faculties and civic responsibility.[100]

Al-Arsuzi's rejection of the primordial Arab identity that al-Husri occasionally gestured toward can be viewed as part of the overall consolidation of Baathism into a specific state- or Party-centered ideology in Syria. In light of his close association with Aflaq, Assad, and other Baathist ideologues, al-Arsuzi reflected their orientation toward the conceptual primacy of the regime or Party, and at times he continued to use emotive phrases such as "family" to refer to this construct. At the same time, however, he sought to temper this rhetoric with a more inclusive and democratic vision of the citizenry. In one notable passage he openly described these concerns as well as the shift that had occurred in his own thought:

> As far as the role of love is concerned, it brings together various individuals and communities. When I came back from Paris I had a racial [Arabist] orientation in my feelings of brotherhood, but this feeling exists in all human beings ... When I reached the stage in which the divisive limits between individuals and communities fall, I became a refuge for everyone and strived for our highest ideal to establish a state that would guarantee its citizens freedom and dignity, be they Armenians, Kurds, or Turks.[101]

Notably absent from this passage, and from most of al-Arsuzi's work, is any rhetoric linking the concept of love to martial sacrifice or physical heroism. It is also strongly relevant to my argument to note his phrasing "When I came back from Paris I had a racial orientation." Al-Arsuzi himself, in this passage, associates the influence of primordialist concepts of national identity with his time spent in European schools.

Al-Arsuzi's later thought was not a complete break with Romantic nationalist outlooks, nor with hierarchical concepts, as he continued to promote views of cultural superiority. However, he conflated these views with civic concepts in a complex fashion, for example writing in one passage:

> The principle of nationalism is based on: (1) Fraternity and brotherhood by nature and the proximity of descent [qarāba bi l-nasab] ... but this is not restricted to racial kinship only, for there is kinship in culture and superiority. Therefore, the nation is not only an extension of the family, but also a larger human construction. (2) The nation is also derived from the principle of common interests. (3) The nation is also derived from solidarity.[102]

A somewhat bumbling attempt to navigate or reconcile conflicting nationalist ideologies can be seen in this material, as al-Arsuzi continues to give upfront deference to the primordialist concept, then quickly tempers it through civic-oriented language. Despite such lingering nods to the fraternal nation, the conceptual directions taken by al-Arsuzi are significant, because he was the first Baathist thinker to introduce foundational concepts of democracy and civic choice. While al-Husri and Aflaq were fundamentally preoccupied with the idea of the nation as a primordial community, al-Arsuzi's later works were devoted mostly to discussions of policy issues and the everyday social and political problems faced by citizens.

Finally, in accordance with this book's larger themes, it would be remiss to ignore the gendered language as it is used persistently even in al-Arsuzi's relatively civic-minded writings. As can be seen in the previous quotations, such language appears to float to the foreground whenever the discourse turns toward Romantic and primordialist ideals, in which the national community is inevitably viewed as a "brotherhood" (*'ikhwa*) and its active members as "sons" (*abnā'*). The civic role of women in these passages is quite obscure, and we will have to look in more detail to ascertain what views these Baathist founders held of women and gender, and the philosophical origins and applications of those outlooks. This question is the topic of the following chapter, in which I analyze how specific concepts of gender were leveraged by the early Baathists as a foundational aspect of the "glue" holding together their nationalist ideal.

## Notes

1 See Frank Salameh. *Language, Memory, and Identity in the Middle East: The Case for Lebanon*. Plymouth: Lexington Books, 2010; Partha Chatterjee. *Nationalist Thought and the Colonial World: A Derivative Discourse*. Tokyo: Zed Books, 1986; Colin Liddell. "The Uses and Abuses of Arab Nationalism: White Nationalist Lessons from Brown Nationalist Failure." *Alternative Right*, February 8, 2015. http://alternative-right.blogspot.com/2015/02/the-uses-and-abuses-of-arab-nationalism.html. Accessed July 10, 2016; Kanan Makiya. *Republic of Fear: The Politics of Modern Iraq*. Berkeley, CA: University of California Press, 1998; and Michel Saba'. *S'ādeh wa Aflaq fī l-Fikr al-Siyāsī l-Orthodoxī*. Beirut: Manshūrāt 'Āfāq Jāmi'iyya, 2005, p. 270.
2 See Craig Calhoun. *Nationalism: Concepts in the Social Sciences*. Buckingham: Open University Press, 1997; Hugh Seton Watson. *Nations and States: An Enquiry into the Origins of Nations and the Politics of Nationalism*. London: Methuen, 1977; and Anthony D. Smith. *Theories of Nationalism*. London: Duckworth, 1983.
3 See Carlton J. H. Hayes. *Historical Evolution of Modern Nationalism*. New York: The Macmillan Company, 1949; Elie Kedourie. *Nationalism*, edited by W. A. Robson. Second edition. London: Hutchinson, 1961; and Anthony D. Smith. *The Concept of Social Change: A Critique of the Functionalist Theory of Social Change*. London: Routledge, 1973.
4 See Ida Blom, Karen Hagemann, and Catherine Hall (eds). *Gendered Nations: Nationalism and Gender Order in the Long Nineteenth Century*. Oxford: Oxford International Publishers, 2000, p. 3.
5 See Smith 1983; Anthony D. Smith. *National Identity*. Reno, NV: University of Nevada Press, 1991; Benedict Anderson. *Imagined Communities: Reflections on the Origin and Spread of Nationalism*. New York and London: Verso, 2006; Ernest Gellner. *Conditions of Liberty: Civil Society*

*and Its Rivals*. London: Hamish Hamilton, 1994; Ernest Gellner. *Language and Solitude: Wittgenstein, Malinowski and the Habsburg Dilemma*. Cambridge, MA: Cambridge University Press, 1998; John Breuilly. *Nationalism and the State*. Manchester: Manchester University Press, 1993.
6 Alexander J. Motyl. "Traditional Political Theory and Nationalism." In *Encyclopaedia of Nationalism: Fundamental Themes*, edited by Alexander J. Motyl. Oxford: Elsevier Science and Technology, 2000.
7 Ibid.
8 Johann G. Herder. *Herder: Philosophical Writings*. Translated and edited by Michael N. Forster. Cambridge: Cambridge University Press, 2002, p. 379.
9 Anthony Smith. *Nationalism*. Oxford: Oxford University Press, 1994, p. 47.
10 Robert Adamson. *Fichte 1852–1902*. Edinburgh: Blackwood, 1881.
11 Johann Gottlieb Fichte. *Addresses to the German Nation*. Translated and edited by Gregory Moore. Cambridge: Cambridge University Press, 2008.
12 Smith 1983, p. 17.
13 See Adeed Dawisha. "Nation and Nationalism: Historical Antecedents to Contemporary Debates." *International Studies Review* 4, no. 1 (Spring 2002): 3–22, p. 7.
14 Ernest Renan. "What Is a Nation?" Lecture at Sorbonne University, Paris, March 11, 1882. Translated by Ethan Rundell. http://ucparis.fr/files/9313/6549/9943/What_is_a_Nation.pdf. Accessed June 12, 2013.
15 Ibid.
16 Ibid.
17 Ibid.
18 For more on pan-Syrianism, see Azmi Bishara. *Syria 2011–2013: Revolution and Tyranny before the Mayhem*. London: I.B. Tauris, 2021, p. 8.
19 Nuanced discussions of pan-Arabism can be found in: Ernest Dawn. "The Rise of Arabism in Syria." *Middle East Journal* 16, no. 2 (1962): 145–68; Muhammad Muslih. "The Rise of Local Nationalism in the Arab East." In *The Origins of Arab Nationalism*, edited by Rashid Khalidi, pp. 167–85. New York: Columbia University Press, 1991; and Eliezer Tauber. *The Formation of Modern Syria and Iraq*. London: Frank Cass, 1995.
20 See Raymond A. Hinnebusch. "Modern Syrian Politics." *History Compass* 6, no. 1 (January 2008): 263–85, p. 265; and Eyal Zisser. "The 'Struggle for Syria': Return to the Past?" *Mediterranean Politics* 17, no. 1 (2012): 105–10, p. 192.
21 Frank Salameh. "The Enigma of the Syrian Nation." *The National Interest*, March 11, 2013, p. 18. http://nationalinterest.org/commentary/the-enigma-the-syrian-nation-8204. Accessed February 15, 2015.
22 Yahya Sadowski. "The Evolution of Political Identity in Syria." In *Identity and Foreign Policy in the Middle East*, edited by Shibley Telhami and Michael Barnett, pp. 137–54. Ithaca, NY, and London: Cornell University Press, 2002, p. 147.
23 Hinnebusch 2008, p. 265.
24 Christopher Phillips. *Everyday Arab Identity: The Daily Reproduction of the Arab World*. London and New York: Routledge, 2013, p. 9. Some

*The writings of al-Husri, Aflaq, and al-Arsuzi*  55

additional examples of this tendency include Dawn 1962, p. 150; James L. Gelvin. "The Social Origins of Popular Nationalism in Syria: Evidence for a New Framework." *International Journal of Middle East Studies* 26, no. 4 (1994): 645–61, p. 650; Muslih 1991, p. 147; and Tauber 1995, p. 427.
25 Thomas Collelo (ed.). *Syria: A Country Study*. Washington, DC: Library of Congress, 1987, p. 20. See also Daniel Pipes. *Greater Syria: The History of an Ambition*. Oxford: Oxford University Press, 1992.
26 Eyal Zisser. "Who's Afraid of Syrian Nationalism? National and State Identity in Syria." *Middle Eastern Studies* 42, no. 2 (2006): 179–98, p. 196.
27 Bishara 2021, pp. 170–200.
28 See, for example, Badr al-Dein Aroudky. "The Syrian National Identity between Problematic and Ambiguous." Harmoon Centre for Contemporary Studies, November 2, 2020. https://2u.pw/5ZVy84. Accessed December 20, 2021.
29 Damascus Centre for Research, www.dcrs.sy.
30 Sadowski 2002, p. 148.
31 For a more detailed biography of Sati al-Husri, see Bassam Tibi (ed.). *Arab Nationalism: A Critical Enquiry*. Second edition. Translated by Marion Farouk-Sluglett and Peter Sluglett. London: Palgrave Macmillan, 1990. For Michel Aflaq's biography, see Norma Salem-Babikian. "Michel Aflaq: A Biographic Outline." *Arab Studies Quarterly* 2, no. 2 (1980): 162–79; and for Zaki al-Arsuzi, see Keith D. Watenpaugh. "'Creating Phantoms': Zaki al-Arsuzi, the Alexandretta Crisis, and the Formation of Modern Arab Nationalism in Syria." *International Journal of Middle East Studies* 28, no. 3 (1996): 363–89. https://doi.org/10.1017/s0020743800063509; and Rahaf Aldoughli. "Revisiting the Ideological Borrowings in the Syrian Nationalist Narratives: Sati 'al-Husri, Michel Aflaq, and Zaki al-Arsuzi." *Syria Studies* 8, no. 1 (2016): 7–38..
32 Paul Salem. *Bitter Legacy: Ideology and Politics in the Arab World*. Syracuse, NY: Syracuse University Press, 1994, p. 49.
33 William L. Cleveland. *The Making of an Arab Nationalist: Ottomanism and Arabism in the Life and Thought of Sati' al-Husri*. Princeton, NJ: Princeton University Press, 1971, p. 85.
34 See Anderson 2006, pp. 273–90; and Blom, Hagemann, and Hall (eds) 2000, p. 3.
35 Herder was particularly enthused by the restoration of a perceived historical German culture and language and argued that one's language defined patterns of thought and ways of being. Although his concept of the nation was defined in racial terms, Herder himself did not argue that one race was superior to another, only that each race should adhere to their own distinctive language, culture, and territory, resulting in a diverse and variegated world (see Herder 2002, p. 379). Unfortunately, in subsequent years other German thinkers such as Fichte developed this view into the perspective that the German nation was culturally superior to others and should pursue political and territorial domination.
36 Renan 1882.

37 Sami Moubayed. *Men and Women Who Shaped Syria 1900–2000*. Seattle, WA: Cune Press, 2006, pp. 437–39.
38 See James F. Goode. *Negotiating for the Past: Archaeology, Nationalism, and Diplomacy in the Middle East, 1919–1941*. Austin, TX: University of Texas Press, 2007, p. 199.
39 Sati Al-Husri. *Mā hiya al-qawmiyya? Abhāth wa Dirāsāt 'ala dhaw' al-ahdāth wa al-nazariyyāt*. Beirut: Dar al-'ilm li l-malāyīn, 1959, p. 31; Sati Al-Husri. *'Abhāth mukhtarah fi al-qawmiyyah al- 'arabiyya*. Volume 1. Beirut: Markaz Dirāsāt al-Wahda al-Arabiyya, 1985a, pp. 15–16.
40 Sati Al-Husri. *Difā'an 'an al-'urūba*. Beirut: Markaz Dirāsāt al-Wahda al-Arabiyya, 1985d, p. 7.
41 Sati Al-Husri. *'Abhāth mukhtāra fi al-qawmiyyah al-'arabiyya*, Volume 1. Cairo: Dar al-ma'ārif, 1964a, p. 249.
42 Sati Al-Husri. "*'Awāmil al-qawmiyya*" (1928). *Free Arab Voice*, January 19, 2010; Sati Al-Husri. *Mā hiya al-qawmiyya? Abhāth wa Dirāsāt 'ala dhaw' al-ahdāth wa al-nazariyyāt*. Beirut: Dar al-'ilm li l-malāyīn, 1959, pp. 55–56; cf. Herder 2002, p. 143.
43 Al-Husri 1928, p. 21.
44 Hayes 1949, p. 30; Frederick M. Barnard. *Herder's Social and Political Thought*. Oxford: Clarendon Press, 1965, p. 58.
45 al-Husri 1928; Mohammed el-Atrache. *The Political Philosophy of Michel Aflaq and the Ba'th Party in Syria*. Michigan: Xerox University Microfilms, 1976, p. 26.
46 Al-Husri 1985a, p. 63.
47 Al-Husri 1928, p. 20; cf. Renan 1882.
48 Al-Husri 1928. This passage is also translated and discussed in Adeed Dawisha. *Arab Nationalism in the Twentieth Century: From Triumph to Despair*. Princeton, NJ: Princeton University Press, 2003, p. 72. Compare with Herder's statement that: "Whoever was raised in the same language, who poured his heart into it, and learned to express his soul in it, belongs to the nation of this language" (Herder 2002).
49 Sati Al-Husri. *Muhadarāt fi nushu' al-fikrah al-qawmiyya*. Cairo: Mataba'at al-Risāla, 1951, pp. 43–5, 66–78; Al-Husri 1959, pp. 7–11, 14, 19, 23, 53.
50 Bassam Tibi. *Arab Nationalism: Between Islam and the Nation-State*. London: Macmillan Press, 1997, p. 146.
51 John Hutchinson. *Dynamics of Cultural Nationalism: The Gaelic Revival and the Creation of the Irish Nation-State*. London: Allen and Unwin, 1989, p. 13; John Hutchinson. "Cultural Nationalism and Moral Regeneration." In John Hutchinson and Anthony D. Smith (eds), *Nationalism*, pp. 122–31. Oxford: Oxford University Press, 1994, p. 122; Friedrich Meinecke. *Cosmopolitanism and the National State*. Translated by Robert B. Kimber. Princeton, NJ: Princeton University Press, 1970, p. 29; Smith 1983, p. 22.
52 Al-Husri 1985a.
53 Tibi 1997, p. 129.

54 Gottlieb Fichte 2008, pp. 50–51.
55 See Renan 1882.
56 Sati Al-Husri. *'Ārā' wa 'ahādīth fī l-tārīkh wa l-ijtimā'*. Beirut: Markaz Dirāsāt al-Wahda al-Arabiyya, 1985c, pp. 23–33.
57 Al-Husri 1928.
58 See Anderson 2006.
59 Sati Al-Husri. *'Āra' wa 'ahādīth fī 'l-tarbīya wa l-ta'līm*. Cairo: Mataba'at al-Risāla, 1944, p. 147.
60 Hutchinson 1989, p. 13; Smith 1983, pp. 21–22.
61 Ernest Renan. 1982. What Is the Nation? http://ucparis.fr/files/9313/6549/9943/What_is_a_Nation.pdf. Accessed December 13, 2012.
62 Yasir Suleiman. *The Arabic Language and National Identity*. Washington, DC: Georgetown University Press, 2003, p. 13.
63 Al-Husri 1959, pp. 59, 61.
64 Thomas Hippler. *Citizens, Soldiers and National Armies*. London and New York: Routledge, 2006, p. 172.
65 Ibid., p. 159.
66 Johann Gottlieb Fichte. *Addresses to the German Nation*, edited by G. A. Kelly. New York and Evanston, IL: Harper and Row, 1968, pp. 28–29.
67 Ibid., pp. 148–50.
68 Al-Husri 1985a, p. 117.
69 Sati Al-Husri. *'Āra' wa 'ahādīth fī l-qawmiyya l-'arabiyya*. Fourth edition. Beirut, 1964b, p. 57.
70 Sati Al-Husri. *'Ahādīth fī l-tarbiya wa l-ijtimā'*. Beirut: Markaz Dirāsāt al-Wahda al-Arabiyya, 1984, p. 15.
71 Ibid., p. 20.
72 Al-Husri 1944, p. 50.
73 Al-Husri 1985a, p. 450.
74 Al-Husri 1928.
75 Al-Husri 1944, p. 147; cf. Renan 1882.
76 Al-Husri 1959, p. 59; Al-Husri 1985a, p. 117; and Al-Husri 1964b, p. 57. Cf. Gottlieb Fichte 1968, pp. 148–50.
77 Moubayed 2006, p. 131.
78 Michel Aflaq. "*Al-Qawmiyya hub qabla kul shay'*." 1940a. http://albaath.online.fr/Volume%20I-Chapters/Fi%20Sabil%20al%20Baath-Vol%201-Ch30.htm. Accessed February 2014.
79 See Fouad Ajami. *The Arab Predicament: Arab Political Thought and Practice since 1967*. Cambridge: Cambridge University Press, 1982, p. 27; and Kanan Makiya. *Republic of Fear: The Politics of Modern Iraq*. Berkeley, CA: University of California Press, 1998, p. 201.
80 Michel Aflaq. "*Al-ma'raka bayn al-wujūd al-sathi wa al-wujūd al-asīl*." 1955a. http://albaath.online.fr/Volume%20II-Chapters/Fi%20Sabil%20al%20Baath-Vol%202-Ch38.htm. Accessed February 2014.
81 Ibid.

82 Michel Aflaq. "*'Ahd al-būtūla.*" 1935. http://albaath.online.fr/Volume%20I-Chapters/Fi%20Sabil%20al%20Baath-Vol%201-Ch01.htm. Accessed February 2014.
83 Michel Aflaq. "*Fī thikrā al-rasūl.*" 1943a. http://albaath.online.fr/Volume%20I-Chapters/Fi%20Sabil%20al%20Baath-Vol%201-Ch33.htm. Accessed February 2014.
84 Gottlieb Fichte 2008, pp. 115–16.
85 Michel Aflaq. "*Ma'nā al-risāla al-khālida.*" 1950a. http://albaath.online.fr/Volume%20I-Chapters/Fi%20Sabil%20al%20Baath-Vol%201-Ch26.htm. Accessed February 2014.
86 Michel Aflaq. "*Al-jīl al-'arabi al-jadīd.*" 1944. http://albaath.online.fr/Volume%20I-Chapters/Fi%20Sabil%20al%20Baath-Vol%201-Ch36.htm. Accessed February 2014. Cf. Gottlieb Fichte 2008, p. 105.
87 See Michel Aflaq. "*Fī thikrā al-rasūl.*" 1943a. http://albaath.online.fr/Volume%20I-Chapters/Fi%20Sabil%20al%20Baath-Vol%201-Ch33.htm. Accessed February 2014; cf. Al-Husri 1928.
88 Michel Aflaq. "*Al-Qawmiyya hub qabla kul shay'.*" 1940a. http://albaath.online.fr/Volume%20I-Chapters/Fi%20Sabil%20al%20Baath-Vol%201-Ch30.htm. Accessed February 2014.
89 Ibid.
90 Michel Aflaq. "A Speech to the Branches of the Syrian Region." 1966. http://albaath.online.fr/English/Aflaq-04-on%20heritage.htm. Accessed February 2014.
91 Michel Aflaq. "*Al-'urūba wa al-'alam.*" 1956a. http://albaath.online.fr/Volume%20II-Chapters/Fi%20Sabil%20al%20Baath-Vol%202-Ch22.htm. Accessed February 2014.
92 Michel Aflaq. "The Party of Radical Change." 1949. http://albaath.online.fr/English/Aflaq-04-on%20heritage.htm. Accessed February 2014.
93 Watenpaugh 1996, p. 365.
94 Michael Curtis (ed.). *People and Politics in the Middle East: The Arab–Israeli Conflict: Its Background and the Prognosis for Peace*. New Jersey: Transactions Publishers, 1977, p. 42.
95 Dalal Arsuzi-Elamir. "Nation, State, and Democracy in the Writings of Zaki al-Arsuzi." In *Nationalism and Liberal Thought in the Arab East: Ideology and Practice*, edited by Christoph Schumann, pp. 66–91. Abingdon: Routledge, 2010, p. 67; Saba' 2005, p. 270.
96 Zaki al-Arsuzi. *Al-Mu'allafāt al-Kāmilah*. Volume II. Damascus: Matābi' al-'Idāra al-Siyāsiyya, 1973, p. 213.
97 Ibid., p. 214; cf. Johann Gottlieb Fichte. *Reden an die deutsche Nation*. Berlin: Zentral- und Landesbibliothek Berlin, 1808, p. 20.
98 For example, Zaki al-Arsuzi. *Baath al-'umma al-'arabiyya wa-risalatuha ila l-'ālam: Al-madaniyya wa-l-thaqāfa*. Damascus: Dar al-Yaqaza al-'Arabiyya, 1954, pp. 15–33.

99 Zaki al-Arsuzi. *Al-Mu'allafāt al-Kāmilah*. Volume IV. Damascus: Matābi' al-'Idāra al-Siyāsiyya, 1974, p. 27.
100 For example, al-Arsuzi 1954, pp. 15–33.
101 Zaki al-Arsuzi. "*Mafhūm al-'insāniyyia fi 'alāqatihā bi-mafhūmay al-'umma wa-l-qawmiyya.*" In *Al-Mu'allafāt*. Volume VI. Damascus: Matābi' al-'Idāra al-Siyāsiyya, 1975, pp. 153–54.
102 al-Arsuzi 1973, pp. 213–16.

# 2

# The centrality of gender constructs in early Syrian nationalist narratives

As elucidated in the preceding chapter, Sati al-Husri, Michel Aflaq, and Zaki al-Arsuzi stand as pivotal theorists in the Baathist Syrian context, each engaging with variations of Romantic nationalism, heavily influenced by their European educational backgrounds. Drawing intellectual inspiration from German and French political philosophers such as Johann Herder, Johann Fichte, and Ernest Renan, these Syrian ideologues crafted their unique and intricate perspectives on Syrian national identity. Their treatises and philosophical doctrines continue to be extensively published and incorporated into the educational curriculum in Syria.

However, a critical inquiry arises concerning the role of gender constructs within these emergent nationalist narratives. An analysis of the writings of these influential Baathist theorists reveals three interlinked gender-centric themes. Firstly, there is a discernible analogy equating the national community to a traditional patriarchal family, delineating specific public roles and relationships for women and men. This stark association of the familial archetype with the state and broader society marks a departure from the Ottoman era and other regional paradigms, representing an import from European Romantic thought alongside other nationalist ideologies. Secondly, the prevalent use of gendered terminology in these texts, referencing the national community and active party members with terms like "brothers" (*'ikhwa*), "men" (*rijāl*), and "young men" (*shabāb*), implicitly marginalizes women by exclusion, relegating them to a passive role. This linguistic choice narrows the scope of women's participation in the national narrative. Finally, the pervasive "muscular" concept in these foundational writings, which valorizes fervent martial engagement as the pinnacle of national virtue and the epitome of solidarity, inherently marginalizes women's involvement.[1] Ultimately, these constructs collectively manifest within the national ideal, forging an archetype of the superior, "willful" man, emblematic of the nation's quintessence both domestically and militarily. This conceptualization not only reinforces gender disparities but also cements a singular, masculinized narrative of national identity and valor.

## Al-Husri: men as the guardians of language and culture

In the theoretical framework of al-Husri, language assumes a central role in delineating the essence or the "soul of the nation," as well as in establishing its parameters of inclusivity and exclusivity.[2] Al-Husri posits that a nation is fundamentally a cultural construct that evolves organically from familial units. This naturalistic perspective on the genesis of nations underscores an inherent, nonelective affiliation with one's nation. The pivotal role of language in cultivating a national identity invites scrutiny into al-Husri's gendered interpretation of linguistic functions.

Al-Husri's theory about the national language can be distilled into four key propositions: firstly, as the quintessential embodiment of the "soul of the nation"; secondly, as an instrument safeguarding the nation's cultural ethos during wartime; thirdly, as a determinant of the nation's political and cultural frontiers, fostering unity among Arab nations through the promotion of Standard Arabic and the curtailment of dialectal variations; and fourthly, as a guardian of national heritage, epitomized as the language of patriarchs.

From its inception, al-Husri's nationalistic ideology is imbued with a gendered comprehension of national affection and allegiance. His ideological stance firmly establishes a paradigm for defining "love" toward the nation (*'umma*) and the fatherland (*waṭan*), where al-Husri analogizes national love with familial affection. This primordial love is likened to a child's devotion to their mother.[3] However, this conceptualization of national love morphs into a compelled, naturalistic sentiment, crafting propaganda about the ideal masculine image. Crucially, national love becomes a vehicle for legitimizing sacrificial death for the nation, interwoven with gendered notions of national membership.

The intricate nexus between notions of patriotic allegiance and masculinity is further elaborated in al-Husri's conceptual framework of social kinship. Al-Husri posits that the crux of kinship (*qarāba*) and lineage (*nasab*) transcends mere blood relations, pivoting instead on the belief in such connections. He argues that "the important thing about *qarāba* and *nasab* is not blood relations, but rather the belief in this relation."[4] He asserts that "spiritual kinship" is cultivated through a convergence of language, history, and education.[5] Nevertheless, while eschewing the racial and ethnic genesis of the nation, al-Husri portrays the nation as a "brotherhood" and a "fraternity of descendants from one father."[6] He maintains that the irrelevance of racial origins in defining the nation is substantiated by his advocacy for intermarriages.[7] Although these perspectives imply a nation culturally forged and sustained via language and intermarriages, al-Husri overlooks the pivotal role of women as guardians of the nation's cultural identity through these unions. Consequently, while intermarriages underscore women's role in demarcating national racial boundaries, al-Husri's depiction of the nation remains predominantly as a "fraternity" and a "brotherhood," founded on fraternal solidarity (*'ikhwān*).[8]

Moreover, al-Husri elucidates the necessity of a singular national language, characterizing it as "a mere requirement for men to contribute politically to the nation."[9] Such views underscore the inextricable link between language and nationalism, integral to the modernization of both the political and social spheres.[10] However, al-Husri perceives this connection primarily in the context of the public domain. Notably, al-Husri ascribes significance solely to the utilization of language within state mechanisms for the establishment and propagation of the national language. This perspective conspicuously omits the vital role of the domestic sphere in replicating language with equal efficacy. Paradoxically, while neglecting the role of women in this linguistic preservation, he asserts that the foremost objective is to promulgate the national language through state apparatus.[11]

As language forms a cornerstone in al-Husri's nation-building ideology, he articulates his discontent with the prevalent use of colloquial Arabic (*al-'arabiyya al-'āmiyya*), arguing that its widespread adoption has fragmented and diluted the sense of national cohesion among Arab nations. Al-Husri advocates for the elevation of Standard Arabic via state machinery,[12] emphasizing the need to bolster the role of "intellectual men" in adopting this linguistic style.[13] His argument overlooks the criticality of minimizing colloquial Arabic in domestic contexts, predominantly managed by women. Significantly, his perspective reveals a discernible bias against women's intellectual contributions to Arabic literature and language of his era.[14]

Al-Husri often emphasized the crucial role of standard Arabic in preserving national heritage, linking it to the cultural and literary legacy of the nation's "fathers" (*'ābā'*) and "grandfathers" (*'ajdād*).[15] In line with his focus on language as a defining element of community, it is vital to observe the gendered nomenclature employed in his discourse on patriotic belonging and unity. For instance, when depicting the nation as a vulnerable, passive entity in need of protection, al-Husri consistently used maternal, nurturing, and communal metaphors (*'umma*). In contrast, when portraying the nation as a bastion of pride, strength, and territorial sovereignty, he predictably referred to it as the "fatherland" (*watan*).[16]

As previously discussed, al-Husri dismissed the notion of race or "blood relations" as the cornerstone of national kinship (*qarāba*), advocating instead for a familial model of the nation grounded in shared cultural, linguistic, and educational ties.[17] While this approach removed racial/ethnic paradigms from his ideology, thus fostering a more inclusive national identity in that regard, al-Husri did not extend similar inclusivity in terms of gender. He consistently imbued the concept of national belonging with gendered connotations, frequently referring to active members of the movement as a "brotherhood" (*'ikhwān*). Additionally, al-Husri closely associated linguistic and cultural cohesion with formal education experiences and the necessity for common frameworks in public affairs. He presupposed that this public and educational sphere comprised predominantly authoritative male figures, starkly differentiating it from the "natural school" of domesticity and maternal care. Despite acknowledging mothers' role in transmitting language to offspring, al-Husri's perspective relegated women's agency in education to the realm of imparting "sentiments," as opposed to "knowledge."[18]

Continuing this exploration of al-Husri's ideologies, it is imperative to consider his treatment of gender roles within the broader context of national identity formation. Al-Husri's conceptual framework appears to entrench traditional gender norms, particularly in the sphere of language transmission and national identity. The dichotomy he establishes between the public and private spheres not only reinforces gender binaries but also implicitly suggests a hierarchy where the public, male-dominated domain is given precedence over the private, female-centric domain. This perspective problematically marginalizes the role of women in the nation-building process, despite their integral involvement in cultural and linguistic transmission within the family unit. Al-Husri's focus on the public sphere and its male-centric dynamics in the propagation of national language and identity reveals a significant oversight in his conceptualization of nationhood. The relegation of women to a secondary role in the national narrative not only reflects a gender bias but also overlooks the potential contributions of half the population in the shaping of national consciousness and cultural continuity.

Furthermore, the critical analysis of al-Husri's theories necessitates an understanding of the historical and cultural context in which they were formulated. The early twentieth century, a period marked by significant political and social transformations in the Arab world, influenced al-Husri's thinking. His emphasis on a unified language and a cohesive national identity can be seen as a response to the colonial and postcolonial challenges faced by Arab nations. However, this historical context does not mitigate the gendered limitations of his approach. By prioritizing a masculine conception of nationhood and overlooking the multifaceted roles women play in the cultural and educational realms, al-Husri's ideology fails to encapsulate the full spectrum of national identity. This gendered bias in his theorization not only constrains the understanding of national identity to a patriarchal framework but also inadvertently perpetuates the marginalization of women's roles in both the public and private spheres. To fully grasp the complexities of national identity, it is essential to recognize and integrate the diverse contributions of all genders, acknowledging that the fabric of nationhood is woven from a multitude of threads, each vital to the integrity and richness of the national tapestry.

In his oeuvre, al-Husri exhibits a notable dearth of engagement with the discourse on gender roles, effectively sidelining the presence and contributions of women. This gender bias is evident in his presumptive address to a male readership and his consistent emphasis on the experiences and narratives of men within the nationalist movement. For instance, in the preface to the second edition of his work, "Pages of the Recent Past" (*Safahāt Min al-Mādi al-Qareeb*), al-Husri explicitly states that the republication of his book would be particularly beneficial "to the young men (*shabāb*) of the present and to the mature men (*rijāl*) of the near future."[19] This language conspicuously underscores al-Husri's intent to foster a sense of collective identity predominantly through masculine terminology, thus aligning the audience of his national discourse squarely with a male demographic. Al-Husri articulates the concept of a shared national history as a catalyst for collective emotions and perspectives, fostering communal recollections of historical struggles and triumphs, alongside a collective belief in a national renaissance and shared aspirations for the future. He posits that this:

> gives rise to shared feelings and views. It leads to collective memories of bygone exploits and past hardships, and to a mutual faith in the awakening and to mutually shared hopes for the future ... Every nation feels its self-consciousness and creates its personality by means of its special history.[20]

This conceptual framework, however, is marred by a gendered limitation, as it intertwines the notion of a glorious present and future with the empowerment and mobilization of men, urging them to cultivate a "spirit of sacrifice and victory" while eschewing sentiments of "discontent, despair, and surrender."[21] The subsequent glorification of martyrdom and sacrifice, as exemplified by male valor, equates national allegiance with physical prowess.[22] This approach reveals al-Husri's envisioning of nationalism as deeply intertwined with the construction of an idealized masculine figure within the nation. To the discerning reader, it becomes evident that al-Husri perceives the nation's attainment of glory as synonymous with the male realization of manhood and masculinity. He argues:

> The man loves the nation under the influence of nationalism, and his heart is attached to it severely, and considers himself part of it, so he becomes happy whenever its glory increases, and suffers if its strength reduces. He aspires to see it strong and developed, and be proud of its glories (*'amjād*) ... and tends to do whatever can be done to defend its existence and its dignity. Besides, the man loves his fatherland (*watan*) under the influence of patriotism ... and seeks to serve it, and does not delay to sacrifice his soul for its sake.[23]

*The centrality of gender constructs* 65

These remarks significantly equate the nation's majesty (*majd*) with a man's fervent love for his country. Al-Husri further postulates that such patriotic and nationalistic sentiments are not only spiritually akin but also comparable to maternal affection.[24] Al-Husri's conceptualization of a "special history" epitomizes a curated historiographical method, wherein selective historical events are meticulously chosen and chronicled within the national consciousness to foster a sense of patriotic identity. This approach to history, culturally engineered and predicated on a mosaic of collective experiences—both pain and joy—prompts an incisive examination into the mechanics of this national narrative construction.[25] Central to this inquiry is the interrogation of the discursive processes through which this national narrative is shaped and propagated. Additionally, it necessitates a critical evaluation of the inclusivity of this narrative, particularly probing the extent to which women's experiences and contributions are integrated or marginalized within this national historiography. This scrutiny unveils the potential biases and omissions in the national historical record, thus challenging the comprehensiveness and representativeness of the national identity as envisioned in al-Husri's framework.

Such representations of national love mirror the dynamics of subordination and coercion prevalent in traditional man–woman relationships. Al-Husri contends that this blend of nationalistic and patriotic love is instrumental in kindling the desire for sacrifice and commitment to national rejuvenation and unity: "We must remember that the nationalist idea enjoys a self-motivating power; it is a driving impulse to action and struggle. When it enters the mind and dominates the soul, it is one of the forces which awakens the people (*al-sha'b*) and inspires them to sacrifice." These expressions convey an overtly gendered portrayal, conceptualizing national membership through the lens of physical sacrifice and struggle. This raises the critical question: who exactly are the "people" (*al-sha'b*) implied to embody the traits of "action" and "struggle"? Furthermore, al-Husri's use of the term "young men" (*shubbān*) reinforces the notion of male superiority as the sole bearers of national faith. This juxtaposition between the affirmation of nationalistic conviction and the capacity for self-sacrifice in the national struggle consequently delineates the parameters of belonging within this ideological framework.[26]

Al-Husri's discourse is deeply imbued with a conviction in the inherent virtue of national faith and patriotism. He posits that the paramount obligation for patriots is to elevate the love of nation above personal self-interest. Al-Husri contends that the most formidable adversary to the nation is not external forces but rather an excessive self-love, which stands in stark contrast to the ideals of "altruism" and "sacrifice."[27] However, the resolution to this perceived "selfishness" proposed by al-Husri warrants critical examination. Advocating for absolute national devotion and a profound love for the nation, al-Husri identifies national education as the sole mechanism for cultivating, disseminating, and fortifying national consciousness. He fervently asserts the transformative power of national education in engendering a generation imbued with national pride.

Echoing the broader trends in his oeuvre, al-Husri's narrative conspicuously omits the mention of women. In his advocacy for the revival of historical grandeur through the establishment of a heroic contemporary ethos, the discourse predominantly accentuates the spiritual and martial struggles of men (specifically, *shabāb* and *rijāl*) in their quest for pride and dignity, and their resistance against sentiments of "despair and surrender." This psychological odyssey, as articulated by al-Husri, is intimately linked to an engagement with Romantic nationalism.[28] The pursuit of an efficacious masculine identity and "strength of character" (*rūh ma'nawiyya*) in al-Husri's works is consistently correlated with martial prowess and militarism: "soldiers, officers, and commanders train themselves to have the spirit of courage, of sacrifice ... and, most especially, the spirit of patriotism."[29]

In his treatises, al-Husri recurrently equates the readiness to combat for the nation and partake in martial valor with the authentic realization of manhood. As elucidated in a subsequent work:

> The young man [*shāb*] loves the community under the influence of nationalism, and his heart is strongly attached to it, and he considers himself part of it, and so he becomes happy whenever its glory increases, and suffers if its strength decreases ... He does whatever can be done to defend its existence and its dignity. The man loves his fatherland [*watan*] under the influence of patriotism ... and he does not delay in sacrificing himself for it.[30]

Al-Husri further delineates a dichotomy between vigorous, heroic masculinity and the pitfalls of dissipation, weakness, decadence, and "selfishness" (*'anāniyya*), which he asserts lead individuals toward self-indulgence. In contrast, nationalism, according to al-Husri, implores a man to dedicate himself to his fatherland and to expend all his energies in service and sacrifice for the nation. In his own words: "nationalism asks the man to love his fatherland, and to serve his nation with all his vital force and to sacrifice everything for its sake!"[31] Al-Husri reiterates this ethos in another publication: "When it [nationalism] enters the mind and dominates the soul, it is a force that awakens the young men [*shabab*] and inspires them to sacrifice."[32] This fixation on fostering masculine vitality or willpower is a recurring motif in al-Husri's extensive body of work.

Throughout his theoretical framework, al-Husri's legacy in formulating a militarized interpretation of culture, history, and education perpetuates hegemonic narratives of physical strength. The symbiosis of militarism and nationalism in his national ideology fosters a solidarity rooted in masculinity among the "brothers" (*'ikhwān*) of the nation. This masculinist paradigm, expounded in al-Husri's national ideology, was subsequently echoed and reinforced in Baathist ideology, rendering al-Husri's doctrines pivotal for comprehending the entrenchment of gender bias in the Syrian context.

In delving deeper into al-Husri's conceptualization of national identity, one notes a conspicuous absence of discourse surrounding women and their role in the fabric of nationalism, willpower, or character strength. This lack of engagement necessitates a more discerning analysis to unearth the underlying assumptions al-Husri held regarding women's roles within his nationalistic framework. A pivotal aspect of this analysis lies in scrutinizing the gendered lexicon al-Husri employs, particularly when he addresses involvement in educational and military spheres:

> The role of these two institutions [the school and the military] ... have many similarities. The first takes the child from the family, and pledges to bring up the individual nationally, socially, and educationally. However, the second [the military] takes the young man from his environment and makes him socialize with other men who are prepared to serve and defend their nation.[33]

In this context, al-Husri's selection of language is notably indicative. He employs inclusive lexicon such as "the child" and "the individual" when discussing national schools, yet markedly shifts to "young men" (*shabāb*) when referring to military service, which he perceives as the quintessence of national unity. This semantic transition highlights a gender-specific viewpoint, distinguishing educational inclusiveness from the uniquely masculine sphere of military involvement. Further elaborating on the nexus between militarism and masculinity, al-Husri expounds:

> [Military training] is a life of activity and fatigue. It strengthens the spirit of young men's activity and movement, and gets them familiar with the roughness of life, and develops their endurance of hardship. More importantly, it develops their manhood [*rujūlatuhum*] ... and the spirit of leadership that the nation needs most.[34]

In another of his works, al-Husri reiterates the importance of military training in creating bonds across different ethnicities, yet his vision does not extend to the inclusion of women in this paradigm of unity:

> The soldier lives, during military service ... with a group of the sons of his fatherland who are from different towns and classes and who hold various beliefs and positions. He lives with them in a system in which they are included without discrimination. He does not live there with the intention of returning to his original personality or of being confined to his family and a life centered in his village. On the contrary, he works for a purpose which is loftier than all

of these ... Is there a need to clarify the seriousness of the psychological and educational effects that occur as a result of these circumstances?[35]

Such gendered presuppositions, characteristic of the era, reveal al-Husri's lack of foresight in envisioning an inclusive role for women within his nationalist schema. His focus on men's heroic acts and the cultivation of masculine vigor was instrumental in shaping a gender-biased military ethos in Syrian society, perpetuating the marginalization and restrictions imposed on women under Baathist governance.[36]

Furthermore, al-Husri's perception of muscular nationalism is evident in his discourse on social hierarchies and professions:

> Every nation, from a social perspective, is composed of three basic classes. The first is the general people [*sawād al-nās*], the public. The second is the upper class, the elite, composed of men [*rijāl*] who run the affairs of the nation and have great influence on conducting these affairs, either through government positions or by virtue of scientific, social, or economic status ... The third class is composed of men [*rijāl*] who occupy a middle status in comparison with the general public and the higher class.[37]

In this delineation, al-Husri employs neutral terminology to describe the most extensive social class but adopts masculine language when referring to the elite and middle classes. This linguistic pattern subtly reinforces a hierarchy where women are implicitly confined to the lower social echelons, with little opportunity for advancement or recognition. Similarly, in his discussions on professional training, al-Husri underscores the significance of educating young men in various fields critical for national progress, conspicuously excluding women from this narrative. The only reference to women in this context is a cursory critique of mothers potentially hindering their sons' pursuit of higher education.[38] While al-Husri advocates for broadening women's education, he envisages this education as confined to traditional domestic skills such as cooking and sewing.[39] Thus, al-Husri's vision of national family predicates women's participation in the public sphere while maintaining, or even reinforcing, their subordinate roles and limited spheres of influence. This approach not only mirrors but also perpetuates societal norms of gender inequality, positioning women as peripheral participants in the national narrative, devoid of significant agency or influence in shaping the nation's future.

## Aflaq: the idealized man of passion

Michel Aflaq's political philosophy has been extensively scrutinized as a seminal influence on the formulation of Syria's political structure.[40] His approach to nationalism, imbued with a militant ethos, is most insightfully unraveled through an analytical dissection of the nationalistic motifs and language present in his seminal text, *Fi Sabeel al-Baath* (Toward the Resurrection). This examination entails a meticulous analysis of Aflaq's extensive array of public lectures, articles, and speeches, spanning the period from 1930 to 1980. The evaluation of his corpus also involves an assessment of the intended recipients of his message. Consequently, this study seeks to elucidate the following inquiries: In what manner did Aflaq endeavor to situate himself in relation to his audience? And what kind of political community was he endeavoring to forge?

In contextualizing Aflaq's rendition of nationalism, his oratory and writings consistently project an image of manhood as the quintessential embodiment of the ideal human. This militant brand of nationalism Aflaq advocates is markedly fixated on exalting the archetype of the man characterized by fervent action. Aflaq's rhetoric, particularly in his early and profoundly influential essay "The Age of Heroism" (*ahd al-butūla*), extols the virtues of "great men"—those imbued with unwavering patriotism and valor, who are primed to spearhead the tangible struggle for Syrian liberation.[41] Aflaq commences this discourse with the proclamation: "Now we close a page of weakness from our history and open a new one ... A page full of patriotism and heroism."[42]

In a subsequent article disseminated a year later, Aflaq further delineated the qualitative disparity between the "revolutionary men" within the Party and those outside its ambit. He postulated that the "nobility of soul" inherent in the superior man of action constitutes the "treasure of life" (*tharwat al-hayāh*), bestowing upon existence its profound significance.[43] Through this narrative, Aflaq constructs a pronounced hierarchical distinction between men who successfully actualize their legitimate masculine identity via martial endeavors, and those who are deficient in such noble character traits or valor.

Another salient aspect of Baath ideology is its dependency on the dynamism and zeal of youth, particularly young men (*'indifā' al-shabāb*).[44] In a distinct discourse, Aflaq articulates a synergistic bond between the nation and its men, stating: "between our nation and our men, there is chemistry, appointment, and a meeting." In a more explicit exposition of this perspective in 1955, Aflaq avows that the activism and fervor of men are indispensable to the nation: "They are the rescuers." This focus on the activism, impulsiveness, and assertiveness of men transcends mere utilitarianism in Aflaq's philosophy. Indeed, his writings often suggest that the construction of masculinity holds as much significance as the construction of the nation itself, as underscored by his repetition of the sentiment: "between our nation and our men, there is a chemistry, an appointment, and a meeting."[45]

Aflaq's conceptualization of manhood is imbued with a distinct definition, underpinned by fundamental attributes (*sifāt 'asāsiyya*) that he deems crucial for delineating men's national allegiance. He accentuates the exalted stature of the nation's heroic past, urging men to not only identify with this illustrious history but also to integrate its essence into their contemporary and future endeavors. More significantly, Aflaq envisages a particular national and moral orientation in these men toward their nation.[46] It is noteworthy that Aflaq's discourse is overtly directed at men, prompting an exploration into how he perceives the sense of belonging and the requisite moral disposition these men should exhibit toward their nation.

In delineating the contours of national belonging, Aflaq underscores the imperative of preserving cultural and traditional legacies. In his oration "Abstract Thinking" (*al-tafkīr al-mujarrad*),[47] Aflaq assigns paramount importance to the role of men in safeguarding the heritage of the nation, conspicuously neglecting the contributions of women in the perpetuation of Arab culture. Moreover, Aflaq is invested in fostering an emotional foundation for the nation, predicated upon the fervent love men harbor toward it.

This approach by Aflaq effectively situates men at the epicenter of national identity and cultural conservation, implicitly relegating women to a peripheral status in the national narrative. The emphasis on masculine emotional connection and cultural stewardship not only marginalizes women's roles but also reinforces gendered dichotomies within the framework of national identity construction. Aflaq's vision thus encapsulates a gendered dimension of nationalism, where the preservation of cultural heritage and the emotional underpinnings of national identity are predominantly, if not exclusively, the purview of men. This perspective, while reflective of the historical and cultural context of Aflaq's ideology, raises critical questions about the inclusivity and representation of all members within the national discourse.

In his theoretical exposition on nationalism, Aflaq espouses a particular ethos that he envisages men should adopt toward the nation. This ethos, as articulated by Aflaq, is encapsulated in the concept of "love," a term he employs to denote a fervent, primal, and profound emotional connection coupled with a sentiment of proprietorship. In his 1940 treatise "Nationalism Is Love Before Anything Else" (*al-qawmiyya hub qabl kul shay'*), Aflaq articulates a parallelism between this profound nationalistic fervor and the affection typically found within the bounds of familial relationships. He posits:

> The nationalism which we call for is love before anything else. It is the very same feeling that binds the individual to his family because the fatherland is only a large household and the nation is a large family ... and as love is always found linked to sacrifice, so is nationalism. Sacrifice for the sake of the nation leads to heroism.[48]

## The centrality of gender constructs

In this discourse, Aflaq correlates nationalism with a familial love paradigm, conceptualizing the fatherland as an enlarged familial structure. This perspective inherently links love with sacrifice, positing that the deep-seated devotion toward one's nation, akin to familial bonds, necessitates sacrifices that culminate in heroism. Such a conceptual framework inherently bears patriarchal underpinnings, as it centers around an active, protective male figure, characterized by martial strength, physical robustness, and combat readiness, while portraying other familial members as objects of protection and control.

This familial analogy extends to the public sphere, rendering women invisible in both domains. The metaphor of the family for the nation ascribes traditionally masculine qualities to societal and national structures. Sheila Katz discusses the patriarchal nature of Aflaq's concept of national love, summarizing its impact on the masculinization of the nation:

> [M]en could become lovers and heroes. Sacrifice ... entailed shahada, the imperative to die for a family/nation ... nationalists interpreted the nation to be a place in which (at least certain) men could consider themselves at home. Dignity at home would be unassailable or, if assailed, defended by brothers. Nationalism became a male affair through masculinized definitions of national community, freedom, dignity, economic opportunity, and security.[49]

Thus, Aflaq's portrayal of the nation as a familial entity focuses on those who perceive themselves as protectors and defenders of the nation, elevating heroism as a fundamental component of national identity. This conceptualization of nationalism, though ostensibly centered around "love," is framed within masculine terms where men are envisaged as the patriots and valiant defenders of the nation. Consequently, this perspective marginalizes the role of women in the formation and sustenance of the national community. Furthermore, Aflaq's familial metaphor is coercive, as he expresses disdain for men who do not align with this national and familial ideal, referring to them as "that distorted, abnormal minority who are in denial of their national role,"[50] demonstrating a rigid and exclusionary stance on national identity and participation.

Aflaq's primordialist perspective on national identity fosters a totalizing worldview, predicated on the inescapability of one's intrinsic identity, which can only be authentically honored or disingenuously betrayed. He articulates in the title of another contemporaneous essay, "Nationalism Is Beloved Destiny" (*al-qawmiyya qadar muhabbab*), the inevitability of this form of identity. Consequently, the "love" and masculine ideals he espouses become imperatives:

> We belong to the nation in the same way that we have our names since we were born, and like our facial features that we inherit from our fathers and

grandfathers. Even though in adulthood we might dislike our names and prefer if we were called other names, we are obliged to accept our name as well as our face ... Why does a man try to change his destiny when he can fulfil every step in his life with patriotism? He should say, "if this is my destiny, then let it be heroic!" ... What kind of man is that who does not feel pride in his nation?[51]

This narrative constructs a deterministic view of national identity, likening it to unalterable personal attributes such as one's name and facial features inherited from ancestors. Aflaq's rhetoric suggests an inherent obligation to embrace this identity, equating deviation from it with a betrayal of one's destiny. Aflaq's preoccupation with men adhering to this paradigm of masculine heroism for the nation borders on the obsessive, as he further elucidates:

> Whenever I think about the conditions of such a man, I writhe with fear of the image of misery engulfing him, and the frostbite of isolation keeping him apart. What narrow horizons surround his world; what a poor soul; what a silly, dull life! He goes through his life not knowing that he is a bough of a tree deeply rooted in the past whose branches grow up through the ages ... All those millions who strove, fought, and wrestled with storms and withstood disasters to lead him forth from the darkness of nonexistence into the light of life, to give birth to him—the unmindful, the forgetful! ... To give him a name by which he is called and features with which he is distinguished, so that he is no longer a nobody, so that when it is time for every nation to vie in boasting, he can say: "I am Arab!"[52]

In these reflections, Aflaq delineates a monolithic conception of belonging, where achieving masculine valor is normative within the national context. He also establishes a dichotomy between men, categorizing them as either heroes or cowards, contingent on their willingness to defend and sacrifice for the nation. A conspicuous aspect of Aflaq's early nationalist doctrine is the exclusion of women from participating in the national discourse. This overwhelming emphasis on masculine valor is further mirrored in the heroes Aflaq routinely evoked as inspirations and symbols of identity for Party adherents. These heroic figures, entrenched in Aflaq's narrative, are invariably male, further entrenching the gendered bias in his conception of national identity and participation. In his own words:

> We were destined to live in the age of weakness, disgrace, backwardness, and division instead of living in the age of Walid or that of Rashid ... Destiny may sometimes be cruel, but it is forever just; it distributes heroism only according to difficulty, and gives glory only according to effort. The heroism of those striving today to liberate their countries from foreign occupation and the threat of division and to extract them from the abyss of ignorance and poverty is no less than the heroism of Qutaybah and Nusayr.[53]

In his historical references, Aflaq frequently invokes warrior heroes and influential figures, such as the caliph Walid or the scholar-jurist Qutaybah, epitomizing images of masculine achievement and impact. These exemplars of male prowess and authority are contrasted with the passionate endeavors of "young men" (*shabāb*), whom Aflaq upholds as paragons for the wider populace (*jamāhīr*) to emulate. Significantly, Aflaq's narratives lack comparable female role models; nor do they acknowledge women's contributions to society.

Aflaq's emphasis on resurrecting a heroic past is intricately linked to the valorization of collective experiences of struggle and adversity by the "masses." His approach to reconceptualizing this heroic past involves rites of sacrifice and struggle that effectively meld historical experiences with contemporary realities. Although the term "masses" suggests a gender-neutral framework, Aflaq's discourse persistently differentiates between active and passive male participants, thereby excluding women from this national narrative.[54] Furthermore, Aflaq posits that pain and suffering are not merely elements of a heroic past but are also fundamental to the nation's backbone. In his article "Arabism and Suffering" (*al-'urūba wa al-'alam*), Aflaq articulates a philosophy where "resurrection is through suffering," and Arabism is actualized through "struggle" and "pain." He states: "The destiny of our Arabism is suffering."[55] However, these notions of national suffering and struggle are inextricably linked to masculinity. Aflaq correlates "the great struggle" of the nation with the achievement of "perfection of manhood" (*rujūla*).[56] In this way, Aflaq's narrative not only imbues national identity with masculine connotations but also defines national struggle and suffering in terms of male experiences. This conceptual framework reinforces a gendered hierarchy in the national discourse, elevating male experiences and contributions while marginalizing or altogether omitting the roles and experiences of women. Consequently, Aflaq's portrayal of national identity and struggle becomes a predominantly male narrative, leaving little room for the recognition or inclusion of women's perspectives and contributions.

As the Baathist Party ascended to prominence and eventually commandeered the governance of Syria, the thematic essence of Aflaq's discourse remained largely unaltered. For instance, in 1956 Aflaq was still deeply engrossed in elucidating the significance of the nationalist struggle in facilitating the attainment of the "perfection of manhood (*rujūla*)."[57] By 1967 this notion had further evolved, culminating in an extensive essay where he posited that martial combat represented the sole avenue through which men could attain a profound sense of self-identity. This motif of sacrifice and struggle continued to underpin the hierarchical structuring of individuals within the national psyche. Aflaq's theoretical framework is marked by a clear demarcation between active and passive men, where he posits that the quintessential attributes of authentic Baathists are sacrifice and struggle.

This perspective is not only demonstrative of Aflaq's hierarchical classification of men within the nation but also conflates "humanity" with manhood. In doing so, Aflaq's narrative not only reinforces a gendered hierarchy within the national context but also implicitly suggests that the true essence of being and identity is intrinsically tied to the male experience and expression. In his own words:

> When activists accept the hard-won struggle and bear the sacrifices and agonies ... they are aspiring that their comrades will follow the road of national struggle in order to establish their nation for their people and their sons ... However, there is an organic link/nexus be-tween the eras of negative struggle and the eras of positive struggle. The achievements of positive struggle are the production of virtues, steadfastness ... and the production of deep human experience by which the fighter acquires through his experience of struggle and adversity ... this is what distinguishes him from the [passive] others ... So struggle is an indivisible unit with both its positive and negative halves ... Therefore, struggle is the true life and I would say its foundation is this active part ... it is the period when the fighter is absorbed and fused with principles, suffering and sacrifice ... It is the only period by which the identity of the fighter is determined alongside his destiny, merit and his originality.[58]

This conflation of manhood with broader human qualities underscores a deeply entrenched gender bias in Aflaq's conceptualization of national identity and the role of individuals within it. Consequently, his worldview elevates the experiences and roles of men, particularly those engaged in struggle and sacrifice, as the epitome of national and human virtue, while marginalizing or overlooking the contributions and experiences of women and other groups in the formation and sustenance of national identity.

Aflaq's hierarchical structuring of national identity is intricately linked to his bifurcated classification of men into passive and active categories. This paradigm essentially situates women in a tertiary category, effectively marginalizing them in the national consciousness to a realm that is not only private but almost imperceptible. In the 1970s, while Aflaq did sporadically shift focus to the necessity for men to pursue education and spearhead the country's technological advancement,[59] he consistently reverted to emphasizing that the essence and activities of combatants (*munādilīn*) were quintessential to defining the Party's ethos: "The living image of the Baath and of the nation can only be embodied by the military man ... he is the life of the past and of the future ... of heritage, authenticity, progress, and creativity."[60]

*The centrality of gender constructs* 75

This propagation of Baath ideology is encapsulated in his speech "About the Arab Message" (*Hawl al-risāla al-'arabiyya*),[61] where he articulates:

> as a belief before anything else ... it precedes any practical knowledge ... It is the nation ... and it is the right of every individual to aspire for chivalry (*murū'a*) and heroism (*butūla*) ... However, as should be noticed, although it is required that each one should aspire for heroism, but not all people are heroic (*'abtāl*).[62]

While Aflaq ostensibly extends his discourse to "all individuals" (*'afrād*), thereby seemingly including both genders, the underlying message ties the fulfillment of one's individual and national role to the pursuit of heroism and chivalry, concepts heavily laden with masculine connotations. In Arabic, "chivalry" (*murū'a*) connotes "perfect manhood," indicating an essentialist linkage between masculinity and the construction of an ideal national identity. The synthesis of "heroism and chivalry" in Aflaq's rhetoric reveals an inclination toward a masculinist national ideal. Concurrently, Aflaq introduces the notion of the Baath's revolutionary character, underscoring the necessity of the revolutionary spirit predominantly within its "young men."[63]

Aflaq asserts that the realization of a man's national identity is symbiotic with the actualization of the nation's identity, positing that "in the achievement of man's national identity, the identity of the nation will be achieved. And the realization of his ambitions and dreams will contribute to public life."[64] He contends that the nation's essence is actualized through the genuine embodiment of patriotism in its members' souls. As such, Aflaq's framework delineates a national identity that is heavily predicated on male experiences and ideals. The valorization of masculine attributes such as heroism, chivalry, and martial prowess not only reinforces a gendered narrative but also implies that the realization of the nation's identity and aspirations is contingent upon the expression and fulfillment of these masculine virtues. This perspective, therefore, marginalizes the roles and contributions of women, rendering them peripheral in the construction of national identity and public life.

In this sense, Aflaq's conceptualization of a revolutionary Baathist identity prompts an analysis of his perception of the Baath generation. It is clear that Aflaq predicates the realization of the nation's identity on inherently masculine characteristics such as heroism, strength, and, critically, militarism. This correlation between the masculine individual and the nation crystallizes a gendered framework of nationalism. In cultivating a tiered, masculinist paradigm within the national consciousness, Aflaq lionizes the military's role. His oration "The Army Is Part of the Fighting Masses"[65] engenders further inquiries regarding the positioning of women within these "fighting masses." Aflaq declares: "I am here to confirm that the Party gives a primary position to the army. In the Baathist ideology and its theorization, the army is very important."[66] In this context, the army emerges as a crucible for the idealization of masculinity, emblematic of traits like heroism, bravery, and sacrifice, typically associated with masculine virtues. The Baathist stance does not merely assign importance to the military; it seeks to embed militarism within societal norms:

> The Baath ideology should take care of those men who enter the army for a short period—the period of military service only—and those who remain in civil life; we should enforce values of militarism into their lives ... This is for the upbringing of the new generation, whether in the military or in civilian life.

Aflaq's rhetoric here bestows upon the values of militarism a pervasive role in society, reinforcing and expanding structures of hierarchy, patriarchy, and valor. By normalizing a military ethos, Aflaq underscores the hierarchical ascendancy of male dominance, aligning it with the cultivation of a masculinity-centric culture. Furthermore, he extends the militaristic paradigm into civilian life, perpetuating patriarchal ideologies. This naturalization of militarism, embedded within Aflaq's theoretical framework, primarily relies on male authority, encompassing both militaristic and domestic domains.

The persistence with which Aflaq continued to extol martial heroism and military training for all men, even after the consolidation of Baathist power, illuminates his perception of this ethos as both an inherently virtuous principle and a crucial mechanism for socialization. The perpetuation of the need to engage in combat, and for men to be ever prepared to confront a tangible adversary, is posited as an objective in its own right. For instance, in his 1974 address "The Army Is Part of the Fighting Masses" (*Al-jaish huwa juz' min al-jamāhīr al-munādila*), Aflaq reiterates his dedication to militarism as a societal and masculine shaping tool:

> I am here to confirm that the Party gives a primary position to the Army. In the Baathist ideology and its theorization, the Army is very important ... Consideration should be given to those men who enter the Army for a short period—the period of military service only—and then return to civilian life. We should enforce the values of militarism into their lives ... This is for the upbringing of the new generation.[67]

In subsequent chapters I will delve into how, congruent with Aflaq's perspectives and those of other prominent Party figures, the culture of militarism indeed became deeply entrenched in Syrian society under Baathist governance, yielding extensive implications. This militaristic emphasis was accompanied by an obsessive focus on cultivating a specific form of manhood, establishing masculine dominion, and prioritizing men's issues and narratives in the national consciousness. Similar to al-Husri's writings, Aflaq's consistent preoccupation with masculinity in his essays and speeches afforded minimal space for addressing women's roles. However, toward the latter part of his career, Aflaq seemingly made attempts at incorporating a more gender-inclusive approach. He began addressing both men and women in his speech salutations and, in certain instances, recognized a role for women as proactive participants in the Party. For instance, in a 1974 speech concerning the Arab–Israeli conflict, Aflaq proclaimed: "When the nation is exposed to great danger, its duty is to mobilize all its forces ... Yes, we should recruit children to face this imperialist Zionism. The nation and its men, women, elderly, and children must all be alert and present to fight in this great battle."[68] Notably, such inclusions of women are presented as a contingency measure, necessitated by urgent circumstances, and mentioned alongside the recruitment of children. In a manner akin to al-Husri's amalgamation of women into the "general" or lowermost societal tier, Aflaq typically perceives women as part of an indistinct mass, contributing in subsidiary roles to the national fabric. This approach underscores a persistent undercurrent of gender biases within Aflaq's conceptualization of national identity and participation.

The nuances of the role assigned to women in Aflaq's rhetoric become more evident in a speech he delivered in 1982. In this rare instance, Aflaq acknowledged the contributions of women to the Baath Party, characterizing them as enablers of the virtues necessary for triumph. He articulated that such devoted women "facilitate the characteristics required for victory and promote the values of heroism and martyrdom."[69] Although this address stands out in Aflaq's corpus for its acknowledgment of women's efforts, it is candid in its implication that women do not inherently possess qualities such as heroism but merely "facilitate" or "promote" these traits—ostensibly through their support and reinforcement of male combatants.

One might posit that in Aflaq's perception, such loyalist women were esteemed more highly than the "distorted, abnormal" men who failed to personify martial valor. However, like these men, women were fundamentally barred from realms of agency and influence within this nationalist framework. Moreover, Aflaq's conditional recognition of women hinges on their endorsement and internalization of male-centric heroism, effectively relegating them to a subordinate role. This dynamic underscores a systemic relegation of women to secondary status, wherein their contributions are valued only insofar as they bolster the ideals of masculine valor and sacrifice. This perspective, while offering a semblance of inclusion, essentially perpetuates and reinforces the gendered hierarchy within the nationalist discourse, maintaining women's roles as auxiliary and their status as dependent on their relation to male paradigms of heroism.

## Al-Arsuzi: consolidating gender roles

In the preceding chapter we examined Zaki al-Arsuzi, distinguished among the Baathist "founding fathers" for his later-career pivot toward a heightened focus on civic volunteerism, pluralism, freedom, and democratic consensus. This shift was particularly striking when contrasted with the enduring primordialist views on national identity espoused by his contemporary, Aflaq. Although al-Arsuzi's evolving perspectives on civics exerted minimal practical impact on the trajectory of the Party under Hafez al-Assad's leadership, al-Arsuzi's foundational role in the Baath movement and his Alawite heritage, which he shared with much of the regime's leadership, ensured the continued relevance of his writings. The scarcity of scholarship on al-Arsuzi can be attributed to restricted access to his early and later works. Nevertheless, his influence on the development of the Baath political framework has been reevaluated following Hafez al-Assad's ascent to power in 1970.[70] This reassessment largely stems from Assad's need for an ideological advocate to consolidate his authority among Baathist adherents. Consequently, during Assad's tenure as the Syrian Regional Commander post the 1963 coup, and as Minister of Defense following the 1966 coup, he actively involved al-Arsuzi in interactions with military personnel, bringing him along to meet soldiers and officers. Assad's engagement with al-Arsuzi revitalized the latter's ideological position, prompting al-Arsuzi to compose extensive ideological profiles on Assad for Baath periodicals.[71]

This ideological gravitation toward al-Arsuzi's national theory is not merely pivotal in the political realm of Syria but also bears significant ramifications for the conceptualization of women within Syrian society. Al-Arsuzi, widely regarded as the progenitor of Baath ideology in Syria, is acknowledged by Dalal Elamir as a foremost figure in introducing concepts of liberalism and nationalism to the Middle East.[72] It is therefore important to interrogate the perceptions of women in his theory. Al-Arsuzi's advocacy for the civic construction of the nation marks a departure from the purely cultural notions of nation formation, advocating instead for the crystallization of statehood through the enactment of democratic principles, free elections, and the safeguarding of liberty.[73]

This civic paradigm transcends the mere realization of a collective cultural identity, aspiring to the institutionalization of these ideals within the state's structure. The salience of al-Arsuzi's political treatises resides in his dedication to articulating a doctrine of a free society, a vision that was not preceded in depth or emphasis by the likes of al-Husri and Aflaq. Al-Arsuzi's political philosophy, therefore, opens a discourse that potentially reconfigures the societal fabric to include a more robust, civically engaged citizenry. Within this context, the inquiry into the placement of women in relation to

*The centrality of gender constructs* 79

the state and society under al-Arsuzi's dualistic approach of primordialistic and civic national conceptions becomes particularly pertinent. The interrogation into his political writings and their implications for women's roles in state-building and societal participation is essential to understand the inclusivity and progressiveness of his political thought. As such, an exploration into al-Arsuzi's political doctrine requires a thorough examination of the space it allocates to women within the evolving narrative of nationhood and statecraft.

In the ambit of al-Arsuzi's political thought, his dedication to forging a concept of a free society is noteworthy, particularly as it diverges from the approaches taken by al-Husri and Aflaq. Al-Arsuzi's preoccupation with this theme represents an unprecedented attempt to construct a theoretical foundation for a society predicated on civic conception. Moreover, Al-Arsuzi's particular focus on philology as a tool for nation-building necessitates a thorough analysis of his nationalistic concepts and linguistic applications. This analysis will seek to unravel how philology underpins his national theory and how it shapes his conception of women within the nation. To this end, the ensuing examination will dissect the language of al-Arsuzi's national theory, scrutinizing his steadfast commitment to the state and democracy as the quintessential instruments for the genesis of a national community. The objective is to explore al-Arsuzi's ideologies concerning women, especially with regard to their inherent qualities, educational needs, and their designated positions within the societal and political hierarchy.

In the context of this section, al-Arsuzi emerges as a distinctive figure among his peers, such as al-Husri and Aflaq, by virtue of his explicit theorizing on the roles of women and men within society. He frequently revisits the metaphor of the nation as a "family," employing this analogy with zeal to delineate civic roles and responsibilities. This perspective, which situates traditional gender roles as cornerstones of national structure, can be interpreted as one of the bedrock tenets of his philosophical edifice. In his analytical exposition "Family" (*'usra*), al-Arsuzi articulates his vision of social roles and their purported inherent "naturalness" within human existence:

> The family as a unit is based on men and women. The man [*rajul*] in this natural entity symbolizes the ideal figure, as he becomes the role model for his sons. The mother, overflowing with emotions, fuels her sons with sentiment. The gentleness of women, and the tendency of men to control things and to seek camaraderie between brothers, is what formulates a family environment that is full of life. In such an atmosphere, the people learn how to carry out their public duties ... The mother blooms with tenderness and mercy, and the father practices what he is naturally born into, which is his inclination for

sovereignty and the administration of justice ... In such an atmosphere, all members of the family enjoy freedom, the freedom to tackle the duties and problems of life.[74]

The gendered diction employed in the passage is self-evident, presenting a vivid juxtaposition: women who "bloom" and "overflow" with a nurturing essence against men characterized by their quest for sovereignty and dominion. However, the text then extrapolates this domestic archetype to the broader canvas of national affairs, where male leaders (*imāms*) are envisaged as the embodiment of power and control, purportedly as a benevolent expression of love and to ensure societal harmony.[75] Al-Arsuzi's idyllic vision, arguably encapsulated by the phrase "everyone happily in their place," perpetuates a patriarchal gender hierarchy, distancing itself from the racialized nationhood constructs he later disavowed.[76] Despite advocating for inclusivity and dignity across ethnic and religious divides, al-Arsuzi remains anchored to a traditional gender binary that posits authority as the exclusive domain of men. "Freedom," within this context—distinct from racial considerations—is conceived as the acceptance and fulfillment of one's predefined role within the social stratification.

Al-Arsuzi's adherence to primordial notions of gender roles is strikingly evident in his staunch resistance to women entering into matrimony outside the national community. His discourse on the necessity of the nation to steer women's reproductive choices is framed within the context of eugenics, invoking the notion of "the evolution of the family towards superior humanity."[77] Al-Arsuzi maintains that this ideology is humanistic in its essence as opposed to being racially motivated. Nonetheless, his preoccupation with the matrimonial selections of women as a determinant of national demarcations is palpable. He characterizes offspring from mixed-nationality unions as "repulsive" (*muqrif*) and destined for cultural and societal disintegration.[78]

In these discussions it is noteworthy that al-Arsuzi's concerns, as articulated in his writings, do not encompass the potential sexual conduct of men. Rather, his emphasis lies exclusively on the imperative to ensure that Syrian women form alliances with men within the national fold. This perspective culminates in practical implications, such as al-Arsuzi's advocacy for policies that prevent Syrian women from conferring citizenship upon their progeny if the father is non-Syrian—a restriction not reciprocally applied to Syrian men with non-Syrian partners. This stance underscores an asymmetrical focus on the agency of women in the perpetuation of national identity, thereby cementing gender-based disparities within the societal framework.

In a discursive excursion titled "Woman" (*mar'a*), al-Arsuzi embarks on a series of unorthodox etymological conjectures to reinforce his essentialist

*The centrality of gender constructs* 81

stance on gender roles. He postulates that the term *sayyid* (male lord or master) derives from *'asad* (lion), thereby emphasizing the man's sovereign role, his responsibility as a provider, and his propensity to "protect his house."[79] By contrast, al-Arsuzi contends that the term *'unūtha* (femininity) etymologically resonates with *sukūn* (stillness and quiescence), suggesting that women possess an inherent predilection for "stability and settlement" and are naturally inclined to "remain in her sacred home."[80] Furthermore, he posits that the Arabic word *'ab* (father) bears phonetic similarity to the English word "up," insinuating that the paternal role is associated with "loftiness" (*i'tilā'*) and "vigor" (*hayajān*).[81] The rationale behind al-Arsuzi's invocation of such distinctive linguistic parallels remains enigmatic, particularly considering his intellectual stature. The leap from alleged etymological origins to ascribed intrinsic attributes appears tenuous at best. It is challenging to view these assertions as anything but a tenuous grasp at any available justification to underpin his preoccupation with reinforcing conventional gender roles. Such arguments, predicated on specious etymological associations, suggest an attempt to utilize academic discourse to validate predetermined gender constructs rather than to engage in a genuine scholarly examination of language and its social implications.

Within the same treatise, al-Arsuzi exhibits a pronounced interest in women's ability to incite sexual desire in men, characterizing this "function" as a fundamental means by which women can bolster the vitality of the nation's men and facilitate their proper integration into society. He posits that women's role in providing sexual fulfillment for men is indispensable in fostering an orderly, morally upright, and intellectually robust public sphere.[82] Al-Arsuzi revisits this motif recurrently throughout his essay on women, expounding on the role of women in appealing to men in such a way as to engender progeny for the nation, and in anchoring men by offering sexual constancy and fidelity. He contends: "The woman completes the terms of her function if she has helped the man to perform his public responsibilities. She will ingrain in him a sense of chivalry and prevent those who lead from descending into shabbiness and villainy."[83] Moreover, he argues that women's sensuality ought to "fire up the man and ignite his imagination, which will turn him into an artist and a hero." Al-Arsuzi assures that this role should be readily embraced by women, as they are inherently "made for love [*hubb*]" and possess a natural "docility" (*wadā'a*).[84] Al-Arsuzi's assertions ascribe a transactional nature to women's sexual agency, viewing it as a mechanism to energize and stabilize male counterparts, thereby ensuring their effective participation in the public and political realms. This perspective implies that the cultivation of male societal leaders is inextricably linked to the sexual and emotional support they receive from women, situating women's worth within the context of their relationships with men and the domestic services they provide.

The romanticized notion that al-Arsuzi presents is not without its problematic facets, particularly in that it ostensibly renders women accountable for the virtuous and vicious conduct of men. This accountability is predicated on the assumption that men's actions and achievements hinge upon the sufficiency of sexual and emotional sustenance furnished by women, thereby inscribing women within a confined, essentialized social function. Al-Arsuzi elucidates the ramifications of this ideology with pronounced clarity: "The practical duties of the woman ... in which she completes her function and accomplishes her identity, are through being a housewife. She should organize everything about the house to make it a perfect place for the man to rest after accomplishing his tiring duties in public life."[85] He further expounds that "the woman does her duties through turning the house into a national fireplace around which her children can learn about the heritage of their grandfathers," and finds her contentment by "preserving her feminine nature and cooperating with the man to achieve what her nature entails."[86] Embedded within these propositions is the unequivocal notion that the quintessence of womanhood is defined through servicing men's needs, enhancing men's comfort, and perpetuating a male-dominated societal structure. Moreover, such contributions are depicted not as voluntary acts performed by equal partners but as obligatory devotions, with women's adherence to their prescribed roles deemed indispensable for the maintenance of men's rectitude and the establishment of a well-ordered, secure society. In this light, al-Arsuzi's conceptualization of ingrained gender roles stands in stark contrast to his espousal of civic volunteerism, democratic participation, and elective national identity. His vision of gender dynamics reveals an inherent incongruity with the principles of democratic agency and individual autonomy that inform his broader civic ideology.

Beth Baron has posited that nationalist movements frequently exhibit a "Janus-faced" approach to gender, advocating for increased political participation from women yet simultaneously imposing stringent constraints on the scope of roles, activities, and behaviors available to both genders.[87] This paradox is manifest in the writings of al-Arsuzi, who made concerted efforts to involve women in the Baathist movement and recognized the importance of integrating their perspectives into state affairs, even while delineating their "natural functions" and "docility" within the same expositions.[88]

The obligation for women, as well as men, to subscribe to and engage in these restrictive gender narratives as a precondition for Party valorization raises questions about the depth of al-Arsuzi's dedication to democratic principles. An intriguing manifestation of these gendered expectations was al-Arsuzi's advocacy for women to adopt a secular dress code, eschewing overt religious symbols—a stance that might superficially be perceived as liberal yet was, in fact, rooted in his belief that such displays of religious identity denoted a deficient allegiance to the male-dominated nationalist movement.[89] Toward the conclusion of this discussion, al-Arsuzi proffers a paradoxical caution: while acknowledging the indispensability of women for the perpetuation of the nation, he simultaneously frames their status as tenuous and contingent upon male benevolence. He contrasts this with the purported innate independence of men, encapsulating this dichotomy with the assertion that "the woman cannot live without the man."[90] This declaration not only underscores the fragile positioning of women within his national vision but also reinforces a gender dynamic that fundamentally undermines the autonomy and equality of women.

Al-Arsuzi's final comments on the inherent independence of men, juxtaposed against his earlier emphasis on their reliance on women for virtuous conduct and self-actualization, may reflect underlying tensions about the nationalist movement's identity as an exclusive "brotherhood" (*'ikhwān*)— a concept and fixation that al-Arsuzi shared with contemporaries like al-Husri and Aflaq.[91] With the Baath Party's evolution from a revolutionary clique to a dominant political power in Syria, it confronted the challenge of integrating a heterogeneous populace into its ranks, both as nascent Party affiliates and as constituents of the national establishment. Al-Arsuzi's fixation on conventional family structures as an analogue for national governance served as a method to navigate the dynamics between nationalist figureheads and the wider public, while also grappling with the evolving public roles of women in a modernizing society. Fundamentally, the intricate discourses dissected in this section are acutely aimed at underpinning and perpetuating social hierarchies that distinguish decisively between those who command and govern and those who affirm and bolster these leaders. This stark delineation implicates the perpetuation of established power structures, wherein the prerogative of leadership and authority is reserved for a select few, while the majority are relegated to roles of acquiescence and support within the prescribed social order.

In his broader oeuvre, al-Arsuzi demonstrates a pragmatic engagement with democracy and civic structures. Yet, akin to his fellow Baathist patriarchs, he encounters a threshold beyond which the notion of granting the populace the autonomy to shape their own futures becomes untenable. For al-Arsuzi this boundary is explicitly intertwined with gender dynamics as well as fealty to the Party line. He articulates that integration into the nationalist entity is contingent upon adherence to Party ideology and the execution of one's predefined function within the national order as delineated by that ideology.

For women, the expectations are explicit: they are to provide Baathist men with both sexual and substantive support, to eschew aspirations for decision-making authority or entry into the echelons of leadership, and to refrain from cultivating allegiances or identities that fall outside the nationalist paradigm. Within such a framework, the liberation and public engagement of women are, at most, theoretical conceits. Women are cast into inherently subservient positions, envisioned as naturally predisposed to fulfill the demands of the Party's male members. This conception of women's roles effectively circumscribes their agency, confining their participation to the private realm of domestic service and support, and precluding their involvement in the public, political, and decision-making spheres of the national community.

Within the cultural phase of national identity formation, the interconnection posited between national and familial affection has facilitated the perpetuation of an identity steeped in the tenets of compulsory militarism and pronounced masculinity. The conceptualization of the nation as an extension of the family unit has been embraced by Syrian ideologues as a foundational metaphor, one which inherently positions the man as both the patriarch within the private domain and the combatant within the public arena. Crucially, this analogy has served to legitimize the transference of patriarchal structures from the familial realm to the public sphere.

While these intellectuals have drawn parallels between familial and national structures, they have each ascribed varied significance to this relationship in their construction of cultural identity. Al-Husri, for instance, relegated the family to a peripheral role within the nation, as evidenced by his approach to language, history, and education. He placed emphasis on the public sphere in fostering nationalistic sentiment, effectively supplanting the familial role with educational institutions and, subsequently, military establishments. Conversely, Aflaq acknowledged the genesis of nationalistic love within the familial setting but overlooked the maternal role in his theorization, instead accentuating physical fortitude as a cornerstone of both the nation and the Baath ideology.

Al-Arsuzi, however, adopted a notably distinct stance, recognizing the integral role of the family within the nation. Nevertheless, this deliberate inclusion of the familial construct within his national narrative further entrenched the subjugated status of women in both societal and familial contexts. Through his engagement with the topic of women, al-Arsuzi rationalized their subordination by objectifying them as possessions of men. He characterized women predominantly as sexual beings and as subordinates to men, a viewpoint that resonates with the broader trend of normalizing militarism and masculinity within the Syrian national discourse, as elucidated by both al-Husri and Aflaq. Additionally, al-Arsuzi's ostensible valorization of the maternal figure as a cultural progenitor imposed constraints and hegemonic control over women's autonomy and choices.

This scholarly inquiry into the entrenchment of gender roles within the foundational narratives of Syrian nationalism is mirrored in the legislative developments postdating the establishment of the Baath state in 1970. The subsequent chapter delves into the manner in which the inculcation and normalization of militarism within the national narrative has sustained a hierarchical structure that impedes the dissolution of gender disparities within the Syrian constitutional and legislative frameworks. Accordingly, this chapter will scrutinize the embodiment of the tenets of muscular nationalism, as delineated in the writings of the Baathist founders, within these state apparatuses, and evaluate the consequent ramifications on the social fabric of Syrian women and men.

The 1973 Constitution emerges as a seminal legal artifact in this discourse, encapsulating and institutionalizing the Baathist philosophy, thereby mandating citizen compliance with its ideologies. Nonetheless, it is imperative to also consider the specific statutes and practices instituted by the Baath regime, which, as will be explicated, frequently diverged from the constitutional rhetoric. The following chapter aims to unravel these inconsistencies and elucidate their implications for the socio-political landscape in Syria, particularly in terms of gender relations and the lived realities of its citizens.

## Notes

1 As discussed in the Introduction, the concept of "muscular" nationalism was coined by Sikata Banerjee. *Gender, Nation and Popular Film in India: Globalizing Muscular Nationalism*. New York: Routledge, 2016 to encapsulate this complex form of romantic masculine identity, which emphasizes men's physical power, heroic sacrifice, passionate loyalty, and militarism as symbols of the national ideal.
2 Sati al-Husri. "*'Awāmil al-qawmiyya*." (1928). *Free Arab Voice*, January 19, 2010. http://freearabvoice.org/?page_id=104. Accessed June 17, 2014.
3 Sati al-Husri. *'Abhāth mukhtarah fi al-qawmiyyah al-'arabiyya*. Volume 1. Beirut: Markaz Dirāsāt al-Wahda al-Arabiyya, 1985a.
4 al-Husri 1928.
5 Sati al-Husri. *Hawl al-qawmiyya al-'arabiyya*. Beirut: Markaz Dirāsāt al-Wahda al-Arabiyya, 1985b.
6 Ibid.
7 Sati al-Husri. *Mā hiya al-qawmiyya? Abhāth wa Dirāsāt 'ala dhaw' al-ahdāth wa al-nazariyyāt*. Beirut: Dar al-'ilm li l-malāyīn, 1959.
8 Ibid.
9 Ibid., p. 67.

10 Ibid.
11 Ibid, p. 73.
12 Sati al-Husri. *Fi l-lugha wa l-'ādāb w 'alāqatuhumā bi l-qawmiyya.* Beirut: Markaz Dirāsāt al-Wahda al-Arabiyya, 1985e, p. 30.
13 Ibid., pp. 29, 32.
14 Salih J. Altoma. "The Emancipation of Women in Contemporary Syrian Literature." In *Syria: Society, Culture and Polity*, edited by Richard T. Antoun and Donald Quanterat, pp. 71–95. Albany, NY: State University of New York Press, 1991, pp. 79–91.
15 al-Husri 1928.
16 For example, al-Husri 1985a, p. 23.
17 Ibid., p. 105; al-Husri 1928.
18 al-Husri 1928, p. 21. A section of this passage on "knowledge" vs. "sentiments," showing al-Husri's presumptions about gender roles in education, is translated and discussed in Chapter 1 of this book.
19 Sati al-Husri. *Safahāt min al-maḍī al-qarīb.* Beirut: Dar al-'ilm li l-malāyīn, 1948, p. 7.
20 al-Husri 1928.
21 al-Husri 1948, p. 70.
22 Ibid., p. 112.
23 al-Husri 1985a, p. 27.
24 Ibid., pp. 27–29.
25 Sati al-Husri. *'Ā'rā' wa dirāsāt fī l-fikr l-qawmī.* Edited by Muhmad al-Rumihi. Second edition. Majallat al-'Arabī, 1985f, p. 19.
26 Ibid., p. 40.
27 al-Husri 1985a, p. 117.
28 Ibid., p. 70.
29 Ibid., p. 63.
30 Ibid., p. 27.
31 Ibid., p. 117.
32 Sati al-Husri. *Muhadarāt fi nushu' al-fikrah al-qawmiyya.* Cairo: Mataba'at al-Risāla, 1951, pp. 238–39.
33 al-Husri 1985a, p. 450.
34 Ibid.
35 Sati al-Husri. *'Āra' wa 'ahādīth fi 'l-tarbīya wa l-ta'līm.* Cairo: Mataba'at al-Risāla, 1944, p. 65.
36 Anders Ahlbäck. *Manhood and the Making of the Military: Conscription, Military Service and Masculinity in Finland 1917–39.* London and New York: Routledge, 2016 has provided a fascinating discussion of the ways in which mandatory military conscription for men can contribute to the consolidation of gender boundaries and hierarchies in the overall society. Ahlbäck's analysis of this phenomenon in early-twentieth-century Finland is strongly applicable to the later evolution of Baathist Syria, as the Party's ceaseless rhetoric of military-based "brotherhood" and solidarity placed women into an outsider role, an experience that I will discuss in detail in the upcoming chapters.

37 al-Husri 1944, pp. 77–78.
38 Sati al-Husri. *'Ahādīth fi l-tarbiya wa l-ijtimā'*. Beirut: Markaz Dirāsāt al-Wahda al-Arabiyya, 1984, pp. 73–82.
39 al-Husri 1944, pp. 89–90.
40 See Mohammed El-Attrache. *The Political Philosophy of Michel Aflaq and the Ba'th Party in Syria*. Michigan: Xerox University Microfilms, 1976, p. 75.
41 Michel Aflaq. "*'Ahd al-būtūla*." 1935. http://albaath.online.fr/Volume%20I-Chapters/Fi%20Sabil%20al%20Baath-Vol%201-Ch01.htm. Accessed February 2014.
42 Ibid.
43 Michel Aflaq. "*Tharwat al-hayāt*." 1936. http://albaath.online.fr/Volume%20I-Chapters/Fi%20Sabil%20al%20Baath-Vol%201-Ch02.htm. Accessed February 2014.
44 Michel Aflaq. "*Al-ma'raka bayn al-wujūd al-sathi wa al-wujūd al-asīl*." 1955a. http://albaath.online.fr/Volume%20II-Chapters/Fi%20Sabil%20al%20Baath-Vol%202-Ch38.htm. Accessed February 2014.
45 Ibid.
46 Michel Aflaq. "*Fī thikrā al-rasūl*." 1943a. http://albaath.online.fr/Volume%20I-Chapters/Fi%20Sabil%20al%20Baath-Vol%201-Ch33.htm. Accessed February 2014.
47 Michel Aflaq. "*Wājib al-'amal al-qawmī*." 1943b. http://albaath.online.fr/Volume%20I-Chapters/Fi%20Sabil%20al%20Baath-Vol%201-Ch35.htm. Accessed February 2014.
48 Michel Aflaq. "*Al-Qawmiyya hub qabla kul shay'*." 1940a. http://albaath.online.fr/Volume%20I-Chapters/Fi%20Sabil%20al%20Baath-Vol%201-Ch30.htm. Accessed February 2014.
49 Sheila H. Katz. *Women and Gender in Early Jewish and Palestinian Nationalism*. Gainesville, FL: University Press of Florida, 2003, pp. 80–81.
50 Michel Aflaq. "*Ma'nā al-risāla al-khālida*." 1950a. http://albaath.online.fr/Volume%20I-Chapters/Fi%20Sabil%20al%20Baath-Vol%201-Ch26.htm. Accessed February 2014.
51 Aflaq 1940.
52 Ibid.
53 Ibid.
54 Michel Aflaq. "*Nidāl al-wahda huwa nidāl al-jamāhīr*." 1957a. http://albaath.online.fr/Volume%20II-Chapters/Fi%20Sabil%20al%20Baath-Vol%202-Ch45.htm. Accessed February 2014.
55 Michel Aflaq. "*Al-'urūba wa al-'alam*." 1956a. http://albaath.online.fr/Volume%20II-Chapters/Fi%20Sabil%20al%20Baath-Vol%202-Ch22.htm. Accessed February 2014.
56 Ibid.
57 Ibid.
58 Michel Aflaq. "*Nafham al-turāth b al-fikr al-thawrī w al-mu'ānāh al-nidāliyya*." 1967. http://albaath.online.fr/Volume%20III-Chapters/Fi%20Sabil%20al%20Baath-Vol%203-Ch04.htm. Accessed February 2014.

59 Michel Aflaq. "*Hizb al-thawrah al-ʿarabiyyah.*" 1970. http://albaath.online.fr/VolumeV-Chapters/Fi%20Sabil%20al%20Baath-Vol%205-Ch08.htm. Accessed February 2014.
60 Michel Aflaq. "*Al-Baathi huwa al-sūra al-haqīqiyyah li l-'umma.*" 1975. http://albaath.online.fr/Volume%20III-Chapters/Fi%20Sabil%20al%20Baath-Vol%203-Ch02.htm. Accessed February 2014.
61 Michel Aflaq. "*Hawla al-risāla al-ʿarabiyya.*" 1946. http://albaath.online.fr/Volume%20I-Chapters/Fi%20Sabil%20al%20Baath-Vol%201-Ch25.htm. Accessed February 2014.
62 Ibid.
63 Michel Aflaq. "*Al-Baath al-'arabī huwa al-'inqilāb.*" 1950c. http://albaath.online.fr/Volume%20I-Chapters/Fi%20Sabil%20al%20Baath-Vol%201-Ch18.htm. Accessed February 2014.
64 Michel Aflaq. "*Al-jīl al-ʿarabi al-jadīd.*" 1944. http://albaath.online.fr/Volume%20I-Chapters/Fi%20Sabil%20al%20Baath-Vol%201-Ch36.htm. Accessed February 2014.
65 Michel Aflaq. "*Al-jaish huwa juz' min al-jamāhīr al-munadila.*" 1974a. http://albaath.online.fr/Volume%20III-Chapters/Fi%20Sabil%20al%20Baath-Vol%203-Ch16.htm. Accessed February 2014.
66 Ibid.
67 Michel Aflaq. "*Qadaruna 'an nuhārib ma'an.*" 1974b. http://albaath.online.fr/VolumeV-Chapters/Fi%20Sabil%20al%20Baath-Vol%205-Ch21.htm. Accessed February 2014.
68 Ibid.
69 Michel Aflaq. "*Wilādat marhala jadīda min al-'umma.*" 1982. http://albaath.online.fr/Volume%20III-Chapters/Baath-Volume%20III-Ch16.pdf. Accessed February 2014.
70 Michel Saba'. *S'ādeh wa Aflaq fī l-Fīkr al-Siyāsī l-Orthodoxī*. Beirut: Manshūrāt 'Āfāq Jāmi'iyya, 2005, p. 298.
71 Ibid., p. 270.
72 Dalal Arsuzi-Elamir. "Nation, State, and Democracy in the Writings of Zaki al-Arsuzi." In *Nationalism and Liberal Thought in the Arab East: Ideology and Practice*, edited by Christoph Schumann, pp. 66–91. Abingdon: Routledge, 2010, p. 66.
73 Zaki al-Arsuzi. *Al-Mu'allafāt al-Kāmilah*. Volume II. Damascus: Matābi' al-'Idāra al-Siyāsiyya, 1973, p. 321.
74 Ibid., p. 304.
75 Ibid., p. 344.
76 Zaki al-Arsuzi. "*Mafhūm al-'insāniyyia fi 'alāqatihā bi-mafhūmay al-'umma wa-l-qawmiyya.*" In *Al-Mu'allafāt*. Volume VI. Damascus: Matābi' al-'Idāra al-Siyāsiyya, 1975, pp. 153–54.
77 al-Arsuz 1973, p. 305.
78 Ibid., p. 307.
79 Ibid., p. 311.
80 Ibid.

81 Ibid., p. 308.
82 Ibid., pp. 311–12.
83 Ibid., p. 312.
84 Ibid., pp. 308, 310.
85 Ibid., p. 313.
86 Ibid.
87 Beth Baron. *Egypt as a Woman: Nationalism, Gender, and Politics*. Berkeley, CA: University of California Press, 2005, p. 2.
88 al-Arsuzi 1973, pp. 314–16.
89 Ibid.
90 Ibid., pp. 314–16.
91 See, for example, al-Arsuzi 1973, pp. 323–24.

# 3

# Implementing masculinism under Baathist hegemony

Following the entrenchment of Baathist dominance in Syria during the late 1960s, the regime embarked on a modernization agenda that underscored the preeminence of state institutions within societal structures.[1] The era commencing in the 1970s witnessed a nuanced shift in Baathist discourse, where notions of communal and cultural coherence began to be paralleled by narratives framing Syria as a geographic state (*watan*), coupled with increasing focus on the formulation of laws and policies. A pivotal juncture in this evolution was the ratification of Syria's first permanent Constitution in 1973.

In examining the subordinated position of women in both the state apparatus and broader societal context, it is imperative to acknowledge the backdrop against which Syrian national identity was being sculpted and institutionalized by an ostensibly secular state. Within this framework, it becomes essential to highlight that scholarly discourse pertaining to constitutions and legislative frameworks in Middle Eastern societies has extensively explored gender biases. These explorations have predominantly revolved around various axes, including religious patriarchy, tribal dynamics, traditional norms, and the evolving social and legal status of women.[2] In the discourse surrounding the historical and political genesis of Syrian legislation, a notable segment of scholars posits that the extant laws, originating under the French Mandate, continue to exert influence.[3] However, such arguments, paralleling broader feminist scholarship,[4] often overlook the intricate relationship between Syria's tumultuous historical narrative—characterized by a succession of military coups d'état from 1949 up until Hafez al-Assad's ascendancy in 1970—and the entrenchment of masculinism within the constitutional and legal fabric.

In this chapter I propose a divergent perspective, contending that the persistence of this colonial legacy within Syrian laws should be ascribed not merely to historical inertia but rather to the solidification of Baathist political ideology and the establishment of a militaristic regime. Within this regime the exaltation of the male warrior archetype becomes a defining template for Syrian citizenship. Consequently, I adopt an alternative analytical approach, positing that masculinism should not be perceived merely as an explanatory variable but rather as a lens for interpretation—a critical instrument within what is termed "ideology critique."[5]

At the crux of this scholarly examination lies the conceptualization of the nation-state as an extension of the familial structure, a paradigm that inherently perpetuates gender-based hierarchies. This conceptual model, wherein the nation is metaphorically envisioned as a family unit, facilitates the transposition of the notion of familial honor to the construct of national honor.[6] Such a metaphorical framing often positions the nation in feminine terms, concurrently emphasizing the role of men as masculine protectors, charged with the defense of both women and the nation. This interplay between *'ird* (honor) and *'ard* (land/nation) intertwines themes of militarism and masculinity. However, this feminine conceptualization of the nation, reinforced by the authority vested in men as protectors and the state apparatus, is a salient feature in Syrian legislation. This feminization narrative extends beyond symbolic representation to encompass the nationalization of women's sexuality and bodily autonomy. It manifests through state control over aspects such as women's fertility and the legalization of violence against women under the guise of safeguarding honor (construed as women's purity).

This patriarchal logic, embedded in Baath ideology, not only establishes hierarchical structures within legal narratives but also casts women as inherently dependent on male guardianship. This patriarchal authority, underpinning the notion of protection, further entrenches the subordination of women and defines their relationship to the state. This dynamic is exemplified in the Syrian nationality law, which precludes women from conferring citizenship onto their offspring. This legislative stance reflects a broader societal and political paradigm wherein women's rights and agency are circumscribed by entrenched patriarchal norms and state policies, underscoring the complex interplay between gender, law, and national identity.

My research has led me to the conviction that there exists a pressing necessity for an in-depth, sustained, and explicitly gender-focused analysis of the complex, multilayered conceptualizations of militarism and masculinism. This chapter, while primarily addressing these themes in the context preceding the Syrian war, traces the perpetuation of martial values from the early inception of Baath ideology in the latter half of the twentieth century. This historical trajectory is pivotal in understanding the construction of a hierarchical, gendered identity, positing the male as the paradigmatic citizen—a theme that will receive further detailed exploration in Chapter 5.

In the current chapter my objective is to scrutinize how the tenets of muscular nationalism, as propounded in the writings of Baathist founders, were operationalized within state institutions, and to assess their resultant impact on the lives of Syrian women and men. A critical document in this analysis is the Constitution of 1973, which played a crucial role in codifying the Baathist perspective and embedding it within the legal framework, thereby mandating citizen compliance. However, it is equally imperative to examine the specific laws and practices enacted by the Baathist regime. As I will elucidate, these often displayed a dissonance with the rhetorical ideals espoused in the Constitution. This dichotomy between constitutional rhetoric and practical enactment reveals the complexities and contradictions inherent in the Baathist approach to governance and gender roles. By delving into these aspects, this chapter aims to uncover the nuanced interactions between ideological constructs, legal frameworks, and the lived experiences of Syrian citizens under Baathist rule.

In my forthcoming analysis I intend to demonstrate that the Baathist regime's preferential treatment of specific masculine identities and the exaltation of the Baathist fighter, central to the rhetoric of the "founding fathers," found continued expression in the formal Constitution through its portrayal of the Syrian state. This explicit delineation of the ideal citizen as a physically robust male warrior within the constitutional framework is indicative of the extent to which the Baathist nationalist vision perpetuated the marginalization of women during its implementation phase. Further, I will explore the impact of masculinist ideologies on the positioning of women within various legislative domains, including penal, personal, labor, and citizenship law, during the nascent stages of Baathist rule. This examination will scrutinize the representation and treatment of women in these legislative texts, prompting the critical question: were women considered equal citizens under the Baathist regime? My argument posits that, despite superficial efforts by the regime to incorporate women's liberation as a tokenistic element within its legitimizing narrative, such overtures were fundamentally undermined by the entrenched gendered framework of muscular nationalism. This resulted in a legal milieu that institutionalized male privilege. Under this system, women were paradoxically expected to demonstrate allegiance and gratitude toward the Party's purported protection, while concurrently being denied the same level of esteem and rights accorded to their male counterparts. This contradiction highlights the inherent disparities in the legal and ideological structures of the Baathist state, revealing a complex dynamic where state-sponsored narratives of empowerment and protection clash with the realities of systemic gender inequality and marginalization.

## The national ideal and the Syrian citizen

To comprehensively grasp the trajectory of Baathism from its theoretical underpinnings to its pragmatic enactment, it is essential to examine the utilization of military power as an instrument for consolidating Hafez al-Assad's dominion. The transformation of the Baath Party into a progressively militaristic entity commenced post its reconstitution in 1962. This metamorphosis was markedly evidenced when the Military Committee orchestrated a coup d'état on March 8, 1963, overthrowing the *infiṣāl* regime, an action that notably garnered support from the Party's civilian leadership, thereby signifying an escalated acceptance of militaristic strategies. By 1966, Assad embarked on a strategic consolidation of his influence within the government, primarily through pivotal military appointments.[7] His successful maneuvers ensured that, by 1969, the appointment of his confidants within military ranks effectively marginalized the radicals to mere custodians of the Party apparatus, while Assad maintained an unyielding control over the army.[8]

The intraparty rivalry reached its zenith during the Black September crisis of 1970, amid the regime's involvement in supporting the Palestine Liberation Organization (PLO). Seizing this critical moment, Assad initiated the Corrective Movement on October 30, 1970, deploying loyalist troops to detain members of Jadid's government, thereby supplanting the radical faction and embedding his adherents within the Baath Regional Command. The internal dynamics of the Baath Party from 1963 to 1970 underscore a fundamental tenet: control over the military apparatus was tantamount to governance control, a realization that culminated in Assad's unchallenged ascendancy to the presidency. This period illuminates the critical role of military influence in the political arena, shaping not only the Party's direction but also the broader landscape of Syrian governance and leadership.

In the intricate process of nation-state formation in Syria, the role of the army, while central, was insufficient in isolation for the nation's modernization. This phase of development involved a deliberate institutionalization of constitutional legitimacy, implemented in a top-down fashion.[9] To encapsulate this phenomenon, one may invoke Hinnebusch's characterization of Syria's state formation as akin to a " 'Bonapartist' regime—a postrevolutionary authoritarian regime standing 'above' classes and presiding over the formation of a strong new state."[10] This period, particularly the 1970s, signifies the emergence and consolidation of the Baath regime, with a pronounced emphasis on the cultivation of state institutions as the primary vehicle for Syria's modernization.[11] The Baath regime's focus on bolstering state institutions notably "increased the degree to which citizens interacted and identified with their state."[12] Consequently, in an era marked by a concerted effort to fortify the legitimacy and sovereignty of the Syrian state, there was a discernible shift from the theoretical tenets of Baathism to a more pragmatic politicization. This transition manifested in the militarization of the state apparatus, with the Baath Party emerging as the predominant political entity in Syria. This strategic shift underscores the intricate relationship between state-building, militarization, and the evolving political landscape, delineating the regime's approach to nation-state development through a combination of institutional strengthening and authoritarian governance.

Raymond Hinnebusch offers a nuanced understanding of the evolution of the Baath state, describing it as a "product of a nationalist party and an army radicalized by the conflict with Israel, developed under Hafiz al-Asad [sic] into a huge national security apparatus designed to confront Israel."[13] This perspective encapsulates the transformation of the Baath regime into a formidable entity, intricately shaped by the dynamics of regional conflict and nationalistic fervor. Under Hafez al-Assad's leadership, the state expanded into an extensive national security structure, strategically engineered to counter the Israeli threat. This development reflects a complex interplay between nationalism, militarization, and geopolitical strategy, underscoring the regime's approach to statecraft in the context of regional tensions and internal Party dynamics.

In the modern history of Syria, dating back to its establishment as a contemporary nation-state in 1920, the landscape has seen the promulgation of over fifteen constitutions. The fluidity and frequent revisions of the Syrian constitution can be largely attributed to the succession of military coups, which utilized constitutional reform as a means of legitimizing their rule. Within this politically turbulent context, the evolution of Baath ideology culminated in the assertion of Syria's political sovereignty. A pivotal moment in this trajectory was the drafting of the first permanent Constitution in 1973, orchestrated under the aegis of Hafez al-Assad amid a prevailing state of emergency. This 1973 Constitution stands as a landmark document, not merely for its permanence but for the significant paradigm shift it represented. This Constitution's enactment was instrumental in the Baath Party's consolidation of power. It not only conferred legitimacy upon the Party but also facilitated the institutionalization of Baathist ideals and values within the Syrian state apparatus. Such institutionalization marked a critical juncture in Syrian history, embedding the Baathist ideological framework into the very fabric of the nation's legal and political structure, thereby shaping the subsequent trajectory of Syrian governance and national identity.

The Syrian Constitution of 1973 presents a compelling study in linguistic dichotomies, particularly in its oscillation between gender-inclusive and distinctly masculine language. Terms like "the people" (*sha'b*) and "the masses" (*jamāhīr*), ostensibly gender-neutral and encompassing both women and men, are set against specific clauses that implicitly assume the default citizen to be male. This linguistic incongruity may be interpreted as an exemplar of what can be termed "false or deceptive universalism," a concept extensively critiqued by feminist theorists, encapsulated in the provocative inquiry "Are Women People?"[14] As explicated in the preceding chapter's analysis of the writings of the Baathist "founding fathers," there exists a palpable omission of women's contributions and roles within the nationalist narrative. This exclusion is intricately tied to an overemphasis on the archetype of the fighter, invariably envisioned as male. This focus on the male fighter's "struggle" and achievements not only marginalizes female presence but also perpetuates a gendered construction of national identity. This gender bias in the constitutional language reflects a broader ideological pattern within Baathist thought, where the valorization of martial masculinity effectively eclipses the recognition and inclusion of women in the conceptualization of citizenship and national identity.

The rhetorical fabric of the founder's writings in Baathist Syria, marked by an emphasis on military valor and the veneration of heroic male figures from a storied past, significantly permeates the Constitution's portrayal of the Syrian nation, its core values, and aspirations. Within various sections of the Constitution, these depictions are often presented in a gender-neutral manner, engendering a certain level of ambiguity regarding the inclusivity of such concepts of heroism and struggle. This ambiguity extends to the associated recognition of citizens' contributions, leading to questions about whether these accolades are universally applicable or predominantly reserved for the feats of men. However, a more scrupulous examination of the text reveals that, while ostensibly elevating a specific brand of masculine identity, these narratives of muscular nationalism are imbued with a tacit yet unequivocal exclusion of women as proactive participants within the national ethos. This exclusion is not merely a matter of oversight but a deliberate construction within the constitutional narrative, which endorses and perpetuates a specific gendered vision of national identity. Such an approach not only marginalizes women's roles and contributions but also reinforces a monolithic and patriarchal conception of national belonging and participation, effectively delineating the boundaries of citizenship and national identity within a distinctly masculinist framework.

The preamble of a constitution typically functions as a foundational narrative, delineating the overarching ethos and fundamental principles that underpin the constitutional community and define state membership. Consequently, a critical analysis of the Preamble of the Syrian Constitution is indispensable for elucidating how the constructs of national identity have been conceptualized and articulated. The Preamble serves as a microcosm of the dominant national motifs propagated within the Constitution, encapsulating themes such as resolve and determination, the ethos of struggle, and the veneration of sacrificial heroism. This constitutional narrative is imbued with the imagery of the idealized Baathist man, replete with references to a constructed ideal of masculinism and heroism. These elements not only glorify a specific masculine ideal but also reinforce male privilege across both the domains of state and society. The Preamble, in essence, offers a concise yet potent encapsulation of the Baathist vision of national identity. It manifests the regime's ideological leanings and priorities, setting the tone for the constitutional document and providing critical insights into the gendered underpinnings of state ideology and national identity construction as envisaged by the Baathist regime. As it states:

> With the close of the first half of this century, the Arab people's struggle has been expanding and assuming greater importance in various countries to achieve liberation from direct colonialism. The Arab masses [*jamāhīr*] did not regard independence as their goal and the end of their sacrifices, but as a means to consolidate their struggle, and as an advanced phase in their continuing battle against the forces of imperialism, Zionism, and exploitation, under the leadership of their patriotic and progressive forces, in order to achieve the Arab nation's goals of unity, freedom, and socialism.[15]

The most striking feature of this constitutional depiction is its portrayal of the establishment of an independent Syrian nation, not as a goal in itself but as a means to fortify a continuous militant resistance against perceived imperialist forces. This perspective highlights the instrumentalization of national sovereignty in the context of an ongoing struggle. The preeminence of the Baath Party within this nationalist paradigm is underscored in the Constitution's Preamble and further articulated in Article 8, which asserts: "The leading party in the society and the state is the Socialist Arab Baath Party. It leads a patriotic and progressive front seeking to unify the resources of the people." This clause not only cements the role of militarism in Syrian societal dynamics but also legitimizes the perpetual dominion of Baathist leadership, albeit ambiguously ascribed to the "will of the people." It is crucial to recall, within this framework, that the ascendancy of the Baath Party was not the result of democratic electoral processes but rather the outcome of a military coup. This historical context lends additional weight to the interpretation that the Constitution's recurrent references to the generic "people" and "masses" inherently exclude women, continuing to position them outside the national narrative. Such language, while seemingly inclusive, operates within a gendered paradigm that privileges a masculinist interpretation of citizenship and national belonging, effectively marginalizing women's roles and identities within the Syrian constitutional and national context.[16]

Within the Syrian milieu the interrogation of gender in the formulation of constitutional identity involves an intricate interplay of textual homogenization, as evidenced by the deployment of generic terms as proxies for human entities. This is compounded by the construction of a distinctly virile identity, anchored in the perpetuation of narratives centered around struggle, heroism, and sacrifice. These narratives engender a specific sense of selfhood, intrinsically linked to maleness. In this context, the concept of "sacrifice" for the nation is inextricably tied to a masculinist paradigm of protection, where the "self" is conceptualized as embodying normative manliness, in contrast to the "other," represented as the subordinate female. This binary division of gender roles is further obfuscated through the authoritative use of terms such as "people," "masses," and "citizens" within the Constitution. These terms, ostensibly universal, raise critical questions about their role in crafting an ostensibly homogeneous national identity. This rhetorical strategy not only masks underlying gender disparities but also reinforces a model of "masculinist protection," underpinned by heroism and sacrifice. Such constitutional framing, therefore, not only delineates but also legitimizes a gendered hierarchy, where the valorization of masculine attributes and roles comes at the expense of recognizing and incorporating the full spectrum of gender identities and contributions within the national narrative.

The ostensible neutrality presented in the Preamble of the Syrian Constitution, achieved through the utilization of generic terminologies, is further entrenched in the correlation drawn between the concepts of "struggle" and the "sacrifice" attributed to the "people" and "masses." A primary concept underpinning the Preamble is that of struggle, which implicitly signals a necessity for masculine protection. This notion serves as an instrumental device in demarcating gender boundaries within the national psyche, thereby augmenting the masculinization of the popular will. This construction prompts a critical inquiry: does the evocation of popular struggle in the Preamble exclusively represent the heroic actions of men?

Although, in a theoretical framework, the "masses" whom the Baathists professed to represent could encompass women, the empirical reality reflects a stark contrast. The individuals actively engaged in militant endeavors, and occupying leadership roles within the Party were predominantly, if not exclusively, men. Addressing these considerations necessitates a meticulous examination of both the linguistic choices employed in the Preamble and the potential associations of the concept of struggle with masculinist characteristics and ethos. This analytical approach aims to unravel whether the language and conceptual framework of the Preamble implicitly enshrine a gendered bias, aligning national identity and agency with a predominantly male narrative and perspective.

The Preamble of the Syrian Constitution emphatically commits to the perpetuation of an archetype of idealized heroism and virility, thereby framing historical narratives within a predominantly male-centric construct. Significantly, while the Preamble proclaims a transcendental authority by asserting that "the masses of our people" in Syria have sanctioned the leadership of the Socialist Arab Baath Party, there exists an inherent irony in this assertion. The proclaimed "revolution" of March 1963, in reality, was a military coup, casting doubt on the authentic inclusivity of women in this historical narrative. This phrasing, thus, intricately intertwines the notion of "revolutionary" struggle with a nostalgic invocation of a glorified past, amounting to an implicit emblem of masculinist virility. This conflation of heroic sacrifice and struggle serves to perpetuate the idealized construct of masculinist protection and militaristic values, concepts that are deeply ingrained in Baathist ideology. The propulsion of this narrative is facilitated by the emphasis placed in the Preamble on the "party's militant struggle." This focus on militaristic ethos is evident in the following excerpt from the Constitution:

> In the Syrian Arab region, the masses [*jamāhīr*] of our people [*sha'b*] continued their struggle after independence. Through their progressive march they were able to achieve their big victory by setting off the revolution of 8 March 1963 under the leadership of the Socialist Arab Baath Party, which has made authority an instrument to serve the struggle for the construction of the United Socialist Arab society. The Socialist Arab Baath Party is the first movement in the Arab homeland which gives Arab unity its sound revolutionary meaning, connects the nationalist with the socialist struggle, and represents the Arab nation's will and aspirations for a future that will bind the Arab nation with its glorious past and will enable it to carry out its role in achieving victory for the cause of freedom of all the peoples.

This constitutional language not only enshrines a gendered perspective within the national narrative but also reinforces the ideological linkage between masculinity, military prowess, and national identity. Such framing situates the concept of heroism within a narrow, gender-specific context, marginalizing alternative forms of contribution and valor, particularly those of women.

The phraseology employed in the Constitution illuminates the core values and foundational principles underpinning its structure. It explicitly evokes the politicized elements of Syrian national identity, such as will and determination. The initial invocation of the popular will of "the people" in the Preamble serves to broaden the scope of the Constitution's sovereignty. Yet, this reference to popular will is predicated on a willingness to sacrifice oneself for the nation, a notion intrinsically linked with attributes of masculine valor. This raises critical questions regarding the precise identity of "the people" as conceptualized within this framework. Furthermore, it is imperative to acknowledge that concepts such as "struggle" (*kifāh*) and "will" (*'irāda*), already deeply embedded in Baathist ideology, receive further institutionalization in the Preamble. The codification of these terms within the constitutional text not only reinforces their significance within the national ethos but also subtly entrenches the gendered dimensions of these concepts. This institutionalization perpetuates a particular interpretation of national identity and citizenship, one that is inextricably tied to militaristic and masculine ideals, thereby shaping the narrative of national belonging and participation within a distinctly gendered paradigm.

The Preamble further justifies the end of militant struggle and claims that the Party's militant struggle reflects popular demands and aspirations: "Through the party's militant struggle, the 16 Nov 1970 corrective movement responded to our people's demands and aspirations. This corrective movement was an important qualitative development and a faithful reflection of the party's spirit, principles, and objectives." The verbiage employed in the text accentuates the endorsement of militarism and the rationale of masculinist protectionism. The conferment of overarching authority upon the Baath Party, characterized by its militaristic disposition, to wield supreme judicial, legislative, and executive power in Syria, underscores a stark absence of a pluralistic and democratic framework. This absence is critically relevant in the context of women's political engagement, as it impedes the development of mechanisms and platforms conducive to advancing women's rights and ensuring equitable representation. As such, this constitutional arrangement not only centralizes power within a singular, militaristically oriented party but also restricts the scope for diverse political discourses and participatory democratic processes. Such a concentration of power, coupled with the ingrained masculinist ethos of the regime, creates systemic barriers to the political mobilization of women. This impediment extends beyond mere political participation, affecting the broader pursuit of gender equality and the challenge of dismantling entrenched patriarchal norms within the societal and political landscape of Syria. The configuration of state power and the embedded gender biases within this structure thus play a pivotal role in shaping both the political opportunities available to women and the broader discourse on gender rights and representation.

The nexus between the institutionalization of a military ethos and the perpetuation of patriarchal power dynamics is a subject that has garnered considerable scholarly attention in various national contexts. Cynthia Enloe, for instance, astutely observes: "militarization puts a premium on communal unity in the name of national survival, a priority which can silence women critical of patriarchal practices and attitudes; in so doing, nationalist militarization can privilege men."[17] This perspective is particularly pertinent in the context of Baathist Syria, where the militarization of society functioned not only to stifle feminist critiques but also to systematically exclude women from the nationalist narrative and institutional structures. The disparity in the inclusion of women within the Party's participatory framework and the broader civic activities is rendered more conspicuous when examining the subsequent sections of the Constitution. Here, male pronouns are interspersed with ostensibly universal language, thereby revealing a gendered bias beneath the surface of seemingly inclusive rhetoric. As it states:

> The exercise of his freedom makes him a dignified human being capable of giving and building, defending the homeland in which he lives, and making sacrifices for the sake of the nation to which he belongs ... The citizen's freedom can be completed only by his economic and social liberation.

This linguistic strategy serves to subtly reinforce the masculine orientation of the state's vision of citizenship and participation, further marginalizing women's roles and contributions within the socio-political fabric of the nation. The Constitution, in this manner, becomes a vehicle for the entrenchment of gender disparities, under the guise of national unity and militaristic valor, effectively perpetuating a patriarchal status quo.

The utilization of male pronouns in historical legal documents, a practice subject to considerable scholarly debate in both Arabic and English contexts,[18] manifests intriguing patterns in the 1973 Syrian Constitution. Notably, these gendered terms are predominantly absent from sections addressing the obligations of citizens and their allegiance to the Party. Instead, they surface primarily in the context of individual rights and freedoms. Determining whether this usage stems from a deliberate choice or an ingrained, reflexive bias remains a challenging endeavor, likely eluding definitive resolution. However, the linguistic differentiation evident in these various sections of the Constitution underscores the nonessential nature of gendered language within its text. The sentence structures could have been constructed in a gender-neutral manner, as exemplified by the hypothetical reformulation: "The citizens' freedom can only be completed through economic and social liberation." The prevailing inclination toward masculine language in contexts pertaining to rights and freedoms suggests a latent comfort with, or presumption of, the rights-bearing citizen as male. This inherent assumption of a male-centric viewpoint is particularly evident in the following excerpt from Article 40 of the Constitution: "All citizens have the sacred duty to defend the homeland's security, to respect its Constitution and socialist unionist system. Military service is compulsory and is regulated by law." In the Syrian Constitution, while Article 23(3) ostensibly addresses the general theme of compulsory military service, it significantly underscores the association between education and the cultivation of a physically robust body, thereby reinforcing the archetype of the male protector. The Article states: "Physical education is a foundation for the building of society. The state encourages physical education to form a physically, mentally, and morally strong generation." This articulation of education is closely allied with the glorification of militarism and embodies the encouragement of patriotism, masculinist protection, and heroism.

The emphasis placed on the development of a physically potent generation is intrinsically linked to Article 11, which delineates the defense of the homeland as a duty primarily reserved for military forces. Furthermore, the syntactic structure employed in this context reflects a discernible prioritization of physical strength over mental and moral fortitude. This lexical choice prompts critical reflection on why there is an explicit focus on fostering physical robustness, as opposed to nurturing a holistic, balanced development encompassing mental, moral, and physical health. The selection of the term "strong" (*qawi*) aligns with a masculinist interpretation of citizenship, predicated on a readiness and capacity to defend the nation. This choice reveals an underlying bias toward a specific conceptualization of citizenship, one that is predominantly framed within the parameters of physical prowess and martial capability. Such a framing not only reflects but also perpetuates the gendered underpinnings of national identity and civic duty as envisioned within the Syrian constitutional context.

The conceptualization of citizenship as delineated in the Syrian Constitution exhibits a pronounced emphasis on physical prowess, thereby establishing an intimate correlation with militarism and the epitome of the Baathist male ideal. This constitutional narrative sanctifies physical strength, intricately weaving it into the fabric of the national identity and associating it with the image of the Syrian warrior. Consequently, the notions of citizenship and "sacred duty" implicitly presuppose that the archetypal Syrian citizen is male. This presumption is further reinforced by the recurrent themes throughout the Constitution, such as "struggle," "heroism," and "physical education," all of which are steeped in martial lexicon and symbolism traditionally and pragmatically considered within the male domain. Women's roles and activities, while potentially encompassed under the broader mandates of defending security and upholding the socialist system, are effectively relegated to a peripheral status in this gendered narrative. They are perceived, at best, as a special category, divergent from the Constitution's primary focus areas like the stipulated compulsory military service. This constitutional discourse, therefore, not only delineates the realm of the idealized citizen within a distinctly masculine framework but also implicitly positions women's contributions and participation as ancillary to the core elements of national duty and identity. Such a gendered construction of citizenship and national duty underscores the deeply ingrained patriarchal biases within the constitutional fabric of Syrian society.

The contextualization of terms such as "struggle," "sacrifice," and "glorious past" within the Preamble of the Syrian Constitution serves to construct a constitutional identity deeply enmeshed with notions of manhood, thereby endeavoring to perpetuate a continuous image of militant identity. Significantly, this articulation of militant struggle, introduced early in the document, implicitly excludes the narrative of women's struggles against colonial and imperial forces. The ambiguity surrounding the conceptualization of women within the Constitution becomes evident when examining the major principles set forth in the Preamble, which states:

> Freedom is a sacred right and popular democracy is the ideal formulation which ensures for the citizen the exercise of his freedom, which makes him a dignified human being capable of giving and building, defending the homeland in which he lives, and making sacrifices for the sake of the nation to which he belongs. The homeland's freedom can only be preserved by its free citizens. The citizen's freedom can be completed only by his economic and social liberation.

As previously discussed, the Preamble establishes the overarching framework for national identity under the purview of this Constitution. While the language ostensibly endorses freedom and democracy in a seemingly egalitarian manner, the employment of certain gender-neutral nouns paradoxically raises questions about the inclusion of women. The subtle yet persistent use of masculine references, juxtaposed with the notion of sacredness, appears to confine the concept of sacrifice and belonging to a framework that aligns with masculinist protection and societal militarization. This consequently amplifies the existing dynamics of privileging masculinity and manhood. In essence, the "sacred" right of freedom, as articulated in the Constitution, is intimately associated with "defending the homeland." Within this framework it becomes pertinent to question the inclusivity of this call to freedom and defense. Does this constitutional envisioning of freedom and its associated duties extend an equal invitation to both genders, or does it inherently lean toward a male-centric interpretation of citizenship and national duty? This inquiry underscores the necessity of critically examining the gender implications embedded within the constitutional language and its impact on the broader societal understanding of gender roles and national identity.

This discourse leads us to an examination of Article 11 of the Syrian Constitution, which delineates: "[t]he armed forces and other defense organizations are responsible for the defense of the homeland's territory and for the protection of the revolution's objectives of unity, freedom, and socialism." In Syria the military comprises a conscripted force, mandating that males serve for two years upon reaching the age of eighteen. This stipulation further perpetuates the ambiguous positioning of women regarding their rights to freedom and democracy, raising critical questions about their recognition as fully realized human beings and citizens. Furthermore, the conceptualization of freedom and humanity within the Constitution is discursively molded by an emphasis on sacrifice, ingrained through the socialization of militarism. The intricate relationship between freedom and the capacity to defend the nation engenders an inquiry into the inclusivity of the term "citizen." Does it genuinely confer equal national membership to women? It is vital to acknowledge that the Preamble draws a connection between freedom and humanity, stating that the "citizen" exercises "his freedom which makes him a dignified human being capable of ... defending the homeland ... and making sacrifices for the sake of the nation to which he belongs." This portrayal crafts a unified conception of citizenship, intertwining the capacity to defend the homeland with notions of freedom, humanity, and manhood. Such a construction of citizenship not only consolidates the conflation of defense capabilities with broader concepts of freedom and human dignity but also underscores a gendered narrative that privileges a masculine interpretation of these ideals. This framework effectively marginalizes alternative perspectives on citizenship, particularly those of women, casting them in a subsidiary role within the national discourse. The constitutional language, thus, not only reflects but also reinforces a patriarchal vision of national identity, where the intersection of freedom, humanity, and civic duty is predominantly viewed through a masculinist lens.

The interplay between constitutional membership, masculinist protection, and militarism is further accentuated in Article 40, located in Part 4 (Freedom, Rights, Duties) of Chapter 1 (Basic Principles) of the Syrian Constitution. This article delineates two "sacred rights":

(1) All citizens are imbued with the sacred duty to defend the homeland's security, to respect its Constitution and socialist unionist system.
(2) Military service is compulsory and regulated by law.

Notably, the characterization of homeland defense as a "sacred duty" for "all citizens" introduces a degree of ambiguity in the gender specification of these citizens. The subtlety of the language used in the second clause further narrows the ostensibly gender-inclusive duty of defending the homeland to men, as implied by the reference to compulsory military service.

This constitutional framing generates an overlap between the perpetuation of masculinist norms and the ostensible equality in constitutional membership between men and women. By contextualizing the male prerogative to defend the homeland as sacred, the Constitution enshrines a symbolic hierarchy, effectively establishing the dominance of one gender over the other. As Pettman observes, the marginalization of women in the state sphere is often linked to "close associations of citizenship with bearing arms and being prepared to kill or die for the state."[19] Similarly, Elshtain highlights the "militarization of citizenship," where women are portrayed as passive "weepers over the tragedies" of war, in contrast to men, who are cast as protectors and guardians, thereby perpetuating a narrative of dependent and submissive femininity.[20] This constitutional rhetoric not only reinforces gender stereotypes but also crystallizes a patriarchal conception of citizenship, where the valorization of martial roles and duties is intrinsically linked to masculinity, further marginalizing women's roles and contributions within the national fabric.

In light of the preceding analysis, an examination of the Preamble of the Syrian Constitution reveals the establishment of a national narrative fundamentally anchored in the notions of struggle, will, and heroic sacrifice as defining characteristics of constitutional membership. This narrative framework invariably shapes the portrayal of women, reinforcing perceptions of their unsuitability for full citizenship status. The early sections of the Constitution, emphasizing a masculinized identity, cast doubt on the apparent gender-inclusiveness of terms such as "people" and "masses," especially when juxtaposed with the mandate of enforced military conscription. The crux of the issue lies not in the concept of conscription itself but rather in the ambiguous deployment of the term "citizens" to predominantly denote men in military roles and in framing the defense of the homeland as a sacred duty, intrinsically linked to human dignity. This association between military service, masculinist protection, and citizenship creates a hierarchical schema within the Constitution, effectively reinforcing gender demarcations in Syrian legal structures. The Baathist Party's militarized ethos, which consistently eclipsed the presence of women and defaulted to envisioning the man as the prototypical citizen, aligns with the broader exclusion of women from political spheres and activities engaged in by the Party's early leaders.

This gendered dynamic is not unique to the Syrian context. Hooper observes that the connections between military service, masculinity, and citizenship have been notably strong in the modern era. Elshtain also discusses the "militarization of citizenship," positing that it confers elevated social status and influence within the state to certain men, predicated on their perceived roles as protectors and guardians.[21] These observations were particularly salient during the institutionalization phase of the Baathist Party in the 1970s and 1980s. During this period, martial perspectives were consistently valorized in key documents, including the 1973 Constitution, while women's existence as citizens was marginalized by the intertwining of military service with the ideal of national belonging. This period marked a significant consolidation of gendered narratives within the constitutional and societal framework, profoundly impacting the representation and participation of women in the national discourse.

## Co-opting women's liberation

Despite its pronounced militaristic and masculinized ethos, and the conspicuous absence of women in its initial leadership echelons, the Baath Party has historically endeavored to project itself as an advocate for women's rights. As early as 1947 the Party's manifesto articulated a rather tepid endorsement of women's equality, stating: "The Arab woman should enjoy the full rights of a citizen, and the Party is struggling to raise her level so that she will deserve to enjoy these rights."[22] This statement is, at best, equivocal, implying that women must undergo an elevation of their "level" to become deserving of citizenship, rather than acknowledging citizenship as an inherent right of every individual under the state's jurisdiction. Furthermore, it categorizes women as a distinct group separate from the Party, necessitating the Party's guidance and paternalistic intervention for their advancement.

This perspective has persistently shaped Baathist rhetoric and policy concerning women across the institutionalization phase and into the present era. It represents a paradigm in which women's liberation is brandished as a token of the Party's modernizing ethos and as a legitimizing feature, particularly in contrast to other regional power structures. However, despite this rhetorical emphasis, tangible progress in enhancing women's rights, autonomy, and representation remains elusive. This approach to women's issues illustrates a superficial commitment to gender equality, serving more as a political instrument for the Party's image than a genuine effort to address and ameliorate the systemic gender inequalities entrenched in the social and political fabric.

In the 1973 Syrian Constitution, the principle of equality among all citizens is ostensibly established as a foundational guideline, seemingly applicable to both women and men. Article 25, for instance, articulates: "The citizens are equal before the law in their rights and duties. The state ensures the principle of equal opportunities for citizens." While this provision suggests a gender-neutral application of rights and duties, as previously discussed, there remain significant ambiguities regarding the conceptualization of the default citizen, particularly concerning gender. The Constitution also explicitly addresses women's rights in Article 45, which states: "The state guarantees women all opportunities enabling them to fully and effectively participate in the political, social, cultural, and economic life. The state removes the restrictions that prevent women's development and participation in building the socialist Arab society." At first glance, this provision appears to signal a progressive stance toward women's liberation. However, several critical nuances warrant attention regarding Article 45. Notably, the Article guarantees not equality or representation per se but rather "opportunities" and the removal of "restrictions." Thus, the focus appears to be on dismantling traditional or non-Baathist power structures perceived as impeding women's advancement. The Constitution does not explicitly commit to ensuring substantive improvements in women's lives or their autonomy.

Furthermore, this framing potentially creates a scenario where women could be held responsible for their own marginalization if the mere elimination of certain formal barriers does not lead to tangible enhancements in their quality of life. This approach implies a superficial commitment to women's rights, emphasizing structural changes over concrete improvements in women's lived experiences. Such a perspective fails to address the deeper societal and cultural factors that contribute to gender inequality, thereby limiting the potential impact of these constitutional provisions on the actual advancement of women's rights and autonomy. Secondly, the stipulated removal of restrictions, as articulated in Article 45 of the Syrian Constitution, is explicitly intended to facilitate women's "development" (*tatawwur*) and to augment their engagement with the Baathist socialist agenda. This provision does not represent an emancipation of women to autonomously determine their paths or to contribute democratically to political discourse. Instead, it presents an opportunity for women to align with and support the Baathist cause and its prescriptive ideals. This emphasis on women's need for "development" resonates with the Party's earlier, more overt assertion that women's "level" must be elevated to meet the criteria of a deserving citizen.

In a vein similar to the 1947 Party platform, Article 45 implies that women's freedom is contingent upon their endorsement of Baathist leadership and attaining favor within the Party's framework. This approach does not grant women the liberty to mobilize independently of the Baathist paradigm, nor does it confer upon them the right to substantive equality. Collectively, these facets of Article 45 illustrate that women's liberation is approached as an instrumental or ideological facet of the Baathist agenda, rather than as an inherent right accompanied by substantive and practical measures. This perspective reduces women's liberation to a tool within the Baathist political strategy, lacking a genuine commitment to the realization of women's rights and agency. It portrays women's advancement not as an end in itself but as a means to further the Party's objectives, effectively subordinating the pursuit of gender equality to the broader aims of the Baathist regime. This approach underscores the instrumentalization of women's rights in political discourse, prioritizing ideological conformity over the actual empowerment and liberation of women.

The Syrian Constitution articulates provisions for the engagement of women in the political arena, asserting: "the state guarantees women all opportunities to contribute effectively and fully to political, social, economic, and cultural life and works to remove the restrictions that prevent their development and participation in building a socialist Arab society." Despite this constitutional guarantee, the actual participation of women in politics, such as their eligibility for candidacy in the People's Assembly, has remained markedly constrained, not surpassing 12 percent. This participation is exclusively facilitated through party candidacy, precluding the possibility of independent runs.[23] The highest political office attained by a woman in Syria was by Najah Attar, who assumed the Vice Presidency in 2006, and previously served as the Minister of Culture from 1976 to 2000. Additionally, Bouthaina Shaaban's career trajectory, transitioning from the presidential translator in 1980 to the Director of the Department of Foreign Information in the Ministry of Foreign Affairs in 2002, and later assuming the role of Minister of Expatriates in 2006, is notable.

However, the relatively low representation of women in political life suggests that the regime's purported advancements in fostering women's political participation were largely superficial. The nominal presence of women in political roles does not equate to their recognition as integral partners in decision-making or in the construction of the political system. Women continue to be substantially outnumbered by men in these positions, with their participation being limited as the regime maintains stringent control over the political landscape. This situation points to a significant gap between constitutional provisions regarding women's rights and their practical implementation, highlighting a disparity between the regime's declarative commitment to gender equality and the actual dynamics of women's political empowerment and representation.

The Syrian regime's deployment of women's rights as a mechanism for legitimization was not paralleled by the enactment of effective legislation; nor did it precipitate any substantial shifts in the entrenched masculinist political culture. This period was marked by a stark contrast between the ostensibly inclusive language of the 1973 Constitution and the realities of legal practices under Baathist rule. For instance, Article 28 of the Constitution asserts: "No one may be tortured physically or mentally or be treated in a humiliating manner." While this clause ostensibly affirms a universal right to protection from torture and humiliation, its practical application revealed significant exceptions, particularly in the context of violence against women, especially when such acts occurred within the family setting. This disconnect between constitutional rhetoric and legal reality underscores a broader issue within the regime's approach to human rights, where formal declarations of rights were undermined by the lack of corresponding legal mechanisms and societal attitudes that perpetuated gender-based violence. The dichotomy between constitutional promises and lived experiences reflects a superficial commitment to the principles of equality and human rights, revealing the instrumentalization of these principles as tools for political legitimacy rather than as foundations for genuine societal reform and protection. This discrepancy highlights the complexities and challenges inherent in translating constitutional ideals into effective legal practices, particularly in contexts where traditional norms and power structures resist transformative change.

The Syrian state's inertia in addressing legal sanctioning of violence against women, under the guise of patriarchal and masculinist protection, is evident in various aspects of its penal laws. Notably, the Syrian Penal Code, established in 1949 and principally influenced by French and Islamic legal traditions, has remained largely unamended under Baathist governance. This stagnation raises critical questions about the extent to which Baath ideology, with its inherent masculinist traits and normalized glorification of militarism and soldiery, has contributed to and reinforced the perception of women as subordinate to men. Furthermore, the persistence of these legal provisions, despite the professed secularism of the Baath state, illuminates how the Syrian state has exerted control over public perceptions of women's political identity. This control delineates the exclusive boundaries of political discourse, legitimizing a masculinist ethos of protection. The Penal Code's omission of domestic violence legislation, particularly within familial contexts, exemplifies this issue. Recent scholarly evaluations of the Penal Code and societal trends in Syria have highlighted the prevalence of domestic violence nationwide.[24] Significantly, this form of abuse is not explicitly prohibited; for instance, spousal rape is not recognized as a criminal offense under the legal definition of rape. Article 489 of the Penal Code specifies:

(1) The man who violently threatened a woman other than his wife to have intercourse with him will be punished for 15 years with hard labor.
(2) The punishment will be not less than 21 years if the victim was less than 15 years old.

By omitting any reference to rape within the marital relationship, this article reflects a deeply entrenched gender bias. It underscores a legal and societal landscape where the rights and protection of women are marginalized, and where the state's approach to women's rights is characterized more by its alignment with traditional patriarchal norms than by a commitment to gender equality and the safeguarding of women's rights and dignity.

While the Syrian Constitution ostensibly affirms the principle of equality before the law for all citizens in terms of their rights and duties, as delineated in Article 25(3), this constitutional assertion stands in stark contrast to the discriminatory practices evident in the Penal Code, particularly concerning matters of adultery. Under Article 473 of the Penal Code, there exists a pronounced disparity in the sentencing of men and women: a woman convicted of adultery is subject to a sentence ranging from three months to two years, whereas a man, only if married, faces a sentence of one month to one year. Further exacerbating this gender-based discrimination, Article 474 specifies that a convicted husband is liable to a sentence of one month to one year only if the act of adultery occurs within the matrimonial home. This differentiation in treatment extends beyond sentencing disparities. The legal framework adopts divergent approaches to adultery committed by men and women, reflecting a gender-biased perspective in its adjudication. According to Articles 473(3) and 475, the criteria for evidential proof in cases of gender-based violence differ markedly based on gender. Men are permitted to present any form of evidence to substantiate their claims, whereas women are constrained to presenting solely written evidence, such as a written confession from the husband.

These legal provisions not only manifest gender discrimination but also illuminate a deeper, systemic bias within the legal system. They underscore a societal and judicial perception of adultery and gender-based violence that disproportionately disadvantages women, both in terms of legal recourse and the broader societal implications of these legal standards. This differential treatment evidences a legal framework that reinforces patriarchal norms and perpetuates gender inequality, contradicting the constitutional ethos of equal rights and responsibilities for all citizens.

Despite the constitutional provisions in Articles 28 and 29 of the Syrian Constitution, which assert the equality of all citizens before the law in terms of their duties and obligations, certain clauses within the Penal Code exhibit discriminatory practices against women. A conspicuous example is Article 548, which affords men legal exemption from punitive measures if they inflict harm or cause the death of their spouse, sister, or any descendants in instances of unexpected discovery of these individuals engaged in adultery or extramarital sexual relations. This provision essentially legitimizes honor killings, rationalizing such acts as justifiable under conditions of extreme emotional disturbance or lack of premeditation.

Moreover, Article 548(2) extends this prerogative to situations where the male individual encounters his spouse, sister, or descendants in circumstances deemed "suspicious" (*mashkūk*). The ambiguous nature of the term "suspicious" grants considerable latitude for interpretation, effectively providing men with broad leeway to justify violent acts. This legislation, in effect from 1949 until its amendment in 2009, essentially sanctioned violence against women within the private sphere. The 2009 amendment, prompted by a surge in honor killings (with 533 reported cases in 2007), adjusted the penalty for such acts to a maximum of two years' imprisonment. However, this revised sanction raises significant concerns regarding its adequacy as a deterrent for such severe crimes. The mere imposition of a two-year imprisonment for the act of killing a woman not only fails to reflect the gravity of the offense but also perpetuates a culture of gender-based violence. This legal framework, even post-amendment, falls short of providing effective protection against such crimes and reflects an underlying normalization of violence against women within the societal and legal contexts. This situation underscores a need for a more rigorous and equitable legal approach that adequately addresses and penalizes gender-based violence, aligning with principles of justice and gender equality.

The prevalence of a culture of gender-based violence in Syria is further underscored by the provisions of the Syrian Penal Code, particularly Article 489, which remained in force throughout the Baathist era and until 2012. This Article specifies that a rapist is subject to twenty-one years' imprisonment if the victim is under fifteen years old, but the sentence is reduced to five years if the victim is older than fifteen. Articles 490–508, which encompass crimes of kidnapping, rape, violent assault, and sexual exploitation of females (both under and over fifteen years of age), are also indicative of the gender-based legal framework. Although these articles suggest a sentencing range of five to fifteen years upon conviction, Article 508 controversially allows a rapist to avoid punishment by marrying the victim, thereby perpetuating a legal framework that tacitly condones such violence.

Additionally, Article 489 of the Penal Code implies a form of legally sanctioned spousal violence by stating that a man who violently coerces a woman other than his wife into intercourse faces a fifteen-year hard labor sentence. This provision implicitly suggests that violence within the marital context is not subject to the same legal scrutiny: "A man who violently threatens a woman other than his wife to have intercourse with him will be punished with 15 years of hard labor."[25] Furthermore, the Penal Code continued to criminalize adultery during the Baathist era, imposing harsher sentences for women compared to men and applying differing evidentiary standards for each gender (Articles 473 and 474). This legislative approach reflects and reinforces entrenched patriarchal norms within the legal system, where women are subjected to more stringent legal standards and greater punitive measures than men for the same offense. Collectively, these legal provisions not only reflect a deeply ingrained gender bias within the Syrian legal system but also illustrate the systemic challenges in addressing and rectifying gender-based violence and discrimination. The legal framework, as it stands, fails to provide equitable protection and justice for women, perpetuating a cycle of gender-based violence and reinforcing the societal marginalization of women.

Additional crucial areas in which actual practice and policy were far removed from the lofty Baathist rhetoric included women's education, economic participation, and right to financial security. Article 37 of the Syrian Constitution posits education as a universal right, stating: "Education is a right guaranteed by the state. Elementary education is compulsory and all education is free. The state undertakes to extend compulsory education to other levels and to supervise and guide education in a manner consistent with the requirements of society and of production." Despite this declaration, the Baathist administration exhibited limited initiative in encouraging women's education beyond elementary level, typically concluding around age fourteen. The Constitution's use of "undertaking" (*takful*) to expand educational opportunities does not imply a firm commitment, and the extension of education is contingent upon the "requirements of society." One societal norm that seemed to influence Baathist policy was the practice of early marriage for women, leading to their withdrawal from education to assume roles as mothers and housewives. Although the regime ostensibly supported women's rights, it did not actively challenge the norm of teenage marriage. In 2003 the Baathist government even expressed reservations against the UN's Convention on the Elimination of All Forms of Discrimination against Women (CEDAW) regarding the treaty's stance on early marriage.

Research by the Syrian Commission for Family Affairs in the early 2000s revealed that the illiteracy rate among Syrian women exceeded 25 percent, attributed to early marriage and pervasive gender stereotypes within the education system.[26] The portrayal of women in state-sanctioned educational materials as passive, submissive, and relegated to the private sphere undermines the Baathist claims of fostering women's opportunities and socioeconomic engagement. This finding is corroborated by a 2008 UNESCO study, which reported that at age fifteen the female illiteracy rate in Syria stood at 26 percent, in contrast to 12 percent for males.[27]

Regarding economic rights and security, the 1973 Constitution asserts: "Work is a right and duty of every citizen. The state undertakes to provide work for all citizens ... The state fixes working hours, guarantees social security, and regulates rest and leave rights and various compensations and rewards for workers." However, the practical realization of these constitutional guarantees in the context of women's employment and economic independence remained largely unfulfilled. The gap between constitutional promises and actual policy outcomes reflects a broader pattern within the Baathist regime, where the rhetoric of equality and rights often failed to translate into substantive changes and improvements in the lives of Syrian women.

In the realm of labor law under Baathist rule, a discernible discrepancy emerges between the inclusive language of the Constitution and its actual implementation. This disparity is exemplified in Articles 89 and 90 of the Social Insurance Law, which remained operative throughout the Baathist era and continue to be enforced. These articles contain distinct provisions for men and women regarding pension entitlements and spousal benefits. A salient feature of this legislation is its stipulation that widows forfeit their rights to benefits from their deceased husband's pension upon remarriage or if they are gainfully employed. Conversely, this restriction does not apply to men who lose their wives.

This legislative framework exerts profound societal implications, particularly in Syria where premature male mortality is not uncommon. The legal constraints imposed on widows serve to disincentivize them from pursuing new personal or economic opportunities. The law effectively penalizes widows for remarrying or participating in the workforce, thereby limiting their financial independence and autonomy. This gender-specific legal approach not only highlights the unequal treatment of women in the sphere of labor law but also reflects broader societal norms that constrain women's economic participation and personal choices. The disparity between the constitutional commitment to equality and the realities of labor law underscores a systemic bias in legal and societal structures, which continue to hinder women's full participation in economic and social life.[28]

The legal framework of Baathist Syria, particularly regarding marital relations and gender roles within the family, manifests deeply troubling provisions. These stipulations are predicated on the assumption that women lack autonomous rights to their romantic and reproductive decisions. This perspective is subtly embedded in the 1973 Constitution, albeit articulated in ostensibly positive, albeit superficial, language. Article 44 of the Constitution asserts: "The family is the basic unit of society and is protected by the state. The state protects and encourages marriage and eliminates the material and social obstacles hindering it. The state protects mothers and infants and extends care to adolescents and youths." A critical aspect of this provision is its conflation of mothers with children, categorizing them as recipients of state protection rather than as active participants in state governance. This categorization does not delineate specific rights for mothers or children but rather relegates them to a dependent status. Additionally, the declaration that the family constitutes "the basic unit of society," coupled with legal norms affirming male dominance within the family, has profound implications for women's autonomy and independent citizenship.

This constitutional framing, whereby the foundational societal unit is one where women are subordinated and lack self-determination, equal rights, and even basic legal protection against physical violence, casts doubt on the

Baathist regime's purported commitment to women's full socio-economic participation. If the fundamental structure of society is predicated on female dependency and limited autonomy, then the regime's claims of supporting women's rights and participation appear exceedingly superficial. This contradiction between constitutional rhetoric and the reality of legal provisions reflects a broader disconnect within the Baathist legal and societal order, where the advancement of women's rights is ostensibly supported yet practically undermined by entrenched patriarchal norms and practices.[29]

Despite the supposedly secular nature of the Baathist regime, the 1973 Constitution retained requirements in Article 3 that: "The religion of the president of the Republic has to be Islam" and "Islamic jurisprudence is a main source of legislation." (The Arabic phrasing used here also presumes that the president is a man.) In practice, the legal framework that was implemented in Baathist Syria devolved many aspects of Personal Status Law and some aspects of the Penal Code to local religious courts, which applied their own interpretations of Islamic jurisprudence (*sharee'a*). While interpretations of this form of law vary widely among different communities and individuals, its application in Syria was generally left to local patriarchs who ignored any modern interpretations of women's rights as well as other provisions for freedom and equality that were expressed in the 1973 Constitution.[30] Such a state of affairs contributed further to rendering the Syrian Constitution an entirely hollow document when it came to actually implementing women's rights, and ensured that women would remain confined to a condition of dependency.

A related, long-standing legal policy under the Baathists can be found in Articles 523 and 524 of the Penal Code, which criminalize both women who use contraceptive pills and vendors who sell or advertise such products. Abortion is also illegal in most cases in Syria, and it carries a lengthy prison sentence both for women seeking abortion and for medical providers. These legal provisions that exert state control over women's reproductive rights and bodily autonomy are bizarrely contradictory with rhetorical statements presented by the Baathist government's Commission for Family Affairs, which has prominently encouraged women to have fewer children as a means of promoting their education and public social engagement.[31] It is difficult to take such rhetoric seriously when access to contraceptives is criminalized. This is a central example of the hypocrisy or instrumentalization of women's rights, in which important concepts of social progress are cynically co-opted as a legitimization framework and a weapon against political opponents, with essentially no commitment whatsoever to actually implement the purported ideals.

Regarding the strategy proposed by the Syrian government's Commission for Family Affairs, their publication outlined a national population program aimed at integrating both direct and indirect measures to influence childbearing patterns. The document delineated:

> The suggested national population program should be based on achieving integration between direct tools (reducing childbearing demand, increasing demand on reproductive health services and new family planning methods) and indirect tools (improving population characteristics), which have an impact on reducing childbearing. Such characteristics include literacy, eliminating school dropout and child labor, encouraging higher marriage age, giving incentive to more women to complete secondary education, and integrating the highest possible number of women into the labor market.[32]

While the report alludes to "new family planning methods," it conspicuously lacks any detailed proposal for legal reforms that would substantively enhance women's access to family planning, such as decriminalizing contraceptive use. The language used predominantly focuses on "encouraging" particular outcomes, such as reducing childbearing demand and increasing educational and employment opportunities for women, rather than advocating for new rights recognition or specific policy initiatives to support these goals. This rhetorical stance effectively portrays an image of advancing women's liberation without providing tangible support. It places women in a position of potential failure and victim-blaming by professing regime support without implementing meaningful material or structural changes. As Dwyer articulates, "[women's] sexuality and how they do or do not control it is deeply implicated in practices of citizenship and transitional power."[33] The Baathist approach to women's autonomy over their sexuality and reproductive rights is notably contradictory. The regime's rhetoric claims to uphold these rights while, in reality, enacting policies that undermine them. This dissonance between the regime's public declarations and actual practices highlights a critical gap in the implementation of women's rights, reflecting a broader pattern of instrumentalization of women's issues for political expediency rather than a genuine commitment to gender equality and empowerment.

In the domain of Syrian nationality law, a particularly conspicuous issue is the prohibition against women transmitting their citizenship to their children or spouses. As previously analyzed, this gender-specific legislation, rooted in racially charged and patriarchal anxieties about women marrying outside the national community, was supported by Baathist founders, notably Zaki al-Arsuzi. This law exemplifies a stark incongruity between the ostensibly inclusive rhetoric of the 1973 Constitution and the realities of Baathist legal practices.

Article 43 of the Constitution declares: "The law regulates Syrian Arab citizenship and guarantees special facilities [i.e., accommodations] for the Syrian Arab expatriates and their sons." While the gendered reference to "sons" ('*abnā*') in this clause is somewhat ambiguous, the practical application of the corresponding law exclusively pertained to paternal lineage. This disparity is illustrative of a broader pattern where ostensibly neutral language fails to disguise the underlying reality of women's exclusion, contravening the Constitution's professed principle of equality before the law (Articles 25 and 26).

The specific legislation that stipulated the paternal-only transmission of citizenship was codified in the Syrian Nationality Act of 1969 and its subsequent regulations issued in 1976, which remain in force.[34] Notably, the enactment of this legislation coincided with the Constitution's discourse on equal rights and the proclamation of "guaranteeing women all opportunities" (Article 45). However, like other legal statutes discussed earlier, the overarching effect of such laws is to cast women in a role of dependency on male family members, thereby undermining their autonomy and denying them the full rights and equality inherent in true citizenship. This legal framework not only reflects a gendered bias in the transmission of citizenship but also underscores a systemic issue within Syrian law where women's rights and agency are curtailed by patriarchal norms and practices embedded within the legal and societal structure.

## Outcomes for women in the Syrian community

As a result of the regime's cynical instrumentalization of women's rights, Syrian women became caught between the Constitutional ideal and the legislative reality. The rhetoric of the Baathists informed them that the nationalist ideal offered liberation, but everyday, real-world experience proved otherwise. This situation was not entirely unique to women, as numerous forms of rights abrogation and exclusion from political and civic participation were inflicted on the overall population during the decades of Baathist rule in Syria. Indeed, the regime operated under a persistent legal doctrine of a "State of Emergency" and martial law, which was declared in 1963 and did not end until the outbreak of the civil war in 2011. The emergency powers that the Party granted to itself under this mechanism essentially negated most of the rights enshrined in the Constitution, such as freedom of expression, affiliation, travel, and assembly.[35] For women, however, these strictures were particularly burdensome, as women had to contend with all of the general limitations on citizens' liberty as well as the frameworks that specifically subordinated their rights to those of men, as discussed in the previous section. Combined with the overall culture of muscular nationalism and militarism that informed the Baathist Party, this created a profoundly suffocating environment for women's personal and political autonomy.

Among other considerations, the Baathist regime has refused to allow women to establish independent feminist political organizations. The Party inaugurated its own women's apparatus in 1967, under the name of the General Women's Union (GWU), which was authorized to pursue issues of concern to women within the overall framework of the Baathist's socialist ideals. The GWU was established by Legislative Decree No. 121 issued by the interim leadership of the Socialist Baath Party four years after it came to power in Syria. The decree defined the Women's Union as "a general organization for the women of the Syrian Arab Republic that includes a number of branches."[36] The decree detailed the organization of the Union, including the objectives that called for its establishment as a public organization for women, which the Union must pursue. These goals ostensibly represent support for women and an effort to empower them in society. They claim to provide working women, who are also housewives, with support at the local as well as at the international level. This direction has been adopted by the Party as a basis for any work, organization, and movement, where the ideas of socialist nationalism act as a starting point, a builder of capacities, and a permanent tool.[37]

The work of the Union has stayed within the professed framework set by the regime: to strengthen the role of women in society and distance them from their traditional functions. For this the Union opened nurseries and organized training courses for women teaching them sewing and other vocational skills. However, the fields that it opened for women were limited and did not change their role in society but reinforced their traditional roles, all the while propagandizing that it was empowering women and distancing them from these roles. Since this organization existed, according to the regime, there was no need for any other women's group. The Union had the power to accept or reject its members, and, for example, it used security reasons to justify its rejection of veiled women. Likewise, it did not accept independent Syrian women in its ranks to prevent them from playing influential roles that brought about real change in society or from demanding reforms that would impact the societal or legal status of women. Most of the Union's women were affiliated with the Baath Party, especially its leaders.[38] The GWU, however, is institutionally and financially beholden to the Baathist leadership. As Kelly and Breslin have documented: "In practice, this [GWU] monopoly excludes dissenting views on government policies and delays action on specific problems, since initiatives and complaints have to filter up through the unwieldly, multi-layered administrative structure of the Baath Party."[39] The GWU has profoundly failed in its mission to influence Syrian politics and society for the advancement of women's equality, as can be seen in the continuation of numerous and extreme laws limiting women's rights (discussed in the previous pages). Along with the Syrian Commission for Family Affairs, which was established in 2003 and has also issued ineffectual statements supporting women's equality, the GWU has remained incapable of even basic accomplishments such as convincing the regime to accept CEDAW's prohibitions against early marriage. Much of the reason for this stagnation on practical issues of women's rights in Syria can be attributed to the stringent top–down authority exerted over these organizations (and indeed over the entire political landscape) by the Baathist Party, which has made it impossible for feminists to exert meaningful institutional pressure.

One outcome of the authoritarian co-option of women's liberation in Syria is that the political representation of women has been abysmal. Although women in Syria have held the right to vote since 1949, their presence and influence in political structures has been negligible. The Party has made a few prominent appointments of women—which it loudly celebrated as a manifestation of its ideological superiority—for example in the selection of Najah Attar as the first woman in the Arab world to hold the post of vice-president in 2006, the appointment of Shahinaz Fakoush as the first woman in the Baathist Executive Bureau in 2005, and the appointment of Samira Almasalmeh as the first woman editor-in-chief of the state newspaper, *Tishreen*, in 2009. During the Party's rule there have also been three women ministers of culture, four women ministers of social affairs and labor, one woman minister of higher education, and one woman minister of expatriates. All of these positions, however, are orchestrated by the regime for its own purposes, and they have all involved women who are passionate Party members and have served essentially as transparent mouthpieces for the Baathist leadership.[40] Meanwhile, women's representation in the legislature, which is a somewhat more robust measure of political equality, has never risen above 12 percent (Table 3.1).

Mia al-Rahbi has closely examined women's participation in the Syrian legislature and concluded that the gradual increase in participation since the 1970s was a political decision orchestrated by the regime through its managed elections, rather than an expression of a genuine shift in social conditions encouraging the entry of women into politics.[41] Regardless of the reasons for this increase, the most recent figures of around 12 percent representation remain middling at best in comparison with other Middle Eastern states as well as globally. Al-Rahbi also characterized the role of women in the Syrian state as one of "silent representation," meaning that despite increasing numbers, these women contribute relatively little to shaping the direction of the regime or its decision-making processes.[42] It should also be noted that Syrian women have almost no presence in the judiciary and in the executive branch, in part because these roles are strongly associated with religious and military leadership (respectively) in which women continue to play little part.

**Table 3.1** Women's representation in the Syrian parliament

| Legislative session | Number of seats | Number of women | Percentage of women |
| --- | --- | --- | --- |
| 1973–77 | 186 | 5 | 2 |
| 1977–81 | 195 | 6 | 3 |
| 1981–85 | 195 | 12 | 6 |
| 1986–90 | 195 | 16 | 8 |
| 1990–94 | 250 | 21 | 8 |
| 1994–98 | 250 | 24 | 9 |
| 1998–2002 | 250 | 26 | 10 |
| 2003–07 | 250 | 30 | 12 |
| 2007–11 | 250 | 31 | 12 |

*Note:* The parliament has not convened from March 2011 up through the date of this writing (November 2022) due to the ongoing civil conflict. The data in this table are sourced from the World Bank.

Perhaps most significantly, the militarized and muscular concepts of masculinity that were instilled under Baathist rule, and the manner in which these concepts were allowed to override the constitutional rights-based order, heralded a cultural shift in Syria in which women increasingly confronted aggression and direct misogyny. Given the geopolitical context of the Syrian case, the chapter has answered an important question as to what Baathism is and how it is used to perpetuate masculinism. The example of Syria thus presents an opportunity to explore how dominant national ideology generates and endorses masculinist ethos and values. Although this chapter is not, strictly speaking, comparative, its findings and insights should have relevance for other countries in the Middle East. Because so much of Syrian politics has, since the beginning of the twentieth century, revolved around defense and militarism, this militant construction of national identity and belonging has elevated men to much more central roles—while women have remained marginal to the national discourse. Militarism has also been central in defining membership of the constitutional community. In other words, the concept of male sacrifice for the nation in the Baathist ideology symbolizes a system based on privileging men and disempowering women. In addition, the state's control over women's sexuality imposes a complicated perception of the rights of motherhood. In the same vein, understanding the intricate nature of the link between Baathism and the logic of masculinist protection and militarism that prevails in the Preamble of the Constitution reflects the hegemonic patriarchy in the state-formation stage. Such a construction of virile manliness explains why Baathism has failed, despite its nominal secularity, to break with tradition when it comes to women's rights. The following chapter will use the lens of popular songs and masculinity performances to show how this Baathist culture seeped into everyday life as the regime's hegemony continued to seize hold of the country.

## Notes

1 See Massimiliano Trentin. "Modernizing as State Building: The Two Germanies in Syria, 1963–1972." *Diplomatic History* 33, no. 3 (June 2009): 487–505, p. 497; Eberhard Kienle. "Arab Unity Schemes Revisited: Interest, Identity, and Policy in Syria and Egypt." *International Journal of Middle East Studies* 27, no. 1 (February 1995): 53–71, p. 67; and Victoria Gilbert. "Syria for the Syrians: The Rise of Syrian Nationalism, 1970–2013." Master's thesis, Northeastern University, 2013, p. 32. www.academia.edu/3432163/Syria_for_the_Syrians_The_Rise_of_Syrian_Nationalism_1970–2013. Accessed June 10, 2016.
2 See Bouthaina Shaaban. *Both Right and Left-Handed: Arab Women Talk about Their Lives*. Bloomington, IN: Indiana University Press, 1991; Fiona Hill. "Syrian Women and Feminist Agenda." In Paul J. White and William S. Logan (eds), *Remaking the Middle East*, pp. 129–51. New York and Oxford: Berg Publishers, 1997; Rania Maktabi. "Gender, Family Law and Citizenship in Syria." *Citizenship Studies* 14, no. 5 (2010): 557–72.
3 Esther Van Eijk. *Family Law in Syria: Patriarchy, Pluralism and Personal Status Codes*. London: I.B. Tauris, 2016, p. 30.
4 Ibid. See Maktabi 2010; and Elham Manea. *The Arab State and Women's Rights: The Trap of Authoritarian Governance*. London and New York: Routledge, 2011.
5 Lee Harvey. "The Methodological Problems of Ideology Critique." Birmingham Polytechnic Research Unit Discussion Paper 19, no. 5 (1983).
6 Ibid., p. 7.
7 Joseph Mann. "The Syrian Neo-Ba'th Regime and the Kingdom of Saudi Arabia, 1966–70." *Middle Eastern Studies* 42, no. 5 (2006): 769–90, p. 756.
8 John Galvani. "The October War: Egypt, Syria, Israel." *MERIP Reports* 25 (1974): 10–20, p. 11.
9 Raymond A. Hinnebusch. "Modern Syrian Politics." *History Compass* 6, no. 1 (January 2008): 263–85.
10 Raymond A. Hinnebusch. *Peasant and Bureaucracy in Ba'thist Syria: The Political Economy of Rural Development*. Boulder, CO: Westview Press, p. 30.
11 See Trentin 2009, p. 497; and Kienle 1995, pp. 53–71, p. 67.
12 Gilbert 2013, p. 32.
13 Raymond A. Hinnebusch. *Syria: Revolution from Above*. London: Routledge, 2001, p. 138.
14 See Helen Irving. *Gender and the Constitution: Equity and Agency in Comparative Constitutional Design*. Cambridge: Cambridge University Press,

2008, p. 47; and Catharine A. MacKinnon. *Are Women Human? And Other International Dialogues*. Harvard, MA: Harvard University Press, 2006, p. 398.

15 Throughout this chapter, the passages quoted from the Syrian Constitution of 1973 are drawn from the English translation provided by the Carnegie Middle East Center, which can be found online at: http://carnegie-mec.org/diwan/50255?lang=en. I have spot-checked this translation against the Arabic version and can confirm that the content and tone of the Arabic is maintained in the quoted material.

16 Michel Rosenfeld. "Constitutional Identity." In *The Oxford Handbook of Comparative Constitutional Law*, edited by Michel Rosenfeld and András Sajó. Online edition November 2012, p. 757. http://dx.doi.org/10.1093/oxfordhb/9780199578610.013.0037. Accessed September 14, 2015.

17 Cynthia Enloe. *Bananas, Beaches, and Bases: Making Feminist Sense of International Politics*. Berkeley, CA: University of California Press, 1990, pp. 57–58; see also Anders Ahlbäck. *Manhood and the Making of the Military: Conscription, Military Service and Masculinity in Finland 1917–39*. London and New York: Routledge, 2016; and Sikata Banerjee. *Gender, Nation and Popular Film in India: Globalizing Muscular Nationalism*. New York: Routledge, 2016.

18 See Terrell Carver and Samuel A. Chambers (eds). *Carole Pateman: Democracy, Feminism, Welfare*. London and New York: Routledge, 2011, p. 67; and MacKinnon 2006, p. 398.

19 Jan Jindy Pettman. *Worlding Women: A Feminist International Politics*. London: Routledge, 1996, p. 17.

20 Jean Bethke Elshtain. "Reflections on War and Political Discourse." *Political Theory* 13, no. 1 (1985): 39–57, p. 42.

21 Ibid., p. 42; Charlotte Hooper. *Manly States: Masculinities, International Relations, and Gender Politics*. New York: Columbia University Press, 2001, p. 36. See also Pettman 1996, p. 17.

22 This is my own translation of the Baath Party's platform as issued on April 4, 1947. The original Arabic text is available online at: www.albasrah.net/ar_articles_2007/0307/dstor-b3th_070307.htm.

23 Ibid., p. 14.

24 Sanja Kelly and Julia Breslin. "Syria." In Sanja Kelly and Julia Breslin (eds), *Women's Rights in the Middle East and North Africa: Progress amid Resistance*, pp. 459–86. New York: Freedom House, 2010, p. 461.

25 Syrian Penal Law.

26 Sawsan Zakzak Fayek Hjeieh and Maya Al Rahabi, "Gendered Constitution Building Process for Syria." Report, SIDA, Sweden, November 2014. www.efi-ife.org/sites/default/files/001%20Gendered%20Constitution%20Building%20Process%20for%20Syria%20Report%20%28November%202014%29.pdf. Accessed June 6, 2015.

27 UNESCO. "The National Report about the State of the Adult Education Development in Syrian Arab Republic Presented to Preparing for the Sixth

International Conference on Adult Education." Report by Abdulfattah al-Obaid, Director of Adult Education, Syria, for Sixth International Conference on Adult Education, Belem, December 1–4, 2009. www.unesco.org/fileadmin/MULTIMEDIA/INSTITUTES/UIL/confintea/pdf/National_Reports/Arab%20States/Syrian_Arab_Republic__English_.pdf. Accessed June 4, 2015.

28 The text of the Social Insurance Law (in Arabic) can be found on the website of the Syrian Parliament, at: http://parliament.gov.sy/laws/Law/1959/work_05.htm. For more details about pension law and gender in Syria, see Nawar Jaber. "Syrian Army Volunteers: Exposing the Regime Without Confusion." *The New Arab*, October 9, 2016. https://2u.pw/5yGihw. Accessed December 15, 2017.

29 Hill 1997, p. 130, discussed this aspect of the Syrian legal landscape extensively, stating that: "In Syria, it would be reasonable to suggest that women experience their 'rights' in terms of their place in a family, and in a co-local, and often confessional, community rather than in terms of their positions as citizens of the state. Since Syrian families and communities of all ethnic and confessional backgrounds are acutely patriarchal, the rights of women within these communities are, for the most part, defined accordingly."

30 Carnegie Middle East Center. "The Syrian Constitution 1973–2012." December 5, 2012. http://carnegie-mec.org/diwan/50255?lang=en. Accessed May 6, 2013.

31 Syrian Commission for Family Affairs. "First National Primary Policy Report on the State of Population in Syria." 2008. Accessed June 5, 2015.

32 Ibid.

33 Leslie K. Dwyer. "Spectacular Sexuality: Nationalism, Development and the Policies of Family Planning in Indonesia." In *Gender Ironies of Nationalism: Sexing the Nation*, edited by Tamar Mayer, pp. 25–64. London and New York: Routledge, 2000, p. 33.

34 The text of the 1969 Syrian Nationality Act (in Arabic) can be found at: www.cdf-sy.org/low/mrsom%20276.htm.

35 The long-delayed end of the "State of Emergency" in April 2011 was an attempt to appease the opposition and end the outbreak of protests that had begun in the previous month. In pragmatic terms this gesture had no real effect, as the Party's security forces continued to implement a violent crackdown on the demonstrations, in the absence of any truly independent judiciary or legal respect for Constitutional rights. For more on this topic and a full accounting of the regime's "Emergency" powers, see the link: www.hrw.org/reports/2007/syria1007/index.htm

36 Contemporary Syrian History, Decree establishing the General Women's Union in 1967. https://2u.pw/fsoew6. Accessed April 10, 2013.

37 Article 4 of Legislative Decree No. 121 stipulates seven main objectives for the establishment of the Women's Union:

- Organize women's capabilities and coordinate their efforts in collective action to achieve the objectives of the revolution in building a unified Arab socialist society.

- Deepen national and socialist awareness, raise the cultural and social level of women in Syrian Arab lands and provide appropriate conditions for the exercise of their rights and the performance of their duties in all fields.
- Work to provide services that reassure women regarding their role as housewives and as active members of society.
- Provide social, health and cultural services to citizens.
- Participate with other grassroots organizations in achieving the objectives and methods of the revolution and in the foundations of grassroots democracy.
- Work with the masses of women and women's organizations in other Arab countries for the liberation of Arab women and find practical means to ensure their effective contribution to the socialist unitary struggle.
- Allow women in Syrian Arab land to play their role in adopting the positions of the revolution and participating in the liberation struggle of women at the international level. Ibid.

38 Enab Baladi. "Women in the Era of Assad between the Women's Union and the First Lady. Intellectual Domestication in the Crucible of Baath." September 25, 2016. https://2u.pw/Q5JiW1. Accessed October 15, 2016; and Syria Women Bloc for Democracy. "Was the General Women's Union the Supreme Hand of the Baath to Paralyze the Syrian Women's Movement?" March 11, 2018. https://2u.pw/nOQXlv. Accessed April 10, 2020.
39 Kelly and Breslin 2010, p. 464.
40 See Euro-Mediterranean Women's Foundation. "National Situation Analysis Report: Women's Human Rights and Gender Equality in Syria," July 2010. https://docs.euromedwomen.foundation/files/ermwfdocuments/5668_2.139.nationalsituationanalysis-syria.pdf. Accessed March 6, 2015.
41 Mia al-Rahbi. "Al-mushāraka al-siyāsyiya li l-mara'a." *Al-Hiwar al-Mutamaddin*, no. 1131 (March 2005), p. 25. www.ahewar.org/debat/show.art.asp?aid=33062. Accessed July 3, 2005.
42 Ibid., p. 30.

# 4

# Constructing the muscular nation in song and performance

As Baathist power became institutionalized in Syria, the regime sought to promote its viewpoints and reshape the cultural outlooks of the populace. This endeavor included the creation and dissemination of patriotic symbols intended for mass consumption, such as public statues, spectacles, and songs. Prior scholars have written extensively about the role of such nationalist symbols in creating hegemony and have discussed the intensity with which totalitarian regimes often enforce participation in symbolic performances as a means of shaping people's lived experiences and subjectivity.[1] In this chapter I will focus on a particular type of nationalist performance that was pervasive in Syria during the height of Baathist hegemony—the reciting of nationalist songs. By examining these ever-present discourses, it becomes possible to see how the muscular nationalism of the Baathists spread through Syrian society and influenced gender identities, gender boundaries, and gendered relationships.

This analytical exploration delves into nationalist songs spanning distinct historical intervals. The initial category, encompassing the early 1970s to 1990, is typified by a lyrical focus centered on the October 1973 conflict with Israel. The subsequent category addresses nationalist songs that were strategically repurposed to fortify the regimes of Hafez and Bashar al-Assad. This reorientation employed the cultivation of a personality cult as a strategic tool for reinforcing their political legitimacy and ensuring widespread public endorsement.

The rationale for bifurcating the nationalist songs into these two categories extends beyond mere chronological demarcation; it also considers the thematic evolution within each group. In the former category the narrative of the nation is constructed around the mobilization of collective identity and solidarity in opposition to Israel. Conversely, the latter category signifies a shift in the use of nationalist songs from unifying themes to instruments of political legitimization, venerating the personas of Hafez and Bashar al-Assad. In both segments the representation of the nation is predominantly framed as a shared male endeavor, characterized by struggle and sacrifice, while the contributions and roles of women in these narratives remain notably unacknowledged. Additionally, the latter group of songs conceptualizes the nation in familial terms, transitioning from a paternalistic governance model to one influenced by a male lover archetype. This portrayal not only reflects a continuation of the patriarchal narrative but also underscores a shift in the symbolic representation of national authority and identity.

Irrespective of the divergent roles embodied by these two distinct clusters of nationalist songs, a prevailing theme is the pervasive dissemination of a masculinist ethos within their rhetorical framework. The utilization of the term "masculinism" in this analysis acknowledges the presence of female performers in the rendition of these songs. However, the central ethos propagated by these compositions extols the archetype of the strong, virile man, a representation that inherently relegates both women and nonconforming men to a subordinate status within the national narrative. As such, to thoroughly dissect and comprehend the intricate nexus between masculinity and national identity as portrayed in these songs, this chapter adopts a dual categorical framework. This framework encompasses an intersectional analysis of gender and masculinism on one hand, and militarism and hierarchical structures on the other. These categories provide the analytical lens through which the songs are examined, offering insights into how notions of gender, particularly masculinism, intertwine with militaristic and hierarchical themes to shape the construction of national identity in these musical expressions. This methodological approach enables a nuanced understanding of the songs' underlying messages and their implications for gender dynamics within the broader context of nationalistic discourse.

Prior research on patriotic symbols in Syria has tended to overlook or minimize their gendered aspects and their specific impact on women's subjectivity and sense of belonging. For example, Lisa Wedeen has published perhaps the most definitive account of Baathist political symbolism, encompassing ceremonies, marches, monuments, newspapers, plays, TV shows, and other cultural expressions.[2] Wedeen did not include nationalist songs in her analysis, which is somewhat surprising since in my experience the singing of songs has been one of the most common ways in which ordinary people engaged with Baathist ideology. Wedeen also put little focus on the gendered aspects of these Baathist cultural productions, which I view as a crucial omission in her otherwise excellent study. In a similar fashion related work by Victoria Gilbert and Miriam Cooke that has robustly explored the use of symbolism in Syrian nationalism has provided minimal insights into the gendered aspects of these discourses and performances.[3] Thus, the current analysis seeks to fill a gap in the literature by examining how patriotic songs emerged as a prominent means of disseminating muscular Syrian nationalism in both its nationalist and gendered dimensions.

## Songs as nationalist propaganda

Scholars have increasingly recognized the importance of performances and imagery in consolidating national identities. For example, Anthony Smith emphasized the "continuous reproduction ... of values, symbols, memories, myths, and traditions that compose the distinctive heritage of nations." Stuart Hall famously argued that nations are "symbolic communities"; while Anne McClintock characterized nations as "elaborate social practices enacted through time, laboriously fabricated through the media ... [and] the myriad forms of popular culture."[4] Symbols such as flags, catchphrases, and recognizable images have frequently played an important role in consolidating the abstract idea of the nation into an accessible practice for mass consumption, resulting in a kind of intervention or adjustment in the cultural practices of a community. Unfortunately, such symbols may frequently reinforce destructive or unjust forms of behavior, heighten in-group boundaries, and enshrine social hierarchies that position certain individuals or groups as less valuable than others.[5]

Baathist Syria is an especially interesting case for analyzing the role of nationalist performances and symbolism in relation to the politics of domination, authority, and coercion. Since it is effectively a one-party state, and since the regime views loyalty to the Baath Party as indistinguishable from belonging to the nation as a cultural entity, the shaping of nationalist culture in Syria has been a profoundly top–down affair. The Party has long tasked state agencies with the goal of overt cultural and political indoctrination, and it has taken a strong interest in both the creation and dissemination of nationalist discourse through media, educational institutions, and a variety of required public performances. As Wedeen noted, "the power of the Syrian state resides not only in its ability to control material resources and to construct institutions of punishment, but also in its ability to manage the symbolic world."[6] This ideological management takes specific forms in the Syrian context, one of which is the production and enforced performance of song. While some aspects of these nationalist performances might be generalizable or similar across different global regions, it is important to note that the ways these ideas play out are always local to each national culture and subculture. Thus, in my analysis I do not mean to suggest a universal theory of nationalist song; such interpretation will need to be left to a broader comparative study. Instead, I focus specifically on presenting the ways in which certain concepts of gender were inscribed by the Baathist regime in their lyrical propaganda efforts, and how these ideas affected Syrians in our everyday lives.

Song can be a powerful means of disseminating cultural outlooks and symbols, particularly when people are required to memorize and perform the songs in a group setting. Carolyn Birdsall has argued that "nationalistic songs and national anthems ... are particularly useful for propaganda, given their ability to harness feelings of optimism and belonging."[7] Shared musical performances are widely recognized for their ability to induce experiences of social solidarity, in democratic as well as authoritarian contexts.[8] Recognizing this, the Baathists placed a strong emphasis on reiterating their nationalist vision and communicating its symbols through the repetition of song. One central locus in which citizens interacted with the Syrian nationalist songs discussed in this chapter was in educational settings, where essentially all schoolchildren were compelled to learn and perform them for frequent celebratory events and national holidays. Before every national event, schoolchildren would have weeks of training after school. This was mandatory for all children during primary school.

In the Syrian context the construction of national identity in edited and planned songs was fully premeditated by Party leaders. We know this because officials representing the Party and *shabibet al-thawra* would enforce these rituals on all schools. There was weekly training where these officials would join the training and ensure that all preparation for national events were going well. Thus, these songs can readily be characterized as purposeful regime propaganda, even if some aspects of their spread may have occurred organically in Syrian society.[9] When analyzing the songs, I will draw from Nickolas Shaughnessy's framework of propaganda as the intentional manipulation of three salient concepts: "rhetoric," "symbolism," and "myth."[10] In the rhetorical sense the song lyrics were intended to persuade and inspire the public with a vision of desirable ideas, behaviors, and attitudes, largely derived from the writings of the Baathist founders, as discussed earlier in this book. In regard to symbols, the songs frequently foregrounded references to imagery that was familiar to Syrians from other state ceremonies and the larger culture, such as the flag, the sword, the eagle, and so forth (explained in more detail below). By linking these symbols together with a repetition of meaning and emotional valence, the songs participated in an intertextual discourse that reinforced and expanded participants' sense of identification with the Baathist ideology. Finally, in the sense of myth, the songs frequently served to establish vague historical narratives, usually incorporating some type of feisty man protecting the nation in a violent fashion.[11] As we will see, these "foundational myths" of

Baathist cultural propaganda closely intertwined men's heroism, muscularity, and social authority with the origins and continuation of the Syrian national community.

## Songs as expressions of patriarchy

Nationalist songs hold a position of considerable prominence across various Arab milieus. The analytical dissection of these musical compositions facilitates the conceptualization of the nation as an entity emergent from a meticulously crafted orchestration of experiences. These experiences are selectively reconstituted through symbolic representations that bestow upon them their distinctive character.[12] Such songs have historically functioned as instruments to legitimize and reinforce the sovereignty of Arab regimes, employing the evocation of a heroic national past and framing struggle as a mechanism to sustain internal cohesion. In the Syrian milieu, the focus on the cultural identity of the nation within the national narrative is particularly striking. Syrian symbolism plays a pivotal role in the Baathist state's strategy, employed to establish channels of cultural and political discourse that serve to concretize the national ethos. The state's promotion of nationalist songs under the Baath regime was strategically aimed at mythologizing the collective experiences of the nation's constituents. This endeavor was designed to underscore the regime's legitimacy and authority, while simultaneously reconstituting and reshaping the collective national memory. The use of these songs as a tool for statecraft in Syria elucidates the intricate interplay between cultural symbolism and political power, highlighting the role of art and culture in the construction and perpetuation of national identities and state narratives.

In considering the impact of Baathist songs on gendered subjectivity, I pose two questions. First, how did these songs position women and men in their concept of the nation's "people"? And second, what ideas about gendered behavior and identity did they encourage in women and men? In regard to the first question, one of the most persistent features seen in these songs is that the singer is presumed to be a man. Women or feminine imagery sometimes appear in the background—in many cases as an abstract representation of the nation itself—but in these appearances women are passive objects in need of protection, not active agents. More often, as was seen in the Baathist founders' writing in previous chapters, women are simply absent from the patriotic songs. This situation reflects a view of gendered nationalism voiced by McClintock, who wrote that "women are subsumed symbolically into the national body politic as its boundary and metaphoric limit."[13] Similarly, when theorizing about the gendered dimensions of nationalism, Victoria Peterson has argued that "The motherland is female but the state and its citizen-warriors are male ... Excluded intentionally from the public domain, women are not agents in their own right but instruments for the realization of male-defined agendas."[14] Similar to these more general analyses, I will argue that the Baathist songs presented a concept of the active citizen who was assumed by default to be a man, with women shown as a passive backdrop, when they are present in the songs at all.

In regard to the second question, I will discuss how the Baathist songs nudged the performer to identify with and recite a particular type of muscular identity, which is associated with men through assumptions about the singer's gender as well as through the symbols and myths that are heralded lyrically. A central aspect of this gendering is the songs' emphasis on men engaged in violent struggle. While most countries have, at one time or another in their history, engaged in military conflict, there is much to be said about the extent that various regimes emphasize such activities in their self-presentation and ideology. War is only one of the many activities in which governments and citizens may engage, but in militarized societies it rises to a central prominence in the social imagination. In the Baathist songs, military violence is persistently foregrounded as a foundation of loyalty and national identity. While it might be expected as a logical outgrowth of the Syrian founders' view that martial conflict leads to the "perfection of manhood,"[15] it is worth noting that this militarized view of society was not inevitable and was not necessarily the desire of most ordinary Syrian citizens. The nationalist songs were intended to alter this state of affairs and to instill such militarized gendered identities and values in the populace. As will be documented in the following sections, the songs persistently, almost obsessively, reinforced the concepts of heroic violence, struggle, and physical sacrifice, while frequently connecting these activities to the "dignity" (*'iza*) and social value of men. In regard to women's proper activities, the songs have little to say at all, other than an insistence that everyone must show appreciation and gratitude toward the actions of muscular protectors.

## Muscular love and belonging

The Baathist anthems conspicuously interweave motifs of violence/aggression with those of love/belonging within the national collective. This juxtaposition engenders a persistent conflation of masculinity, martial engagement, and romantic sentiment. After the rise of Hafez al-Assad to power, there is a discernible perpetuation of the emotive and robust nationalist paradigm established by the Baathist founding fathers, now intricately linked to the Syrian state and its leadership structures.

*The muscular nation in song and performance* 129

For instance, in a widely broadcast speech announcing the 1973 October War against Israel,[16] the conceptualization of the "homeland" as a cultural and ideological construct assumes a central position. In this address, al-Assad accentuates national belonging by consistently referring to Syrians as "brothers" and articulating a shared cultural fate. "I address in you the authentic soul of Arabism," he asserts, "the soul of sacrifice, heroism ... I address in you your love of the homeland, to which you have been born." Within the framework of galvanizing support for Syria's war efforts, this speech imbues an emotional connection with the state and its territory as an innate and elemental characteristic of all legitimate citizens. This rhetoric situates emotional allegiance to the nation as a foundational aspect of citizenship, intrinsically tied to the state's political and military ambitions. The fusion of cultural identity with state loyalty, particularly in times of conflict, underscores the state's effort to mobilize collective sentiment and nationalistic fervor in support of its geopolitical objectives, thereby reinforcing the conflation of patriotic duty with militaristic engagement.

In a 1980 oration marking the seventeenth anniversary of the Baathist coup,[17] Hafez al-Assad alluded to the valorous exploits of the "grandfathers" (*'ajdād*), concurrently articulating the regime's aspiration to cultivate "a society dominated by love, because this land does not have anything but love." These pronouncements, evocative of a deep-seated, primordial connection to the state, are remarkable for their enduring resonance and influence within Syrian society, exerting a compelling influence that extends into the contemporary epoch. Such references to ancestral heroism and the espousal of love as a foundational societal principle illustrate a strategic blending of historical veneration and emotive rhetoric. This amalgamation serves to reinforce a collective national identity anchored in a shared, glorified past, while concurrently framing the state's ideological objectives within the context of affection and communal cohesion. The persistence of these narratives in Syrian discourse underscores the effectiveness of such rhetorical devices in maintaining a continual and pervasive engagement with the state's ideological constructs, exerting a profound and lasting impact on the national consciousness.

An insightful avenue for understanding the evolution of nationalist rhetoric during the Hafez al-Assad era is found in the examination of romantic songs that received the regime's endorsement and dissemination. Imbued with themes of profound emotional ties and selfless heroism, these musical narratives remained firmly anchored in the primordialist tradition, while simultaneously positioning the Syrian state as the epicenter of collective affection. Four songs, originating from the 1973 war against Israel, continue to resonate in contemporary Syrian culture, often performed by schoolchildren and in large-scale public demonstrations. These compositions draw on motifs of maternal affection for the nation, envisaging the relationship between the state and its citizens as akin to that of a mother and her child.

The initial pair of songs nurtures an emotive linkage between the nation and its populace, characterized by their unwavering and unquestioned dedication to sacrifice. The subsequent songs issue stirring calls to arms, thereby glorifying the ethos of military culture and valor. The entrenchment of militarism, masculinity, and physical strength within these songs is intrinsically intertwined with the concept of national belonging. For instance, the song "Your Flags Are Forever High, Oh Syria" (*Rāyātek bil-'Ali ya Sūriyya*), penned in 1973 amid the turmoil of war, commences with the fervor of an impassioned lover, manifesting an explicit devotion and adoration for the nation. The lyrical narrative commences with the vocalist declaring:

> You are my land and my country, oh the best of countries.
> You are my eternal love, oh the sun that shines tenderness.
> It is we who have protected you, our fatherland,
> Against all the betrayals and stabs of the time.[18]

From the title of this song, one can discern the function of the flag as a symbol of the nation's glory.

While the above stanza evokes the prospect of a glorious nation of brotherly comrades, this glory is closely linked to men's ability to guard and preserve the nation. These lyrics demonstrate an interesting mixture of the nation conceived as "the sun that shines tenderness" (generally associated with femininity) and the nation as "fatherland." The appeal to family attachments continues as the lyrics go on to state:

> We opened our eyes learning to love and build you.
> We have grown up learning to be proud of you.
> We raised our flags so high, oh Syria,
> And for you we sang and composed poetry, oh Syria.

Love for the nation is presented here as analogous to the journey of growing up and the primordial sensations first experienced between parents and children. The naturalness of this love is accompanied by the action taken by the child, in raising the flag to honor the parent. In performance contexts this song was most often associated with ceremonies in which male soldiers lifted the flag. Hence, there is a close association between the activity of carrying or raising the Syrian flag and men's role as passionate protectors of the nation, conceived here as honoring one's parents.

The most famous call to ultimate sacrifice that espouses both love and sacrifice to the nation—a fixture in almost every Syrian school and commonly played on TV and in theaters—was *Biktub Ismek ya Blādī* ("I Engrave Your Name, Oh My Country"). This was written in 1973 by Ellie Shwairy and later adopted by many Arab countries. The song was chosen to be featured in one of the most famous plays in the Arab world, *Kāsak ya Watan* ("A Toast to the Homeland"). This is a socio-political tragicomic play, written by the Syrian poet and writer Mohammad al-Maghout. The play starred Dureed Laham, who sang the song, and the play was repeatedly broadcast every Eid. This song adamantly and repeatedly calls for the ultimate sacrifice for the nation. The song has been canonical in Syrian public culture where it was aired on official Syrian channels in both religious and secular celebrations such as Eid holidays or independence days throughout the rule of Hafez and Bashar al-Assad. In *Biktub Ismek ya Blādī* the performer displays a devotion that exceeds even familial ties:

> On the sun that never sets,
> I engrave your name, oh my country.
> Neither my love for money nor for my children
> Would exceed my love for you.

The metaphor of inscribing the homeland's name upon the sun serves to reiterate its perpetual splendor, epitomizing a profound expression of patriotic devotion. However, this affection is gauged by the extent of a man's willingness to relinquish not only his financial resources but also his progeny. The concluding line of the verse articulates an intense, unparalleled ardor for the nation, transcending all other forms of affection:

> Oh, my country, the most faithful of all countries,
> Poems are written for you, and you deserve them.
> May you eternally be shining and bestowed with glory and laurels.
> [Heroes defend you] … with their swords glowing, while your sun never sets.
> There is no love like your love.[19]

The central conceit here of engraving the name of Syria on the "sun that never sets" conveys a certain form of muscular action—marking one's territory so to speak—which is further reinforced by the image of heroes with glowing swords. The gender of the beloved nation is again somewhat ambiguous. While the sun as a symbol could possibly be regarded as masculine or feminine, the nation is also described as bestowed with "glory and laurels," honors that are traditionally associated with men. The lines in which the masculine speaker places his love of the nation above that for his children, and the final conclusion, "There is no love like your love," appear to be a targeted rejection of traditional attachments in favor of this amorphously gendered romantic connection. Fraternal solidarity, in this interpretation, wins out over other attractions, and women disappear from the scene.

The song "Oh, My Beloved Syria" (*Sūriyya ya Habībatī*), penned by Mohammad Salman and performed collaboratively with Najah Salameh and Mohamad Jamal in 1973, emerges as a paradigmatic response to the concurrent Egyptian–Syrian offensive against Israel in October of that year. Emblematic of war-induced emotions, it resonates with themes of dignity and honor. Given the historical milieu, the intertwining of heroism and sacrificial duty is not only understandable but also timely. However, a nuanced analysis of the song's title reveals a compelling personification of the homeland as a feminine lover. This personification extends beyond mere nationalistic sentiment, delving into the realm of romantic or amorous attachment, thereby reinforcing the nation's embodiment as an object of intimate affection.

> You have brought me back my dignity.
> You have brought me back my identity,
> Oh, my beloved Syria.
> By war and fighting [*kifāh*], by the blazing fire of the wounds,
> The way towards freedom is lighted,
> Oh, my beloved.
> … sky and land are all sacrificed for and protected.
> Our blood is sacrificed for them all,
> And our heroes protect them all.
> Our Baath goes on forward
> To achieve its great glory.[20]

While the previously discussed songs were somewhat vague in their martial elements, these lyrics are overt in their emphasis on war, fighting, wounds, and blood. One of the major functions of this song is to create solidarity and a "we" feeling among Syrians. The lyrics further indicate the unity of the group where the relationship of the individual to the group is performed at imposed rallies by the regime. The precise activities that are involved in "protecting" the nation, and the identification of the singer with soldiery, are thus clarified. This blood and sacrifice are offered in the name of romantic attachment to the nation, vaguely gendered, and the relationship between the singer and nation is described as the source of his identity and dignity. In this sense, the process of identity construction is synonymous with active participation in war, reflecting the muscular concepts of the Baathist founding fathers (especially Michel Aflaq; see Chapter 2). The nexus of masculine brotherhood and violence is announced even more emphatically as the song continues:

> Now, now and only now, I am an Arab,
> I have the right to my father's name.
> "Who is your father?" I may be asked.
> "Who is my father?"
> … He is the bullet of a gun,
> That achieves freedom for the proud nation,
> Oh, my beloved.

Using the first-person pronoun in the first line shows gratitude that "only now" can the fighter reclaim the name of his father. This reclaiming of dignity is conditional upon the heroic act of sacrifice. Heroism is connected to the question of who deserves the name of his father. This filiality can only be realized by the bullet of a gun, which in turn stands for action and militarism. Moreover, the repetition of "who is my father?" is even more significant as it emphasizes the paternal lineage of both the nation and the family, and consequently legitimizes patriarchal authority and domination in the national imagining. More importantly, the expression "now … I have the right to my father's name" indicates the right of citizenship. Arguably, this reflects the prejudice of Syrian laws against women, who are not permitted to pass their nationality to foreign spouses or to the children of such a marriage. In this cultural spectrum, belonging and membership are correlated not only with heroism and chivalry but also with patriarchy. The emphasis on military fraternity here is juxtaposed against the almost incidental refrain "Oh my beloved," which seems to appear almost as an afterthought gesturing toward broader inclusion or the instruction of an outsider. It might be useful to ask who the "beloved" is here—is it the land, an ideal, a population, a woman? Perhaps it is all of the above, everything that the singer presumes to co-opt and speak for. The predominant concern, however, is the achievement and recognition of the singer's muscular identity and patrimony, that is, his earning the right to the name of his father. The notable repetition of the line "who is my father?" places an emphasis on this question, underlining the performer's search for a name, identity, or social position. Such identity, the song specifies, is to be found in the use of weapons.

Finally, "Oh My Beloved Syria" ends with a specific call to engage in battle to reclaim the land of Palestine:

> The course of action has not yet finished, oh our nation
> Till our usurped land is returned.
> The orphaned daughter of the exodus is living in tents,
> Calling, "Oh, beloved Syria."

The vocabulary used, such as "action," "now," and "bullets," shows an upbeat revolutionary spirit that appeals to brotherly solidarity. This convergence between action and freeing the land inculcates a monolithic perception of national struggle as measured by men's sacrifice and actions. More importantly, the dominant image of the orphaned daughter in exile captures the loss of patriarchal leadership in both the family and the nation; her suffering is doubled as she has lost her land and her father, her home and her nation. The feminization of the nation captured in the image of the helpless daughter in the tent portrays male fighters as heroic. Such a symbiotic relationship between helplessness and heroism naturalizes the dominant binary opposition of passive females and active males. This will further create a god-like image of those male warriors who, by their militant actions to protect this daughter, are rescuing both the familial and the national spheres. Hence, this juxtaposition of active men and passive women reinforces an essentialist perception of women's roles in both private and public spheres.

The "exodus" here refers to the time when more than 700,000 Palestinian Arabs fled or were forced to leave their homes during the 1948 Palestine War. Describing the Palestinians as an "orphaned daughter" further clarifies the gendered aspects of the Baathist outlook—as this population has lost their political estate and dominion, they are gendered as women and are in need of rescue or protection. Such need in turn justifies and reinforces the militant identity of the Baathist fighter, inscribing a naturalized symbiotic relationship between helpless/passive women and violent/active men. The term "daughter" highlights the pervasive familial aspect of the Baathists' rhetoric; by rescuing this beloved daughter the male fighters can imagine themselves to be securing both the familial and the national spheres.

## Muscular education and memory

The Baathists were particularly intent on constructing a unified version of history, centered around certain imagined communal experiences of pain and perseverance. As discussed in the previous chapters, the Party's founding fathers emphasized the education (or indoctrination) of young Syrians through instilling these stories of a shared identity, a heroic/tragic past, and a glorious destiny. Suleiman has pointed out that "For the nationalists, the past is the storehouse of old glories, common suffering, dim memories, and other distant and authenticating voices."[21] By plundering this storehouse of the region's past, the Baathists co-opted various symbols and myths and rearranged them to suit the Party's goals. Many of the resulting narratives showed up in patriotic songs that were used in educational contexts and foisted upon Syrian youths to memorize and perform.

One song targeted toward a younger audience was called "I Am Syrian and My Fatherland Is Arab" (*'Ana Sūrī wa-'Ardī 'Arabiyya*). The lyrics to this song include the standard "blood and soil" themes of the homeland, the glorious past, and violence, in a simplified and yet morbid form:

> I am Syrian and my Fatherland is Arab.
> My sky, my fatherland, and my water are glorious.
> I swear, and my pledge will be witnessed, that I will sacrifice myself for the glory of my flag.

The eagle is still flying high hugging your glory, oh Syria!
Our past will ever be glorious and we will always be the defenders of our land.
In peace, we are basil, and in the battlefield our blood will spread its aroma.[22]

One of the central impacts of this song is to project an image of unity and continuity—the past is collectively shared, and its battles, attributes, and identities will continue indefinitely into the future. The eternal nature of this community sets up a sharp distinction between those who belong and those who do not, and this distinction is linked to the willingness to shed blood. The image of the eagle seen here and in additional songs below is derived from Syrian cultural history. It is widely recognized in Syria as a symbol of physical power and of the military; thus, the veneration of the eagle in this song further ties its concepts of national belonging to martial engagement.

In a similar song called "I Am Syrian, Oh How Blessed I Am" (*'Ana Sūrī ah ya Niyyālī*), the imagery of the flag and the eagle are associated not only with violence but more specifically with the actions and concerns of men:

Wave, oh our flag, wave up high.
Precious is your eagle, oh our precious fatherland ...
These heroes are the men of the revolution.
Though the sun shines, it is still not reachable ...
They fought France with slingshots, and said "oh invaders get out!"
My father and grandfather said, "listen, the sand of the country is precious to the soul."
All these Arabs call to the boys saying, "I am the strong one, may God protect you."[23]

The image of shining sun in this account represents the longed-for completion or attainment of the nation, which is the goal of the Baathist struggle but remains out of reach due to colonization, oppression, and the general fallen state of Syrian society. The key to reaching this blessed perfection, or at least honoring it and getting closer to it, is physical warfare. The virtues of such conflict are embodied in the heroic men of previous generations who fought off the colonizers "with slingshots," indicating that even with absurdly primitive weaponry, their physical strength and courage was such that their cause prevailed. Finally, the fathers and grandfathers are seen as calling out to the current young men, enjoining them to follow in their martial footsteps and to believe in the strength of the nation. This appeal enshrines the image of a masculine national belonging that transcends time, in which the men who participate are conceived as infinite, revolutionary, and courageous. The representation of the national struggle against France in this song is in fact a rather selective approach toward Syria's history—one in which military men are the only protagonists. The presence of women, either on the battlefield or anywhere else, is rendered invisible. In reality, even some recognition to a wide range of educated men and women at that time is completely missed.

As discussed in Chapters 3 and 4, the Baathists regarded military training as an intrinsic part of a man's education and as directly continuous with schooling. The resulting centrality of militarism in young men's lives and in their developing self-consciousness had significant repercussions in the mainstream Syrian culture. This normalization of the military ethos encouraged men to value aggression, coercion, and hierarchy as an approach toward life, and to be always ready to fight. A song targeted toward youth called "The Line of Soldiers" (*Saff l-'Askar*) conveyed this ethos:

> Teach me to fight, oh soldiers,
> Using the gun and the cannon.
> Here I am, in the land of my grandfathers.
> Who duty once called upon.
> So witness and hear, oh mountains;
> Here I am, ready![24]

By requiring young men to recite these lyrics, the Baathists hoped to generate enthusiasm among the recruits as they entered their mandatory military service. The song offers young men a belief that such activities are not only noble but socially central and eternal, making the men eligible for recognition, admiration, and reward. More broadly, the song promotes a perspective in which all men are expected to identify with the military outlook, in which the roles of soldiers and teachers are blurred together, and in which ordinary husbands and fathers should always stand ready to fight. The centering of this outlook is highly gendered and it promotes a patriarchal view, with the land inevitably portrayed as belonging to the "grandfathers," while grandmothers or other women are not mentioned at all.

The song continues on to describe the very existence of the nation as emerging solely from the dedicated actions and violence of military men:

> The line of troops will stay up all night
> Soldiers, camped along the mountains.
> With their hands, their fatherland they've built,
> And willingly they have gotten ready to kill.
> They've gone early to the threshing floor
> To plant it all with men ready for war.
> At your borders, my fatherland, here I am
> On full alert to be a faithful guardian.

The imagery here of fighting men being planted like crops throughout the land, and ever standing watch to defend the borders, epitomizes a vision of the nation as an insular and closed space of rigid patriarchal dominion.

While the song speaks of dedication and faithfulness, this is not merely a service or job performed to enhance freedom in the community; rather, it is a claim of ownership, possession, control, and the expectation of recognition. Soldiers are not merely contributing to Syrian society but have singlehandedly built it. The fatherland is theirs. Meanwhile, the need to sow the land with men ready for war can be seen as a justification for muscular behaviors and outlooks in everyday life, and as a legitimization of men's aggressive control in both the private and the public spheres.

Another popular Baathist song oriented toward the militarization of young men was called "I've Saddled the Horse" (*Shaddet l-Hijin*). The focus here is again on men's constant readiness for war, as symbolized by a horse that is ready for travel:

> I've saddled the horse for the trip.
> Like wheels, its legs are moving quickly.
> If you choose war, our enemy, then be ready for our bullets,
> As they are prepared and waiting to be fired.
> Beware of attacking the lions,
> For you won't face only death.
> Oh God, you are the One who drives worries away,
> So please shoot our enemies accurately,
> So that the goal is hit precisely.
> Oh, young men, let's put on our headscarves [*kaffiyehs*]
> And be ready to guard and secure our homeland.[25]

The horse here is presented as a symbol of agency or activity, showing the mobility of military men as they constantly scout across their land and prepare for conflict. Again, this indicates the prerogative of dominion and a sense of physical mastery and freedom from constraint associated with soldiery. The lion is also a symbol of such mastery and is known for being the "king of the land," a top predator who is unlimited by other creatures and can go where he wills. (The lion refers specifically to the ruling Assad family and regime loyalists; the name Assad means "lion.") This song also invokes a religious perspective, indicating that God supports the Baathist cause and will punish the souls of those who fight against it. The final verses make it very clear that the presented role of masterful guardian is available only to men, both through the use of the term "young men" (*shabāb*) and through the reference to the *kuffiyeh*, a traditional men's headscarf. Invoking the kaffiyeh in this fashion provides a reference to the past and to cultural tradition, linking the activities of the Baathist soldiers to the heroes and patriarchs of previous eras.

Taken all together, the songs discussed here were a call for young men to adopt a muscular and militarized outlook and to regard Syria as their rightful dominion through the vehicle of the Baath. They are a continuation, in a more abbreviated and accessible form, of the Baathist founders' views that Syrian masculinity and men's pride needed to be revitalized through military training, as discussed in the previous chapters. The impact of these ideas' spread was to normalize muscularity broadly among Syrian men and to consolidate a sense of entitlement associated with the indispensability and superiority of such masculinity in the national imagination. In these representations women, as well as all types of nonmilitary civil society work, appear to hardly exist at all, except perhaps as part of the land to be owned and claimed.

## Leader, father, and lover

A significant category of Baathist songs emphasized the veneration of Hafez al-Assad—and later of his son Bashar—who were presented as the ideal representations of manly willpower, courage, and dominion in all aspects of life. Previous scholars have noted that the consolidation of Baathist power in Syria was closely associated with the growth of an Assad personality cult, but these studies have tended to leave out the centrality of gender ideologies as they were associated with the Assads.[26] I view the image of Assad in Baathist culture to be a central keystone for understanding the connection between muscularity and militarization in the public sphere and men's behavior in the private/personal sphere, because Assad was regarded as a paragon of both roles, often simultaneously.[27]

In the song called "Bassel's Father, Our Leader" (*'Abu Bassel Qā'idnā*), Hafez al-Assad was honored both as a military commander and as the father of his first son (Bassel al-Assad was expected to succeed Hafez but died in a car crash in 1994, leaving the position to his younger brother, Bashar). By succinctly combining the terms "father" and "leader," the song draws a direct parallel between the head of state and the head of a family:

> Father of Bassel [*Abu Bassel*], our leader, with your forehead always uplifted,
> May you be endowed with safety as you fight for our land
> Against all the stabs of the evil night.
> Father of Bassel [*Abu Bassel*] you are a hero to everyone,
> Wielding the sword of justice.[28]

One of the reasons for this song using a form of address that emphasizes Bassel may have been to increase the public's recognition of the heir's name, thus helping to pave the way for his eventual planned ascension to power. More broadly, however, the song creates a synergy between the roles of commander and father, linking these two aspects of gendered identity. The man's role as a hero and commander to his family and as a hero and commander to the nation are essentially the same. Interlinking these constructs creates an association in which loyalty to the regime is viewed as ancillary to the continuation of patriarchy in the family, and vice versa.

The song continues on to praise Hafez at length, while tempering its military imagery through references to domesticity, nature, and the blessings of God:

> The light of your faith has shone on us,
> And in your eyes, God's gravity we always find ...
> Oh, birds of sky sing to you
> And teach you the chants of victory ...
> Oh, flowers of the land show you their smiles,
> And endow you with their precious scent ...
> Oh God, please on Assad bestow your assistance,
> So that his home stands firm.

The success of the political leader and warrior is tied to the strength of his home, and presumably to the lineage that he transmits to his son. Thus, loyalty and support of patriarchy in the private sphere is indistinguishable from the Baathists' national agenda. This construction articulates a specific perception of a national community that feels empowered when the traits of the heroic male fighter and patriarchal father are foregrounded and glorified as the center of society.

The Baathist song "The Father of Men" (*'Abu r-Rijāl*) lauds Hafez as having renewed Syrian men's confidence and effectiveness:

> Long live Hafez al-Assad, forever.
> He is the father of men [*rijāl*] and of competence.
> With flags and dignity,
> It is always sublimely protected.
> With strong hands and awakened eyes ...
> Our days are full of cheerfulness and victory,
> And our dignity has emerged from his steps.[29]

The song is unambiguous about the perceived need to restore masculine stature in Syria, which was regarded as being humiliated or dissipated under foreign rule. It is also clear that flags and military victories are viewed as the way to accomplish this. Important symbols here include the "strong hands" and "awakened eyes," which speak to men's sense of agency and dominion. The situation or needs of Syrian women are not addressed.

"May You Be Protected for Your People" (*Tislam Li-Sha'b*) continues the theme of general praise for Hafez, with incidental lines that characterize Syria as a country of men:

> You are the hope of millions.
> You have raised our flags, oh Hafez,
> And mustered our dignity.
> May you be protected for your people, oh Hafez.
> Syria is the country of free men [*rijāl*].
> Syria is the country of revolutionaries ...
> As long as Hafez is our leader, be proud and pleased, oh Arab people.[30]

As already emphasized, the nation is perceived as an extension of the family, yet the role of women is disregarded. A striking example of this gender bias is in defining Syria as the country of "free men" and "revolutionaries," which casts women as outsiders. Clearly, women are overlooked in this patriotic song, and the leader–people relationship is identified with the father–son relationship that is marked by superiority and hierarchy. While this patriarchization of the nation legitimizes dominance and coercion, it also affirms the limitation of women in national imagining.

While women might presumably be included in the "millions" and in the "people," they do not appear in the song as active agents or owners of the nation in the same fashion as do "free men." All of these patriotic Baathist songs show a persistent obsession with men's stories, men's dignity, and men's freedom, linked to dominion and possession over the land, while women's stories do not appear.

Similar phrasing can be found in the song "May God Protect You, Oh Assad" (*Hamāka Allahu ya Assadu*), which celebrates Hafez's muscular characteristics and achievements:

> You are the lion [*'asad*] of attitudes and firmness.
> You have revealed and showed us the ways to our dignity,
> And, by our dignity, you maintained our unity.
> May God protect you, oh Assad.
> Our souls and bodies are ready to be sacrificed for your sake ...
> April was the torch of our Baath, when darkness was defeated.
> Glory was in its highest point in March;
> October is the blazing fire of our achievements.
> Thus badges of honor decorate our chests.
> Assad, the proud leader, guides his people
> Through the way to dignity.[31]

In this song the celebration of April refers to the founding of the Baath Party (April 7, 1947). March is honored as the date when the Baath overthrew the previous Syrian government, which was regarded as corrupt and elitist

(March 8, 1963). October refers to the surprise attack by a coalition of Arab states that initiated the 1973 Arab–Israeli War (the date of this attack, October 6, is still marked as a national holiday in Syria). Together, these victories are seen as demonstrating Hafez al-Assad's character and leadership, and as being emblematic of "firmness," "dignity," "pride," and "honor." Such muscular characteristics and preoccupations are embodied by Assad as a role model, and as such they are presented as an image for the rest of the nation's men to follow.

Following the death of Hafez al-Assad in 2000, Bashar al-Assad, Hafez's second son, ascended to prominence. Prior to this juncture, Bashar remained relatively obscure to the Syrian populace, with his ascendancy to leadership unforeseen until the untimely death of his elder brother, which preceded Hafez's passing by a few years. Characterized by a soft-spoken demeanor, lacking significant military achievements, and having been immersed in ophthalmology studies in London before being summoned back as the successor, Bashar's profile was unorthodox for a leader. Upon assuming the presidency, he distinguished himself as the youngest head of state in the Arab world. The stern, paternal archetype, synonymous with his father's rule, proved incongruous with Bashar's persona. Consequently, post-2000 Baathist propaganda shifted, portraying him as a youthful, romantic figure. This portrayal amalgamated the robust rhetoric of martial prowess and safeguarding with elements of poetic gentleness.

In the wake of Bashar al-Assad's ascension in June 2000, the official Baathist narrative began to tentatively explore more civic-oriented conceptions of nationhood. This shift aligned with the intellectual reformist wave, known as the "Damascus Spring," that emerged between 2000 and 2001. This period marked a brief liberalization in the Syrian political landscape, infusing the national discourse with notions of intellectual and civic reform, albeit within the confines of the prevailing political structure.[32] This initial phase of civic rhetoric was swiftly supplanted by a reversion to the regime's archetypal romanticized vernacular and authoritarian stance, as Bashar al-Assad perceived a potential jeopardy to Baathist dominance. Post-2001, the rhetorical trajectory of Bashar al-Assad suggests that the civic-oriented elements present in his inaugural discourse might have been a transient deviation, potentially an expedient response to the exigencies of power transition.[33] It is plausible to argue that this inaugural address was emblematic of a unique political and social milieu, necessitating a veneer of civic formality and a nod to legalistic norms.

Conversely, it is conceivable that Assad's initial inclination toward a more of civic conception of national belonging was impeded by an imminent existential threat, particularly as fundamentalist groups rapidly sought to exploit any perceived lacuna in authority. Regardless of the underlying causes, Assad's subsequent key addresses in 2003, 2005, and 2007 indicate a reinvigoration of primordial and masculinist tenets in the conceptualization of the nation–citizen relationship. Each of these speeches, coinciding with significant political milestones and garnering extensive attention, has since been inducted into the informal canon revered by the regime's adherents.[34] This resurgence of a romanticized paradigm in the interaction between the Syrian state and its citizenry becomes particularly conspicuous in Assad's second inaugural address, starkly contrasting with the tenor of his 2000 inauguration speech. Following his reaffirmation as president in another public referendum, which faced widespread criticism and featured Assad as the sole candidate, his acceptance speech unequivocally abandons the earlier civic notion of national identity in Syria. Instead, the rhetoric pivots to emphasize affective bonds, with Assad endeavoring to resurrect the cult of personality associated with his father and to portray himself as a fervent devotee of the populace.

This negative shift toward Romanticized masculinism and conceiving the nation as a locus of familial ties was overtly celebrated in producing songs that optimize the love of the leader. These lyrical discourses in the Baathist songs took an interesting turn. This turn highlights another notable facet of the patriarchal construct, in which the passionate affection and generosity of the lover melds with men's expectation of dominion and violent control. The most notable example of this trend is the song "We Love You" (*Minhibbak*), which was used pervasively by the regime during Assad's public appearances and campaigns. The song displayed a passionate relationship of affection between the leader and the masses:

> We are all your kin and your people;
> In prosperity and adversity, we would be beside you.
> We support you, so go on …
> We love you, oh very great man.
> We love you, oh symbol of our homeland.
> We love you, oh man with a very big heart.
> Your heart is as big as our homeland.
> We love you because you have emerged among us,
> And we are similar to you.
> We love you because you are our leader, unifier, and lion
> Forever, forever, forever.[35]

It is no wonder that the idea behind repeating the phrase "we love you" is to institutionalize ultimate obedience and submissiveness. On the representational level, Bashar al-Assad's cult registers the paradox between the "you" and the "we"—that is, the leader and the people. This cult personifies state formation in Bashar al-Assad, but it is based on the internalization between the leader and the people. The rhetoric here emulates Assad's authority and simultaneously works to represent the connection between the masculinized leader and the feminized masses.

The song does not only define the superiority of Bashar al-Assad but also masculinizes national belonging and identity as they become synonymous with the leader's personal image. The incorporation of the love between leader and people obscures the definition of membership. Such authority, symbolized by political leadership and familial patriarchy, casts women as submissive in the private and public spheres. The creation of a romantic relationship between the nation and the leader, therefore, perpetuates women's subservience to a male-dominated nationalism, familial hierarchy, and a masculinized belonging. Thus, the idea behind repeating the phrase "we love you" is to embody loyalty and submission. The enforced affective relationship is centered around requiring the song's performers (and by extension audiences) to display encouragements for Bashar to stand strong and to "go on" in his actions to command the nation.

The following verses of the song elaborate in more detail the identity of speakers who love and support Assad:

> We are the dearly held promise, the guardians of the nights.
> Oh, man with the uplifted forehead, we are the sun that shines, the sword that glows;
> We are the determination that never gives up.
> We are the government that provides education; we are the symbol of love.
> Oh, guardian of our people's dignity, we love you. We love you.
> We are the eye that never sleeps, always awake to guard the homeland [al-Shām].
> Whatever hardships we may face, we love you.

The recurrent utilization of the pronoun "we" in the text is indicative of the multifaceted roles and identities ascribed to the entities encompassed by this term. However, the scope of "we" is predominantly circumscribed to the functions of guardianship and combat. The construction of "we" within this specific milieu is imbued with the endeavor to forge an idealized masculine image, as evidenced through references to the military and the sword. Such linguistic choices unequivocally underscore the masculinization of "we," connoting physical prowess and strength.

Echoing the thematic elements of earlier songs, the identity encapsulated by "we" in these lyrics is distinctly skewed toward robust, masculine activities and symbols—such as protecting the homeland, exercising authority, enduring adversities, and embodying the role of "the sword." While the gender of the vocalist is not explicitly mentioned in the lyrics, in practice, the song has predominantly been performed by male artists. This continuation in performance tradition aligns with the perpetuation of masculinized motifs of "dignity," sovereignty, and patriarchal heritage, mirroring those prevalent during Hafez al-Assad's tenure. This thematic continuity reflects a persistent cultural and ideological underpinning that underscores and valorizes masculine authority and strength within the societal and national narrative.

## The national anthem

Michael Geisler has astutely noted that national anthems emerged as a distinctive cultural innovation during the nineteenth and early twentieth centuries. They were conceived as instrumental mechanisms for encapsulating and disseminating notions of patriotic allegiance, serving as a countermeasure to the societal fissures engendered by modernity.[36] A significant number of global national anthems have been subjected to critique for their portrayals of belonging and identity that effectively marginalize specific segments of the citizenry. In response to these critiques, there has been a recent trend toward revising some of these anthems to foster a more inclusive representation of national identity. This trend reflects a growing recognition of the need to reconcile national symbolic expressions with the evolving dynamics of pluralistic societies.[37]

In the context of Syria, the national anthem, penned in 1938, has remained unaltered during the Baathist period. This anthem, like numerous Baathist compositions, was profoundly influenced by the writings and ideological underpinnings of Sati al-Husri, Michel Aflaq, and Zaki al-Arsuzi. Their work, imbued with a potent atmosphere of nationalist zeal, significantly shaped the anthem's thematic essence. Titled "Guardians of the Homeland" (*Humāt al-Diyār*), the anthem foregrounds themes akin to those prevalent in later Baathist lyrics—militarism, paternalistic stewardship, and sovereignty. Furthermore, the anthem serves as a foundational source for much of the symbolism and narrative tropes employed in subsequent Baathist songs. It encapsulates motifs of a resplendent historical legacy and the reclamation of pride or dignity. The convergence of these themes in the anthem is emblematic of the broader cultural and political ethos of the era, underscoring a collective identity interwoven with martial valor, historical reverence, and nationalistic pride. The opening verse of the anthem encapsulates these themes, articulating:

> Guardians of the homeland, upon you be peace.
> Our ever-proud souls refuse to be seized.
> The land of Arabism is our sacred home,
> And the throne of our sun will never set.[38]

It is a recurrent theme in national anthems to emphasize military events and wartime narratives. However, this particular anthem is distinguished by its pronounced emphasis on the concept of military "guardians" as both the exclusive audience and the definitive embodiment of the collective "us." In this composition the privilege of belonging and the pride associated with the homeland are exclusively bestowed upon those who assume the role of sentinels. The anthem effectively omits any mention of other citizen groups, thereby elevating the guardians to a position of singular significance within the national identity. This pervasive military ethos and the aspiration to reclaim dignity through assertive, physical means find further resonance in the subsequent verses of the anthem. These verses not only reinforce the central theme of martial guardianship but also articulate a vision of national identity that is inextricably linked to the vigor and valor of the military. This narrative underscores a perception of national pride and identity as fundamentally contingent upon the strength and vigilance of its military protectors.

> The flutter of our hopes and heartbeats
> Are depicted on the flag that united our land.
> Did we not use the black of every man's eye,
> And the ink of martyrs' blood, to write to the heavens?
> ... Our spirits are defiant and our past is glorious,
> And the martyrs' souls are our guardians.
> Walid is from us and so is Rashid,
> So how can we not prosper and build?

The celebrations of soldiery, violence, and martyrdom here are bracketed by references to the historical figures of Walid and Rashid, both of whom were male warriors who forged dynasties based on bloodshed. These figures, though hailing from a very different time and a different political culture, are regarded as "us" in the Syrian nationalist imagination, and are presented as aspirational models. Meanwhile, women and other ordinary, nonmilitary citizens of the current era are not addressed. This myth-making aspect of Baathist cultural production was a highly selective process, identifying heroes and symbols that could be associated with the desired muscular outlooks, and presenting those outlooks to Syrian men as the path to belonging and security. As for women, these nationalist discourses did not provide any path to recognition at all, and no security other than through supporting the stories and agendas of men.

In the corpus of songs examined, the nation is metaphorically construed as a familial construct, epitomizing the interconnection between masculinist traits and the conceptualization of men as both political and patriarchal custodians. This framework facilitates the demarcation of gender roles within both public and private domains. Consequently, these songs have ascended as a salient medium within the discourse of national identity, catalyzing a collective experiential understanding of struggle, adversity, and communal hardship. This musical narrative is instrumental in propagating notions of patriotism and nationalist consciousness, characterized by a pronounced inclination to exalt a national identity that selectively venerates achievements, predominantly in the realms of military prowess and physical fortitude. This selective glorification not only reinforces a specific vision of national identity but also shapes the public consciousness in a manner that emphasizes and valorizes martial achievements and physical strength as core components of national pride and identity.

The analytical examination of these nationalist songs facilitates a reimagining of the past as a narrative replete with sacrifice, concurrently engendering an emotional milieu imbued with camaraderie and militaristic zeal. This revivalist approach to national history is selective, often emphasizing certain aspects while omitting others. Central to this selective historical representation is the portrayal of heroic figures from the past, whose depictions are often intertwined with the glorification of physical strength, a theme that inadvertently contributes to the marginalization of women. These propagandistic musical compositions have typically been utilized as tools to foster and intensify identification with the regime. Prior to 2011 the demonstration of allegiance to the regime constituted a component of a performative act, meticulously rehearsed and repeatedly enacted. This practice served to mirror and reinforce the ideological and value structures espoused by the Baath Party. Thus, these songs functioned not merely as cultural artifacts but as instruments of political and ideological affirmation, embedding the Party's values into the collective consciousness through a blend of historical narrative and emotive appeal. As such, these nationalist songs facilitate a reconceptualization of history, portraying it as a saga of sacrifice while simultaneously cultivating an emotional environment steeped in the ethos of comradeship and militarism. These compositions are replete with allusions to glory, heroism, and sacrifice, often equated with the valorous acceptance of death in service of the nation. Such narratives predominantly propagate military virtues, thereby contributing to a masculinist construction of national identity and belonging.

In the context of songs that idolize leadership, their symbolic content serves to mythologize figures such as Hafez and Bashar al-Assad as paragons of national heroism, fostering a collective sentiment of reverence within the community. This amalgamation of the personas of Hafez and Bashar al-Assad with the state apparatus itself becomes emblematic of national unity and belonging. Consequently, adherence to this veneration becomes a defining criterion for citizenship, intertwining personal identity with the collective narrative of state and leadership. This phenomenon underscores the role of symbolic representation in shaping and defining the parameters of national identity and citizen allegiance within the framework of state-propagated nationalism.

While a significant proportion of the Syrian populace might contend that these songs were not earnestly internalized, often eliciting a degree of cynical response to their mandated glorification,[39] it is undeniable that they constituted an ingrained and consistent element of Syrian political culture. However, it is critical to consider the complex efficacy of these songs beyond their immediate contexts and the implications this has for individuals aligned with the Baath regime. These martial and emotive songs, born out of conflicts and a potent personality cult, played a pivotal role in reinforcing specific facets of Baath ideology. They were characterized by spiritual connotations tied to the nation, predominantly symbolized by the masculine readiness to sacrifice life for national causes. This pervasive narrative went beyond mere sacralization of the nation; it elevated men as the sole custodians and leaders of the national ethos. In doing so, it constructed a hierarchical and hegemonic framework for national belonging and identity. This framework not only delineated the boundaries of national identity but also implicitly defined the parameters of allegiance and participation within the Baathist political and cultural milieu.

Amid the burgeoning discourse on the escalating violence in Syria—encompassing a spectrum of issues from sectarian strife and terrorism to human trafficking and the refugee crisis—the international community's engagement with these challenges has been notable. However, there remains a conspicuous oversight in academic inquiry, specifically regarding the role of symbolism in the realm of masculinism and gender biases. This gap in scholarly attention suggests that the songs analyzed herein not only offer insights but also serve as a catalyst for further research into the construction of Syrian national identity and belonging prior to the upheaval of 2011. The forthcoming chapter aims to illuminate additional facets of political symbolism employed by the Baath regime. This exploration will delve into the ways these symbols were not only utilized to legitimize state authority but also strategically mobilized as instruments of endurance during wartime. Understanding the production and mobilization of political symbols is crucial, particularly in deciphering how they contribute to the formation and evolution of identities. This is of paramount importance in the context of the Syrian Uprising, as it provides a framework to comprehend the dynamic and emergent nature of Syrian identity, particularly as it disentangles itself from the entrenched hegemony of Baathist institutions. This line of inquiry is vital in mapping the shifting contours of national identity amid the transformative forces of conflict and political upheaval.

## Notes

1 See, for example, Michael E. Geisler (ed.). *National Symbols, Fractured Identities: Contesting the National Narrative.* Hanover, NH: University Press of New England, 2005, p. xv; and Max Fisher. "Here's North Korea's New Official Song, with Creepy Music Video." *The Washington Post*, May 7, 2013. www.washingtonpost.com/news/worldviews/wp/2013/05/07/heres-north-koreas-new-official-song-with-creepy-music-video/?utm_term=.6f241673e136. Accessed January 20, 2014.
2 Lisa Wedeen. *Ambiguities of Domination: Politics, Rhetoric, and Symbols in Contemporary Syria.* Chicago, IL, and London: University of Chicago Press, 1999.
3 Victoria Gilbert. "Syria for the Syrians: The Rise of Syrian Nationalism, 1970–2013." Master's thesis, Northeastern University, 2013. www.academia.edu/3432163/Syria_for_the_Syrians_The_Rise_of_Syrian_Nationalism_1970–2013. Accessed June 10, 2016; Miriam Cooke. *Dancing in Damascus: Creativity, Resilience, and the Syrian Revolution.* New York: Routledge, 2017.
4 Anthony D. Smith. *Nationalism: Theory, Ideology, History.* Cambridge: Polity, 2001, p. 18; Anne McClintock. "'No Longer in a Future Heaven': Women and Nationalism in South Africa." *Transition* 51 (1991): 104–23, p. 104. For more on the roles of symbolism in national identity formation, see Eric Hobsbawm and Terence Ranger. *The Invention of Traditions.* Cambridge: Cambridge University Press, 1983; George Mosse. *The Nationalisation of the Masses: Political Symbolism and Mass Movements in Germany from Napoleonic Wars through the Third Reich.* Ithaca, NY, and London: Cornell University Press, 1975; Benjamin Curtis. *Music Makes the Nation: Nationalist Composers and Nation Building in Nineteenth-Century Europe.* Amherst, MA, and New York: Cambria Press, 2008; and Benedict Anderson. *Imagined Communities: Reflections on the Origin and Spread of Nationalism.* New York and London: Verso, 2006.
5 A. Cohen. *The Symbolic Construction of Community.* London: Routledge, 1995, p. 16.
6 Lisa Wedeen. *Authoritarian Apprehensions: Ideology, Judgment, and Mourning in Syria.* Chicago, IL: University of Chicago Press, 1999, p. 32.
7 Carolyn Birdsall. *Nazi Soundscapes: Sound, Technology and Urban Space in Germany, 1933–1954.* Amsterdam: Amsterdam University Press, 2012, p. 42.
8 Chang-Tai Hung. "The Politics of Songs: Myths and Symbols in the Chinese Communist War Music, 1937–1949." *Modern Asian Studies* 30, no. 4 (1996): 901–29, pp. 903–05 has discussed this phenomenon in the context of Communist China. For additional prior scholarship that analyzes the role of songs in nation-building projects outside of Syria, see George Revill. "Music and the Politics of Sound: Nationalism, Citizenship and auditory Space." *Environment and Planning D: Society and Space* 18, no. 5 (2000): 597–613; Marina Frolova-Walker. *Russian Music and Nationalism: From Glinka to Stalin.* New Haven, CT: Yale University Press, 2007; Benedikte Brincker. "Introduction

to Themed Section on Classical Music and Nationalism: Studies into the Political Function of Art." *Nations and Nationalism* 20, no. 4 (2014): 603–05; Rebecca Wagner Oettinger. *Music as Propaganda in the German Reformation*. London: Routledge, 2001; and Philip V. Bohlman. *The Music of European Nationalism: Cultural Identity and Modern History*. California: ABC-CLIO, 2004. One notable aspect of this prior scholarship is that it has seldom addressed how nationalist songs reflect and reinscribe gender ideologies.
9 See Wagner Oettinger 2001, pp. 9–10, for a discussion of the spread of musical propaganda.
10 Nicholas Jackson O'Shaughnessy. *Politics and Propaganda: Weapons of Mass Seduction*. Manchester: Manchester University Press, 2004, pp. 4–6.
11 Esteban Buch, Igor Contreras Zubillaga, and Manuel Denis Silva (eds). *Composing for the State: Music in Twentieth-Century Dictatorships*. London and New York: Routledge, 2016, pp. 9–10, have discussed the ways in which nationalist music tends to emphasize the mythic past as a way of promoting norms in the present.
12 McClintock 1991, p. 104.
13 Anne McClintock. "Family Feuds: Gender, Nationalism and the Family." *Feminist Review* 44 (Summer 1993): 61–80, p. 62.
14 V. Spike Peterson. "Gendered Nationalism: Reproducing 'Us' versus 'Them.'" In *The Women and War Reader*, edited by Lois Ann Lorentzen and Jennifer Turpin, pp. 41–49. New York and London: New York University Press, 1998, p. 44.
15 This quote is from Aflaq 1956a. See the discussion in Chapter 2 of this book.
16 Hafez al-Assad. "Speech by Syrian President Hafez al-Assad during the October 1973 War." YouTube video, posted by "Ba7ebbek Ya Masr," October 19, 2016. www.youtube.com/watch?v=iGSiQvV_B4U. Accessed January 2, 2019.
17 Hafez al-Assad. "The Immortal Leader Hafez al-Assad (I am First and Foremost a Farmer, the Son of a Farmer) a Humane Speech." YouTube video, posted by "ALI HASAN," March 8, 2015. www.youtube.com/watch?v=tduY8lxBXFc. Accessed January 2, 2019.
18 National song, *Rāyātik bil-'Ālī ya Sūriyya*.
19 National song, *Biktub Ismek ya Blādī*.
20 National song, *Sūriyya ya Habībatī*.
21 Yasir Suleiman. *The Arabic Language and National Identity*. Washington, DC: Georgetown University Press, 2003, p. 28.
22 National song, *'Ana Sūrī wa 'Ardī 'Arabiyya*.
23 National song, *'Ana Sūrī ah yā Niyyālī*.
24 National song, *Saff l-'Askar*.
25 National song, *Shaddet l-Hijin*.
26 See Wedeen 1999, pp. 16–17; Marwan M. Kraidy. *Reality Television and Arab Politics: Contention in Public Life*. Cambridge: Cambridge University Press, 2010, p. 27; and Gilbert 2013.
27 Fiona Hill. "Syrian Women and Feminist Agenda." In Paul J. White and William S. Logan (eds), *Remaking the Middle East*, pp. 129–51. New York and Oxford: Berg Publishers, 1997, p. 129, provides a valuable discussion of

links between political personality cults and patriarchy in the family domain. The cult of Assad discussed here can be seen as another example of this trend.

28 National song, *Abu Bassel Qā'idnā*.
29 National song, *'Abu r-Rijāl*.
30 National song, *Teslam l sh-Sha'b*.
31 National song, *Hamāka Allahu ya Assadu*.
32 See Rahaf Aldoughli. "Securitization as a Tool of Regime Survival: The Deployment of Religious Rhetoric in Bashar al-Asad's Speeches." *The Middle East Journal* 75, no. 1 (2021a): 9–32. https://doi.org/10.3751/75.1.11, pp. 125–40.
33 Bashar al-Assad. "President Bashar al-Assad's Speech at the People's Assembly after Taking the Oath as President of the Republic 07/17/2000." YouTube video, posted by "Syria RTV," July 10, 2013. www.youtube.com/watch?v=ATC54C4eiPo. Accessed April 4, 2015.
34 Bashar al-Assad. "President Bashar al-Assad Inaugural Address." Peoples Assembly, July 18, 2007. www.mideastweb.org/bashar_assad_inauguration_2007.htm. Accessed May 11, 2016.
35 National song, *Minhibbak*.
36 Geisler (ed.) 2005, p. xxv.
37 For example, Canada and Austria have both recently altered the words of their national anthems so that they are more gender-inclusive (see Helen Pidd. "Austrians Look Forward to New National Anthem." *The Guardian*, October 31, 2011. www.theguardian.com/world/2011/oct/31/austrians-national-anthem-new. Accessed April 21, 2016. Germany changed its national anthem after the end of the Nazi era, Iraq adopted a new anthem after the fall of Saddam Hussein, and South Africa did the same after the end of apartheid.
38 Author translation.
39 See Wedeen 1999.

# 5

# War and muscular revival after 2011

Amid the violence and repression that has spread across Syria since 2011, it might be asked how the Baath Party has continued to maintain its domination over much of the country's populace. It is undoubtedly true that political loyalty has been influenced by the regime's manipulation of religious identities, as well as by coercion, fear, securitization, and material patronage. These aspects of Syrian loyalism have been well studied by other scholars.[1] What is less documented is the way in which the regime has leveraged a reinvigorated masculinist identity politics as a means to instill heartfelt, passionate loyalty among its supporters. Such emotive patriotism is evident in the public demonstrations of support for Bashar al-Assad that have regularly occurred during the interminable conflict, and in performative displays such as loyalists piercing their fingers to vote for Assad's presidency in blood, as discussed in the Introduction. Returning to these dynamics in the current Syrian conflict, this chapter emphasizes the ideological aspects of loyalist support and the intersections of masculinism and state power.

The previous chapters have shown that during the rise of Baathism and in the period of its hegemony, the muscular concept of the nation was cultivated by the regime primarily as a means of forging a common identity and building bridges among Syria's diverse religious and ethnic communities. More importantly, unlike pre-2011 nationalist songs, which were usually officially sponsored, recorded, and distributed by the regime, these recent exemplars have no clear authorship. They are not sung by notable celebrities; in most cases the singers and authors remain unknown and are not regarded as particularly important in the surrounding media discussions. Lyrics are frequently lifted from one song and inserted into another, and closely similar songs appear with varied arrangements, singers, instrumentation, videos, and performance contexts. When reviewing this material, I found it quite difficult to trace the variations back to a particular origin or author, as the extensive recycling makes it nearly impossible to identify who first produced the songs. It may be possible that Bashar al-Assad's regime has played some role in instigating or supporting aspects of this cultural production, but the spread and popularity of the content and its constant reworking in loyalist media cannot be attributed to top–down coercion. If some of these loyalist videos are a product of a modern "astroturfing" campaign, then it is a highly successful one in the sense that the content has been eagerly adopted, adapted, modified, and spread by regime supporters.

Here I will show that after the outbreak of civil war, this muscular identification yielded tremendous benefits for the regime, since many loyalists came to view its survival as equivalent to the survival of their privileged gendered identities. Such associations were strongly promulgated by the regime from the top down both before and after 2011, but the period of civil conflict also saw a notable rise in "spontaneous" or bottom–up productions in which ordinary loyalist citizens took it upon themselves to recreate the muscular rhetoric, spectacles, and performances to which they had become accustomed during the earlier period of Baathist hegemony. The conflict period thus further shows the extent to which the muscular nationalist rhetoric of the Baathists was internalized and impactful in the everyday lives of Syrians.

During the course of this book, I have shown that the ideal of the muscular Baathist citizen-soldier underwent a process of consolidation and hardening over the years. In the early emergence of Syrian nationalist thought (c. 1940–70), concepts of militarism and muscular manhood were propagated within a broadly revolutionary, philosophical, and anti-colonial spirit. During the regime of Hafez al-Assad (1971–2000), they increasingly morphed into an authoritarian personality cult that retained and exacerbated all of the troubling aspects of the Baathist movement while enacting few of its positive communitarian goals. Emerging from a questionable but aspirational idealism, the muscular concept soon veered into the realm of applied indoctrination, fanaticism, and domination. Thus, for several decades Syrians grew up amid the constant, enforced repetition of ideologies such as "the heroic man," "our glorious past," "killing for the nation," and "protecting honor." The transfer of power to the youthful Bashar al-Assad in the year 2000 initiated hopes among some Syrians that the regime would shift toward greater openness and personal freedoms, but the anticipated ebb in authoritarianism never arrived. Instead, Bashar doubled down in his insistence on Syrians' loyalty and affection, and the regime continued with propaganda and required performances that even further consolidated a Romanticized view of fealty and attachment between the regime and its men.

The 2011 Syrian uprisings and the subsequent civil war were to some extent a conflict over these mandated identities. When demonstrators took to the streets, they specifically contested the regime's rhetoric of brotherhood and militant belonging, often by creating their own subversive variations of

Baathist songs and slogans and by presenting these nationalist performances as an object of distaste. A central example of this trend is the common chant "We don't love you! / We don't love you! / Go away with your Party!" This opposition chant was set to the rhythm of the patriotic campaign song "We Love You" (*Minhibbak*), which was discussed in Chapter 4. Other canonical songs such as "I Engrave Your Name, Oh Syria" (*Biktub Ismek ya Blādī*) and "Syria, Oh My Love" (*Sūriyya ya Habībatī*) were used by the opposition groups after changing their lyrics. Such use of previous regime songs does emphasize the extent to which indoctrination and socialization processes enforced by the regime still has its impact on citizens' attitudes and behaviors.

Meanwhile, however, loyalist factions in Syria went into overdrive to reproduce, revive, and recirculate the Baathist rhetoric of muscularity, blood, and brotherhood, with an increasing edge of anger and fear. As the institutions of the state began to break down, loyalist took it upon themselves to stage their own independent productions of these Baathist scripts, many of which found a home on the YouTube internet platform (one of the primary forms of media consumption in Syria). These videos circulated widely among loyalist groups, on social media, online platforms, and during weddings. The songs were performed by amateur singers and were often set to stock video footage of battles. I focus specifically on how masculinity has become a significant aspect of the loyalist image during the Syrian civil war in newly produced songs and performances.

When I embarked upon my study of Syrian songs after war, the trope of masculinity appeared to be a rather fixed stereotype of Baathist national identity. However, when mounting criticism of regime loyalists began to spur, I started to understand that framing loyalism as a frame is rather a complex of interrelated aspects of identity. As a start I consider these lyrics as a discursive project of reinvented national identity, and a malleable point of negotiation for a newly constructed "other" in Syrian popular culture. While the Baathist masculinism trope serves as an objectified model of identity whose meaning has been located in specific imposed national aspect, post-2011 songs do not show only a continuation of masculinist trope but also a banality in producing symbols of subjectivity.

Such performances cannot be explained in purely materialistic or coercive terms, as the individuals who created and shared them received little pragmatic reward from the regime for their enthusiasm. I argue that these bottom–up repetitions of the Baathist rhetoric during the civil war are ground in a felt need to re-entrench and affirm the gendered and politicized psychological identity matrixes into which many Syrians were inducted during their formative years. I also emphasize the ways in which this constructed "primordial" logic is ensnared in romantic (often erotic) narrative fantasies about "love" and "sacrifice" for the passive, objectified nation that is viewed as being under one's protection.[2]

Another important aspect of my analysis is the role of symbols in maintaining loyalist identities and supporting regime survival. Graeme Gill and Luis F. Angosto-Ferrandez significantly argue that the creation of symbolic discourse is shaped by "multivocality" where competition over who determine the symbolic order became a site of contention.[3] Michael Billig and David A. Butz have written extensively about how symbols can serve to mark national boundaries of inclusion and exclusion, helping to identify the lives and practices that are considered legitimate.[4] To some extent, as I will describe below, Bashar al-Assad has intentionally made himself into the ultimate symbol of cultural power and loyalty, existing alongside the other symbols of the regime such as flags and insignia. Meanwhile, however, loyalist factions in Syria continued to reproduce and circulate such discourses, with an increasing edge of anger and fear. Given the near total breakdown of civic institutions in Syria over the past decade, the continuation of nationalist songs and loyalist demonstrations during this period has to be understood at least in part as an ideological echo of nationalism "from below." These actions cannot be explained in purely materialistic or coercive terms, as their proponents generally receive little pragmatic reward for such enthusiastic displays.

Instead, I argue, they represent a continuation of the politicized psychological identity matrixes into which many loyalists were inducted during their formative years. The sheer repetitiveness of these songs' lyrics (as I will show in more detail below) and their emphasis on the stock images of the omnipresent, adored leader, the heroic male soldier, and the romantic glory attained through dedication to the cause present an almost desperate effort to reinscribe privileged identities that are under threat in a time of social conflict. I emphasize how these symbols are continuously circulated in nationalist songs and rhetoric in loyalist circles to reinforce the emotional resonance and personal impact of certain national ideals. These texts will provide an empirical grounding for discussing the symbols and cultural concepts that are prevalent in loyalist discourses and their role in shaping the contours of political identity.

In the following sections I will focus on a close analysis of seven nationalist songs that were wildly popular among regime loyalists from 2012 to 2020. The features of these songs and their spread—the sheer repetitiveness of the lyrics; the constant reinterpretation and free association conducted by various performers; and their emphasis on stock images of the omnipresent, adored leader, the heroic male soldier, and the romantic glory attained through dedication to the cause—present an almost desperate effort to reinscribe the privileged Syrian identities that were under threat in a time of social conflict. Lisa Wedeen has argued convincingly that public participation in Syrian regime rituals during the period of Baathist hegemony should not be regarded as a sincere sign of acceptance or loyalty.[5] However, the continuation and heightening of such displays during the more recent period of civil conflict indicates that many individuals truly internalized the previously mandated rhetoric and continued to view it as central to their sense of identity and belonging. Songs and other patriotic displays spontaneously produced and circulated by regime loyalists after 2011 are demonstrations of agency, which in this case were targeted toward the reinscription of challenged identities.

When selecting these songs for analysis, I focused on their popularity and prevalence, as demonstrated by the number of views on YouTube. Unlike pre-2011 nationalist performances, which were almost always officially state-sponsored and were recorded and distributed by the regime, these recent exemplars have no clearly identified authorship and were not performed by celebrities. Further demonstrating their impromptu nature, lyrical phrases are frequently lifted from one song and inserted into another, and closely similar songs tend to appear with varied arrangements, singers, instrumentation, videos, and performance contexts. I have divided the songs into two sections: first, those that emphasize the role of the muscular fighter as a venerated and privileged protector; and second, those that emphasize devotion and duty to nationalist comrades and leaders. Nearly all of the songs include elements of both themes, but this organization serves as a means of discussing these focal points of the Baathist muscular construct.

## Authoritarian survival and performativity

A great deal of scholarly literature in the political science field has examined the nature and formation of authoritarian institutions. The majority of this scholarship focuses on material coercion and the actions of ruling elites.[6] These issues are undoubtedly important for understanding the rise and sustainability of authoritarianism, but it is also important to consider how socialization is propagated under these regimes, and the ground-level impact of political spectacle on citizens' behaviors and attitudes. To the extent that such questions have been analyzed in the Syrian context, scholars often fall back on reductive notions of sect, ethnicity, and patronage as an explanatory framework for the country's power dynamics.[7] Departing from such customary lenses, this chapter invites a rethinking of the logic of loyalty in Syria in regard to the basic ideological question of "How can masculinism be used as a tool of authoritarian survival?" In the following sections I emphasize the relatively overlooked issue of constructed primordialism in the Syrian political culture, examining how the regime's rhetoric and loyalist support foregrounds and reinscribes a romanticized view of national belonging and identity. These emotive identity politics, I will argue, provide much of the "glue" that has allowed loyalist support for the regime to continue cohering even after more than a decade of brutality and war.

A common argument in studies of public attitudes toward civil liberties is that education and political communication influence the level of citizens' support for such political norms.[8] This dynamic model of exposure and acceptance is intimately linked to the process of socialization, and it can be applied to authoritarian contexts as well as democratic ones. Some studies have shown that regimes seek to link their preferred political narratives to other values held by the populace, which can help to promote regime legitimization and acceptance among broad swaths of the population.[9] As such, these broader values become conceptually linked not only to a general political philosophy but also to a specific party or leadership tradition.[10] Such arguments are conceptually convincing, though it is often difficult to empirically study the impact of such rhetoric in authoritarian regimes, since the usual methods of surveys and interviews cannot be considered reliable when people may be afraid to state their sincerely held views or to voice political criticism. It is also very difficult to gauge the long-term impact of the partisan reinscription of societal norms, since it is unknown how such norms may have fared in alternative political environments.

It is important to distinguish between different possible reactions to the inscription of authoritarian ideologies, which may range from extreme identification to subversion to overt resistance. In her early work, for example, Lisa Wedeen has emphasized the distinction between sincere loyalty and ritualistic performance in the pre-2011 Syrian context, arguing that "citizens in Syria are not required to believe the cult's flagrantly fictitious statements and, as a rule, do not. But they act *as if* they do."[11] She further concludes that the "effects of Assad's cult, although powerful, are also ambiguous … [the appearance of loyalty] demonstrates *only* that people are able and can be brought to recite the slogans."[12] By focusing on the role of coercion, Wedeen in this early work leaves little room for analyzing the internalization of such regime-sponsored ideologies. After the outbreak of civil war in 2011, however, it has become less possible to believe that declarations of regime loyalty are purely staged.

In her second, post-2011 book on Syrian politics, Wedeen gives a greater credence to "political ambivalence" and the internalized fantasy of a stable and orderly society that some individuals may believe is obtainable through loyalism. As a result, Wedeen argues, many Syrians find themselves adopting a "neutral" or "grey" (*ramādī*) position to retain access to material benefits, or even becoming fervent loyalists who support Assad as an emblem of the secure society. Thus, in Wedeen's estimation, Syrians' identities lurch between "desires for reform and their attachment to order," as individuals react to the glamorous, stable, and modern image of the nation presented by Assad.[13] While there is much to commend in this analysis, I would suggest that it retains too much emphasis on material aspirations, while minimizing the affective and identity-oriented dimensions of loyalist support.

Against this backdrop, the current chapter draws from Judith Butler's analyses of political judgment as a performative display and a profound locus of symbolic political action. According to Butler, political behavior is fundamentally shaped by political discourse and by repetitive social action.[14] From such a perspective, we would expect that participation in endless loyalist spectacles under the Baathist hegemony could not help but have an impact on subjective experiences and outlooks. I argue that Syrian subjects in Syria have been pervasively exposed to a political culture that discursively glorifies sacrifice, emotive attachment, and heroism, and that such experiences have a strong and meaningful impact on the shape of the current conflict. Adopting Butler's theorization of the production of political life as "foreclosed by certain habitual and violent presumptions,"[15] this analysis is based on the view that the development of Syria as a modern nation-state under the Baathists has instilled a performative and internalized link between emotive sentimentalism and regime loyalty. In my previous research I have discussed the foundations of militarism and nationalism in Baathist Syria prior to the current war, and highlighted how this emotive national ideology was linked to the sustainability of authoritarianism.[16] The current chapter extends these perspectives to evaluate how the regime has "harvested" the legacy of emotive identifications to survive through the current conflict, by drawing on constructs such as heroic national violence, killing for the nation, and defending the honor of the nation.

Rather than emphasizing the metaphysical autonomy or internality of subjects, Butler prioritizes social discourse and performance as the origin of action; in other words, the formation and reproduction of subjectivity is "not a doing by a subject who might be said to pre-exist the deed."[17] This perspective complicates the view of the relationship between authoritarian power and subjective response; in the context of Syria it requires, at a minimum, that we give more attention to the impact of public performance in shaping political affiliations and the contours of the conflict. Butler's analysis is also extremely useful in the Syrian context in that she emphasizes the dynamics of passionate attachment and the psychological or affective aspects of power.[18] My outlook combines this perspective with scholarship on political legitimization, which Shaar defines as "a system's ability to persuade members of its own appropriateness." Like Butler, Shaar places a strong emphasis on the role of symbols and performances in shaping citizen's internalized behaviors and subjective experiences.[19] Performative rituals and scripted behaviors can also be viewed as *communications* between a governing regime and the population, through which legitimized actions and subjectivities are reinforced. I will argue that the role of Romanticized primordialism in loyalist texts and performances (as well as oppositional performances critiquing or rejecting these constructs) is vital to understanding the entrenched nature of the Syrian conflict and its broad-reaching political dimensions.

## Songs of heroism

One of the most common themes that can be found in Syrian loyalist songs during the civil war years is the glorification of the masculine soldier as an honored protector of the nation and its people. While this theme is also common in pre-2011 Syrian nationalist songs (as well as in similar patriotic rhetoric worldwide), during the war these songs began to place an ever-increasing emphasis on the masculinity of the heroes, often using terms such as "manliness" (*rujūla*), "fathers" (*'ābā'*), and "chivalry" (*butūla*) multiple times per stanza. While in the past this gendering stood as a default background assumption and issue of concern in Baathist cultural production, here it became even more centered in a fraught and fiercely contested fashion, as though it were an identity that needed to be forced into the listener's consciousness. I would suggest that the anxious foregrounding of muscular manhood in these productions indicates an attempt to reinscribe an identity that was perceived as being under siege.

Perhaps the most popular Syrian loyalist song at the time of this writing (early 2023) is called "May God Save Our Army" (*Allah Mhayyī l-Jesh*). There are at least two primary versions of this song in circulation, with somewhat different lyrics and arrangements.[20] The different versions are abundant with masculinist gratifications, and they make no mention of women fighters at all, despite the fact that the regime began recruiting women into the military in 2014.[21] Instead, women are presented as passive objects to be "protected" and controlled. One version of the song, which is highly unusual in that it gives voice to a woman's presumed outlook—albeit voiced by a male singer—displays the support and gratitude that loyalists expected to receive from women:

> Hail Syria and its heroes
> Hail the Army and its great men ...
> May God hail and cherish the son of my nation
> Who is protecting my honor [*sharafī*] and my children.[22]

The presumptive leveraging of women's support in such lyrics is representative of the manner in which Bashar al-Assad's regime has instrumentalized "feminist" symbolism and representation to prop up a broadly patriarchal state institution. Actions such as patriotic statements made by Asmaa al-Assad (Bashar's wife) on International Women's Day have persistently served as media opportunities to demonstrate eroticized support for male leadership. In some cases they also serve as attempts to launder the regime's reputation, especially among potential international audiences.[23] It is interesting how in this version of the loyalist song the voicing of such women's support is casually replicated by the male performer, without missing a beat. Perhaps the rhetorical form of such feminine support has become so codified that it is now spoken as an abstract invocation or gesture. Apart from such brief passages that display the presumed, one-dimensional support of women for male fighters, these songs are inescapably voiced from a man's perspective, and they display an obsessive focus on calling out men's "greatness" and strength.

"The Army of the Homeland" (*Jesh l-Watan*) is a similar song that has played a prominent role in loyalist marches and demonstrations, especially during Assad's reelection in May 2021. This song is even played at weddings in Latakia and Tartous, where most Alawites live, as their public social media profiles show. Again, there are multiple versions of this song in circulation, with somewhat different lyrics, arrangements, performers, and presentations.[24] They all emphasize the glory of nationalist fighters in masculine terms, both through direct references to men and through allegories such as "flashing swords" and "bulging muscles." One version starts with:

> This is the Army of our nation ...
> It is my brother and your brother
> It is my father and your father
> It has made our nation proud
> Full of manliness and magnanimity ...
> It is my name and your name
> It is my blood and your blood
> It is the symbol of manliness and heroism
> Their twisted forearms protect us from enemies.

The overtly gendered language of "brothers," "fathers," and "manliness" here grounds the lyrics in the logic of masculine protection, and thus links the nationalist cause directly to the presumed domestic leadership roles of men. It also conflates the survival of the nation with the survival of these types of domestic gender ideologies.

Another notable feature of this song is that it continues on to describe violent encounters between the paragons of the nationalist army and those who would resist them, and when doing so it presents the perfidious and "illegitimate" opposition using strongly gendered idioms. The song thus invests tremendously in a muscular hierarchy where enemies of the nation are portrayed as unmanly, and therefore undeserving of love, belonging, and veneration. This was clear from the song's footage and images as they show the regime's army blasting off the location of the opposition areas. Another important aspect in this song is that it turns into a romanticized version when one stanza is sung by a female singer. The female singer Rahaf Zabalawi starts its stanza with "manhood and dignity" (*rujūleh w karāmeh*) in a way to reinforce that this army provides the true meaning of manhood, continuing with words such as "with love we sing to it." It is striking that while the male singer emphasizes in his part lyrics of the strength of the fighters' physique, the female singer uses more emotional expressions to demonstrate attachment to the army.

The popular song "Oh, My Mother, My Syria" (*Ya 'Immi Ya Sūriyya*) merges familial imagery with the muscular fantasy of being honored and loved for one's violent actions. While this song entails themes of devotion and sacrifice, its primary emphasis is on the nobility and veneration of the "son," with the mother's role limited to providing such recognition and witness:

> Oh, my mother, oh Syria
> Hide your tears
> We give you our souls
> We give you our precious blood
> Oh, my mother, your son has changed his address
> He is now in heaven
> He always said: Syria is soul and blood.[25]

The gender dichotomy in this song's language remains consistent—the "we" who act as devoted agents are sons (not daughters) of Syria. While the protector has sacrificed his life, he does so, one might say tragically, in order to affirm his gendered identity, his belonging, and his nobility, in the knowledge that his glory will be seen and remembered. The nation is constructed in the son's vision as a woman who pours tenderness upon those who protect her. Similar to the writings of Sati al-Husri, as discussed in Chapter 2, it is striking in these songs how the common loyalist representation of Syria as the "fatherland" (belonging to or controlled by the fathers) morphs into the image of a supportive mother or female lover when it is called upon to bear passive witness to a soldier's heroism.

There are many additional songs in the current Syrian loyalist culture that emphasize the muscular glory of fighters. Their poetic quality may vary, but their lyrics are largely interchangeable. One of these songs, called "Millions and Millions of Syrians" (*Malayīn Malayīn al-Sūriyyīn*), describes the agency and heroism of men who take it upon themselves to stand up for the nationalist cause. It is in such songs where popular legitimacy as a masculinist construct is even more reinforced in Syrian popular culture. The song thus invests tremendously in a muscular hierarchy where enemies of the nation are portrayed as unmanly, and therefore undeserving of love, belonging, and veneration.

This song is remarkable, even more than the others discussed here, for its adoption and adaptation by various unknown singers and ordinary people. There are even versions in circulation that have been modified to incorporate completely different causes, such as support for the Lebanese group Hezbollah.[26] Such versions were even popularized as a response to oppositions' claims that the regime is jeopardizing the sovereignty of Syria by calling Hezbollah to intervene in Syria. The song also implicitly has a sectarian tone where Hasan Nasr Allah, leader of Hezbollah, has become a symbol of sectarianism for many Syrians after the 2011 war.

The sturdiness and power of fighting men are likewise celebrated in "We Challenge" (*Mnithaddā*), which glorifies a combative stance:

> We challenge all the world
> We are your people, oh Syria
> We are your men
> We fear nothing
> We will never surrender.[27]

When comparing such discourses to the pre-2011 songs discussed in Chapter 4, the difference that stands out the most is that the rigidity of the muscular nationalist identity and its boundaries of exclusion and inclusion have ossified. While there have always been such hierarchies in the Baathist imagination, and while there is a great deal of thematic similarity and continuity between the wartime corpus and the songs of prior decades, the recent popular productions show a more emphatic antagonism toward outsiders. They display what we might call "stubborn" muscularity, in which glory is associated with a refusal to give up or give in regardless of logic or circumstance. As the preservation of muscularity and masculine privilege became ever more detached from the lofty communitarian and anti-colonial goals of the Baathist founders, it gradually became its own raison d'être, and it has now exploded into a reflexive hostility toward the "internal enemy" (that is, any Syrian opposing the regime, and/or any personal doubts about the cause). This is evident in the increasing prevalence of terms such as "treacherous" (*ghāder*) and "enemy" (*"aduww"*) in the lyrics, as well as in the angry tone of the productions. The nationalist songs in the years of conflict have become increasingly focused on rejecting and destroying such dangers, by locating and expunging any sign of "weakness" or "cowardice."

Another song that hails the army and its strength is "Raise Your Arms Higher" (*Allī l-Slāh*). This song features almost the same imagery and footage of old recorded videos of soldiers' training. Most probably, this footage was recorded before the war and was recycled and reused for many other videos. This highlights how such songs did not have a high budget for their production. The song starts with its emphasis on the precious role of the army in protecting the nation:

> Raise your arms higher and higher
> The Syrian army, who is like you?
> No power can defeat you …
> You are the only one that can reclaim our land

The song depicts the soldiers as wild and energetic, uncompromized and unbounded by any means. This romanticized depiction of Baathist mythologies is further enhanced by constructing the "other." This "other" post-2011 is constructed as everyone that opposed the regime. The popularization of this heroic Baathi identity is further preserved by depicting those from the opposition as "treacherous" (*khawwān*): "You should know, oh you treacherous, that our Syrian army will protect us."

The videos that accompany these songs on social media are almost exclusively composed of borrowed footage of male soldiers engaged in physical exercises, practicing hand-to-hand combat, or using military equipment (launching artillery, shooting rifles, etc.). The impact of these activities on the opposition is not shown; instead, the visual emphasis is on the physiques and confident actions of the regime soldiers.

## Songs of devotion

The glorification of the fighting man's heroism and power in loyalist songs is dovetailed by his unconditional commitment to military comrades and leaders. Similar to the songs of heroism, post-2011 discourses in this category show an increasing emphasis on distinguishing between those who are loyal and those who are not. They also highlight the continuing shift in Syria toward an authoritarian personality cult, in which there is little distinction between the cause, the nation, and the leader. As noted above, this phenomenon is not new in Syrian political culture; it was also perpetuated during the rule of Hafez al-Assad, who sought to forward himself as a personal embodiment of the Arabist political philosophy and the national destiny.[28] However, during the rule of Bashar al-Assad, and particularly after the outbreak of the civil war, the personality cult has become essentially all that remains of the regime's governing philosophy. The songs of this period present loyalty to Bashar not as the embodiment of a larger political ideal but rather as an end in itself, centered around the ethos of muscular solidarity and the annihilation of anything that might undermine its power.

The songs of devotion to Bashar al-Assad and to other comrades in the cause are suffused with the language of love and service. They demonstrate the aspect of the militarized masculine identity in which the value of the self is grounded in concepts of hierarchical duty. They also, perhaps, serve as a projection of the affection and admiration that loyalist men believe they are owed from women and other subordinates, as a reward for participating in the gender construct and serving as "protectors" and paragons of the nation. In expressing their devotion to Bashar al-Assad, it might be argued that the singers are also suggesting the contours of the love and acceptance that they themselves should receive. In some cases the affective overtones of these songs border on the homoerotic (a claim that their producers would vehemently reject); at the very least, one can say that they draw from the rhetorical realm of romantic passion as a means of expressing powerful emotional bonds and the desire for belonging. In the song "Oh Bashar, Who Is Like You?" (*Ya Bashar, Mitlak Meen*), the singer emotes:

Whatever happens
We are your millions of soldiers
To you, we pledge ourselves
To you is our love
To you is our blood
To you is our soul
To you is our loyalty
Our sky, land, and water to you only
God wants you, we want you, all of Syria wants you![29]

It is worth noting that some lines of this particular song are taken from a highly canonical ballad written in 1973 in the context of the Arab–Israeli War.[30] However, the words have been changed to replace devotion to the pan-Arab cause with devotion to the person of Bashar al-Assad. Thus, the romantic themes that were once borrowed to symbolize emotional attachment to a political ideal have now been borrowed again to express passionate devotion to the person of the president.

In a similar loyalist song, called "We Want to Preserve" (*Bidna Nhāfez*), Bashar is described in various lines as the "the hope," "the spring of humanity," "beloved of millions," and "master of the proud ones." The song continues on to explain:

The people choose you
The people love you
And your people
Do not want anyone but you![31]

The romanticized language in these songs may appear strange when considered in an analytical framework, but it served an important purpose in reinforcing a type of emotional attachment that locates the nationalist identity construct as a value beyond all reason. During the time of war, such words tend to blur political and ethical judgment and can be used as a tool of mobilization. The passionate identification of oneself with the leader and with one's "brothers" who serve the nation is not something that remains in the realm of rhetoric. It is expressed in actions, in killing, in hostility to outsiders, and ultimately, as many of the songs proclaim, in blood.

The passionate identification of oneself with the leader and with one's "brothers" who serve the nation is not something that remains in the realm of rhetoric. It is expressed in actions, in killing, in hostility to outsiders, and ultimately in blood. In 2021, as Bashar al-Assad stood for a new presidential election, scenes of patriotic regime loyalists piercing their fingers to vote "yes" in blood went viral on social media and in the country's news blogs.[32] From concepts of love and devotion, when abstracted from real personal relationships, exaggerated to all-consuming proportions, and tied to hierarchical gendered roles and insider/outsider dynamics of belonging, is derived an irrational political affinity grounded not in civic philosophies or pragmatic materialism but rather in the preservation of identity. The nature of the "love" between the leader and his people is not one that tolerates disagreement and diversity, nor is it measured by civic rights and accountability. It is a construct imagined as eternal, involuntary, and sacrosanct, though in reality it fluctuates with the whims and impulses of the moment.

These words succinctly combine three points that convey the outlines of primordial nationalist loyalty. First, the leader–people relationship is about maintaining personal and familial ties, based on emotional attachment and "love." Second, these ties of love serve as a measure of the leader's legitimacy and the consent of the governed, replacing the integrity of legal and civic processes. Third, the benefits of citizenship and belonging are predicated upon an individual's readiness to demonstrate unconditional love for the nation and its leader. While seeking to emphasize affective bonds as a means of generating support, this language diminishes the civic notion of national membership. It presumes an involuntary love for the nation and its leader, and implicitly excludes anyone who may not feel such intense bonds of emotional loyalty.

These lyrics show that this trope of masculinity in Syrian public culture is rather ubiquitous and monolithic. This exemplifies the continuity of a banal construction of masculinist national identity even when feelings are heightened in times of political crisis. Representations of hegemonic masculinity began to gain prominence in post-2011 war by an exaggeration of aspects of stereotypical masculinity such as strength and other physical demands—however, most importantly, as juxtaposed with other soldiers from the opposition. While this representation of Baathist masculinity seems to be concrete and corporeal—in other words, present fixed aspects of muscular loyalism—it is important to take into consideration that at the time of writing this chapter, lots of mounting criticism among the Assad loyalist base has begun to show dissatisfaction with the regime's war tactics, and more men are defecting from the army.

This chapter presented a textual analysis of loyalist songs in the context of the Syrian civil war, emphasizing the ways in which an irrational attachment to masculinism is linked to the consolidation and continuation of support for the regime. Privileged and militarized concepts of masculinity have long been reinforced by the Baathist state as an aspect of forging national identity, and during the civil war years, the maintenance of this masculine identity concept has become one of the foremost pillars around which loyalist support is organized. The related discourses, which promote a violent and exclusionary nationalist politics as a way to reaffirm manliness, appear to no longer require the active coercive intervention of the Syrian state, and are now instead recycled and recirculated autonomously by regime supporters "from below."

While this book did not discuss the institution of the military and its role in Syrian politics, it is worth noting that Hafez al-Assad originally came to power through a military coup, and that the Baathist regime relied heavily on the army in consolidating its early dominance and control over the populace.[33] For many years public support for the army was mandatory in Syria, and military parades and performances were a regular spectacle. During the later years of the regime, this militarism began to take on more of a rhetorical and hegemonic character, as opposed to a direct application of coercive force. As the analysis in this chapter has shown, however, the shaping of the body politic around an ethos of militarized masculinism results in a continuing reservoir of potential violence that is always ready to reemerge when needed to defend the construct. For those who can conceive of belonging in no other terms, there is an existential attachment to the masculinist identity construct and an unwavering willingness to shed blood to preserve it. The continuation of these masculinist identifications in Syria has had a drastic negative impact on the prospects for a peaceful transition to inclusive democracy.

Perhaps most importantly, the perception of love is closely integrated with the muscular ideal and with the expectation that men who participate in this ideal would receive admiration and reward. Similar to an overexcited suitor, Syrian loyalists believed that their claims to chivalry, protection, and sacrifice must merit reciprocation, support, and affection—but without bothering to ask the rest of the country's citizens if they would like to participate in such an arrangement. Ultimately, the Romanticized concept of muscular identity served to evacuate other Syrians' ability to choose, replacing the consent of the governed and the integrity of legal and civic processes with an increasingly angry insistence on inescapable and primordial patrimony, enforced when needed through violence against anyone who would question it.

## Notes

1 See, for example, S. N. Abboud. *Syria: Hot Spots in Global Politics*. Chichester: John Wiley and Sons, 2018; Rahaf Aldoughli. "Securitization as a Tool of Regime Survival: The Deployment of Religious Rhetoric in Bashar al-Asad's Speeches." *The Middle East Journal* 75, no. 1 (2021a): 9–32. https://doi.org/10.3751/75.1.11; Rahaf Aldoughli. "What Is Syrian Nationalism? Primordialism and Romanticism in Official Baath Discourse." *Nations and Nationalism* 28, no. 1 (2021b): 125–40. https://doi.org/10.1111/nana.12786; Nader Hashemi and Danny Postel. *Sectarianization: Mapping the New Politics of the Middle East*. Oxford: Oxford University Press, 2017; Fanar Haddad. *Understanding 'Sectarianism': Sunni-Shi'a Relations in the Modern Arab World*. London: Hurst, 2020; Simon Mabon. "Saudi Arabia and Iran: Islam and Foreign Policy in the Middle East." In *Routledge Handbook of International Relations in the Middle East*, edited by Shahram Akbarzadeh, pp. 138–52. Abingdon: Routledge, 2019; Maya Mikdashi. "Sex and Sectarianism: The Legal Architecture." *Comparative Studies of South Asia, Africa and the Middle East* 34, no. 2 (2014): 279–93; and Yassin al-Haj Saleh. *Impossible Revolution: Making Sense of the Syrian Tragedy*. London: Hurst, 2017.
2 Klaus Theweleit. *Male Fantasies*. Volume 1. Minneapolis, MN: University of Minnesota Press, 1987, p. 52.
3 Graeme Gill and Luis F. Angosto-Ferrandez. "Introduction: Symbolism and Politics." *Politics, Religion & Ideology* 19, no. 4 (2018): 429–33. https://doi.org/10.1080/21567689.2018.1539436.
4 Michael Billig. *Banal Nationalism*. London: SAGE, 1995; David A. Butz. "National Symbols as Agents of Psychological and Social Change." *Political Psychology* 30, no. 5 (2009): 779–804. https://doi.org/10.1111/j.1467-9221.2009.00725.x.
5 Lisa Wedeen. *Ambiguities of Domination: Politics, Rhetoric, and Symbols in Contemporary Syria*. Chicago, IL, and London: University of Chicago Press, 1999, p. 17.
6 Beverly Crawford and Arend Lijphart. *Liberalization and Leninist Legacies: Comparative Perspectives on Democratic Transitions*. Berkeley, CA: University of California, 1997; Herbert Kitschelt, Zdenka Mansfeldova, Radoslaw Markowski, and Gabor Toka. *Post-Communist Party Systems: Competition, Representation, and Inter-Party Cooperation*.

Cambridge: Cambridge University Press, 1999; Mark R. Beissinger and Stephen Kotkin. *Historical Legacies of Communism in Russia and Eastern Europe.* New York: Cambridge University Press, 2014.
7 Geneive Abdo. *The New Sectarianism: The Arab Uprisings and the Rebirth of the Shi'a-Sunni Divide.* Oxford: Oxford University Press, 2017; Raymond A. Hinnebusch. "Identity and State Formation in Multi-Sectarian Societies: Between Nationalism and Sectarianism in Syria." *Nations and Nationalism* 26, no. 1 (2020): 138–54. https://doi.org/10.1111/nana.12582; Christopher Phillips and Morten Valbjørn. "'What Is in a Name?': The Role of (Different) Identities in the Multiple Proxy Wars in Syria." *Small Wars & Insurgencies* 29, no. 3 (2018): 414–33. https://doi.org/10.1080/09592318.2018.1455328.
8 See V. O. Key. *Public Opinion and American Democracy.* New York: Knopf, 1961; Philip E. Converse. "Information Flow and the Stability of Partisan Attitudes." *Public Opinion Quarterly* 26, no. 4 (1962): 578–99. https://doi.org/10.1086/267129.
9 John R. Zaller. "Diffusion of Political Attitudes." *Journal of Personality and Social Psychology* 53, no. 5 (1987): 821–33. https://doi.org/10.1037/0022-3514.53.5.821.
10 Beissinger and Kotkin 2014.
11 Lisa Wedeen. "Acting 'as If': Symbolic Politics and Social Control in Syria." *Comparative Studies in Society and History* 40, no. 3 (1998): 503–23, p. 506. https://doi.org/10.1017/s0010417598001388.
12 Wedeen 1999, p. 521.
13 Lisa Wedeen, *Authoritarian Apprehensions: Ideology, Judgment, and Mourning in Syria*, Chicago, IL: University of Chicago Press, 2019, pp. viii, 27.
14 Judith Butler. *Bodies That Matter: On the Discursive Limits of "Sex."* New York: Routledge, 1993, argues that the production of a gendered subject requires a "regularized and constrained repetition of norms" (p. 95), and that gender itself is "a kind of becoming or activity… [through] an incessant and repeated action of some sort (p. 112). This perspective requires that we take seriously the impact of public political ritual on the subjective experiences and identities of the participants.
15 Judith Butler. *Gender Trouble: Feminism and the Subversion of Identity.* New York: Routledge, 1999, p. viii.
16 Rahaf Aldoughli. "Interrogating the Construction of Masculinist Protection and Militarism in the Syrian Constitution of 1973." *Journal of Middle East Women Studies* 15, no. 1 (2019a): 48–74, pp. 58–60.
17 Butler 1999, p. 25.
18 Ibid., pp. 2–7.
19 See ibid., p. 21; Wedeen 1999, p. 9.
20 For all of the popular songs and performances discussed in this chapter, the best way to locate renditions is to search for the song's name (in Arabic) on YouTube. Like most internet content, the posted material is somewhat ephemeral, and it tends to shift over time as new performances become popular and as older ones fall into obscurity and are sometimes taken down. At the

time of this writing, some of the most-watched renditions of "May God Save Our Army" could be found at the following links: www.youtube.com/watch?v=LmMtKpBWO88; www.youtube.com/watch?v=1pKEV28bitw; www.youtube.com/watch?v=hz-wevv-2zI. Accessed September 4, 2022.

21 *Al-Arabiyya* produced a report on loyalist women fighters in the Syrian Army, which can be accessed at: www.youtube.com/watch?v=s5f2U6DzykY. Accessed August 15, 2022. While the upper echelons of the Assad regime sometimes draw attention to these women for propaganda purposes, the ordinary rank-and-file loyalists discussed in this chapter appeared to ignore their existence completely.

22 This version of the song was found at: www.youtube.com/watch?v=TnAPzNgnqxo. Accessed August 20, 2022.

23 An example of loyalist media propaganda highlighting female support can be seen at: www.youtube.com/watch?v=JM5hXJ5Aaw4. Accessed August 24, 2022.

24 At the time of this writing some of the most-watched versions of "The Army of the Homeland" were found at: www.youtube.com/watch?v=DBxFXxuGvKg; www.youtube.com/watch?v=wd_riPJd_WU; www.youtube.com/watch?v=YUj_KOdDFVw; www.youtube.com/watch?v=qKlcRBo0m_c. Accessed August 25, 2022.

25 The version of "Oh, My Mother, My Syria" analyzed here was found at: https://youtu.be/qS1arOuHVZw. Accessed September 10, 2022.

26 The version of "Millions and Millions of Syrians" discussed here was found at: www.youtube.com/watch?v=8_3CDrVF7vA. Accessed September 12, 2022.

27 Popular renditions of "We Challenge" at the time of this writing included: www.youtube.com/watch?v=z0FhxoHfaFc; www.youtube.com/watch?v=iOYLggrJDQw; www.youtube.com/watch?v=-rKhXvGhzAI. Accessed September 14, 2022.

28 See Wedeen 1999, p. 37.

29 The lyrics discussed here for "Oh Bashar, Who Is Like You?" are taken from a version of the song found at: www.youtube.com/watch?v=ckALkT0gIAM. Accessed August 3, 2022.

30 The ballad is titled "Oh My Beloved Syria." For further discussion, see Rahaf Aldoughli. "Interrogating the Construction of Gendered Identity in the Syrian Nationalist Narrative: Al-Husri, Aflaq, and al-Arsuzi." *Syria Studies* 9, no. 1 (2017): 65–120, p. 146.

31 These lyrics for "We Want to Preserve" were taken from a video found at: www.youtube.com/watch?v=3Faq9qYA9Ic. Accessed June 15, 2022.

32 An example can be seen at: www.youtube.com/watch?v=uq9aE_KN19c. Accessed December 17, 2021.

33 Yezid Sayigh. "Militaries, Civilians and the Crisis of the Arab State." *The Washington Post*, December 8, 2014. www.washingtonpost.com/news/monkey-cage/wp/2014/12/08/militaries-civilians-and-the-crisis-of-the-arab-state/?utm_term=.912536e221d8. Accessed May 10, 2016; Adham Saouli. *The Arab State: Dilemmas of Late Formation*. New York: Routledge, 2012; Nazih Ayubi. *Over-Stating the Arab State: Politics and Society in the Middle East*. London: I.B. Tauris, 2009; Adeed Dawisha. *Arab Nationalism in the Twentieth Century: From Triumph to Despair*. Princeton, NJ: Princeton University Press, 2003.

# Conclusion: Citizen activism and prospects for reform in postwar Syria

In this book I conceive *Romanticizing masculinity* as having three constituent parts: (1) a set of constructed beliefs about what makes an ideal citizen; (2) a degree of readiness to pursue those beliefs through sacrificial heroism; and (3) a range of doing this through imposing a gendered conception of nationalism that excludes women. The conceptualization of Romantic masculinity has foregrounded the historical trajectory of the gendered constructs traced in the writings of Syrian nationalists, which were derived primarily from European Romanticism. These ideological borrowings, a "foreign" intellectual trend that was influential in shaping the nationalist thoughts of Syrian ideologues in the early twentieth century, affected the imagined construction of gendered binaries in the cultural and legislative spheres in the Syrian nation. This book has provided the impact of such an established link between the early nationalist trajectory of the Syrian state and early European nationalist ideologies. More importantly, providing such critique of borrowed Romantic masculinity shows the widespread view that the subordination of women in Syria cannot be reduced to tribalism, Islamism, or authoritarianism only.

When I think about my experiences in Syria, the first thing I see in my mind's eye are the pervasive statues of the late Syrian president, Hafez al-Assad, in military attire—there's one in almost every city square. There is also another side to Syria, however, composed of numerous men and women who do not feel a great affinity or easy identification with patriarchal and muscular outlooks. In recent years the impact of the COVID-19 pandemic, combined with new sanctions in the form of the United States' Caesar Act, which targets overseas sources of income for the Assad regime, have contributed to a reduction in military conflict and a renewal in anti-regime civic activism. Bashar al-Assad has been forced to resort to new strategies to prop up his regime's finances, including chasing his cousin Rami Makhlouf—a Party loyalist and one of Syria's most wealthy individuals—for hundreds of millions of dollars in unpaid-back taxes, as well as revising the military service laws to allow greater numbers of men to pay "exemption fees" to avoid military service.[1] These factors have contributed to a reduction in violence. Many elite Party supporters are starting to feel uncomfortable with the war, and for the first time, fairly large numbers of Syrian men can evade military service by paying a fee, without necessarily having to leave the country.[2]

For some men, this abatement of the warrior stereotype has contributed to an identity crisis. In a recent roundtable discussion that I conducted with several dozen men who had fled conscription and were living in the UK, many of the men expressed a sense of anguish for failing to defend the nation. Some concluded that they were not worthy of being Syrian without the honor of carrying arms for their country. Echoing the Baathist rhetoric that I presented in previous chapters, one of the roundtable participants told me: "I feel like I have failed my mother ... Syria is our mother." It's worth noting in this regard that Syria has always levied "exemption fees" for well-off men in the diaspora who could afford to send payment to stay in the regime's good graces, and that within Syria it has not been uncommon for men to pay bribes to avoid military service. The recent expansion of these arrangements simply indicates that the regime is more concerned about cash flow than it is about fresh cannon fodder. However, while these arrangements provide a source of relief for financially stable men who are not eager to engage in military violence, it often comes with the added cost of self-doubt linked to the pervasive association of muscularity with men's belonging and self-worth that has been perpetuated under the Baathist rule. Syria, after all, is still a country where the Constitution dictates military service as a "sacred duty" for men and where failure to serve is often regarded as emasculating. This has led to a situation where, at the very least, most Syrian men feel a need to apologize for not living up to the muscular standard.

The regime has relied heavily on these well-established scripts to retain men's support and to avoid the question of why men should have to fight, or have to pay fees to avoid fighting. Bashar's wife, Asmaa al-Assad, for example, reinforced this narrative of muscular belonging when she met with a group of voluntary women soldiers in March of 2018, praising these women by comparing them favorably against men who evaded conscription. Her remarks include statements that describe women dying in battle as a form of "equality":

> Your presence in the battlefield marks a new victory and a whole new age ... When you are able to sacrifice your soul for the nation, this is the new age and this is the real equality between men and women ... You have now proved to the whole world that you are a human being.[3]

The undergirding view in such rhetoric is that fighting and martial sacrifice for the nation not only are defining features of men's privilege over women but also the very definition of a "human being"—an identity that has largely been reserved for men but that may now be extended to some loyalist women, at least for rhetorical or performative purposes. Bashar al-Assad's speeches in recent years have similarly come to discuss almost nothing other than muscular honor and fighting, cajoling the "brothers" (*'ikhwa*) to defend the nation with arms (*difā'*) and heroism (*butūla*). Since 2021 Bashar has increasingly blurred the distinction between those who support him politically and those who are willing to fight for him militarily.[4] However, while this rhetoric of nationalist muscularity has become only more intense, the actual calamitous economic and material situation on the ground in Syria has cast doubt on the construct's value and provided more wiggle room for those who do not see themselves reflected in it.

At the time of this writing, the unfolding tragedy in Syria is being compounded by a major earthquake that has devastated already-neglected infrastructure and claimed thousands of lives. In such a catastrophic event, one would think that nationalist ideology would at least temporarily be reduced to a secondary topic. When addressing the tragedy, however, Bashar al-Assad has taken every opportunity to bluster on about the militant nationalist struggle and the heroic sacrifice of Baathist fighters, even when visiting a hospital where Syrians wounded and displaced as a result of the earthquake were seeking assistance.[5] Such single-minded obsession with the muscular ideal is the hallmark of a regime that has very little else to offer—that, as I have suggested in this book, has come to predicate its entire identity and survival on the vision of a romanticized struggle. For Syrians who desire a more stable, safe, and prosperous country, we must look elsewhere: to civic leaders and ordinary people who resist such identification and to trends that can lead us away from the legacy of muscularity and patriarchy.

### The impact of mobilizing women as fighters

As noted in Chapter 5, the Baathist regime began mobilizing small groups of women security agents and fighters after the outbreak of the civil war in 2011. This is an expansion of the previous minor roles that the Party held out to women as security guards and wardens (*sajjānāt*), primarily for monitoring and searching women detainees, and also for conducting surveillance and investigations of women. Reports have indicated that after the outbreak of the civil war, such women security agents were often quite brutal in their support for the regime, for example by assisting in the beating and torture of children and mothers, and inflicting pervasive humiliation and verbal insults on women prisoners.[6] The first commando battalions for women in the Syrian army were formed in 2013. They included hundreds of women soldiers, who were trained and assigned to frontline tasks including direct armed confrontations and sniper operations.[7]

There are a variety of reasons why the Assad regime began to mobilize women into the military. As can be seen in Asmaa al-Assad's comments quoted earlier in this chapter, the Baathists viewed these all-women fighting units as a sort of public-relations event, which allowed the regime to present itself as "progressive" or pro-women, while also shaming men who did not want to fight for being outdone even by women in the arena of muscular fervor. While the number of women soldiers in the Syrian army has remained quite small, the attention given to them in media coverage and in certain propaganda efforts (especially those aimed at Western audiences) has been extensive. Unfortunately for the regime's efforts, the celebration of these units has been tarred by a continuous string of scandals involving officers' mistreatment of the women soldiers, including frequent sexual assaults and sexual harassment.[8]

Another motivating factor for the regime was the belief that women could help make up for an increasing number of men who had defected or fled from military service. The mobilization of women coincided with additional changes in the Baathists' military recruitment, such as requiring university students to serve and the creation of contracts that forfeited soldiers' pay if they disengaged or retreated from combat.[9] The shift toward opening the army to women soldiers may have cynically taken into account the fact that military defection and disobedience among women is less common, as women soldiers tend to have fewer external prospects and are more materially dependent on the social ties and security that are breached in defection.[10]

Regardless of these regime motivations, the prominently advertised role of women as soldiers during the past decade has weakened some of the assumptions behind the patriarchal muscular construct. To the extent that the role of martial "protectors" and "heroes" is open to women as well as men, much of the gendered hierarchy and the presumptions of gendered reward for men's participation in these discourses tends to collapse. This may help to explain the hostility and attacks with which male soldiers have greeted the women's units, and it has contributed to the overwhelming sense that Romantic muscularity is in "crisis" and disintegrating in Syria today.[11] When women do not remain in their assigned place as supportive wives and mothers to be owned and controlled, men may begin to wonder what exactly they are fighting and sacrificing for, prompting a reconsideration of the entire landscape of national identity and human relationships.

## Women in civic, charitable, and religious organizations

As protests and demonstrations began to escalate across Syria, the regime took steps to control the Syrian street again. This took many forms, including violent repression, but one of the most nefarious aspects of the Baathist assault on civil society was its efforts to infiltrate and control popular and religious organizations. Such control extended to women's-movement organizations, the majority of which are still under the leadership and supervision of the regime today. The Baathists sought to direct the women's movement in a way that would support its presence at the grassroots. For example, before being officially dissolved by the Party in 2017, the General Women's Union in Syria distributed increasingly boisterous loyalist propaganda, referring to the opposition as a whole as "terrorists" who were seeking to push back women's rights. During the conflict many members of the Union joined the newly formed women's military brigades, while others visited military checkpoints and made speeches offering their blessings for the president's actions, which they predictably described as "heroic."[12]

Al-Qubaysiat, a prominent Islamic Syrian women's organization, also has close ties to the regime, which promoted its work within the larger public religious sphere. The Qubaysiat leader Salma Ayyash was appointed to a prominent role in Syria's Ministry of Religion, where she stated that Bashar al-Assad was responsible for "mov[ing] women's religious work from homes where darkness and fog prevailed, to mosques where there is light and rightness."[13] With such ties to the regime, it is unsurprising that Qubaysiat leaders have been supportive of Assad throughout the war, often appearing alongside him during religious commemorations and helping to organize Party rallies and celebrations.[14] In my personal experiences in Syria, Qubaysiat members have proven to be reliably enthusiastic about the regime and its policies, going far beyond the "minimum affirmation" to express devout confidence in the Baathists' rhetoric and actions.

Similar co-option can be seen in the charitable and relief sectors. A great deal of internal and international aid in Syria is channeled through the General Trust for Development, which was founded by the Party in 2007 and is closely overseen by Asmaa al-Assad. The distribution of aid by the Trust's various programs is linked to its role as an incubator of populist support, for example by organizing public marches and events honoring wounded loyalist soldiers in conjunction with providing them with medical services and material aid. The Trust has in some cases served as a means for the regime to get around international sanctions and to launder foreign investment and aid money for political support. One particularly egregious instance of this is UNESCO's collaboration with the Trust on a project nominally related to Syrian culture and traditions, which served to organize UN and private funding that the regime leveraged for its propaganda and normalization efforts and for its overall solvency, as documented by Karam Mansour.[15] In addition to co-opting a wide swath of aid programs through the General Trust for Development, the regime has also infiltrated previously independent organizations such as the Tamayoz Orphan Care Project, which was essentially seized by the government in 2013. The group's existing funds were taken and some administrators were arrested, while others fled the country, and leadership of the charity was handed over to al-Qubaysiat. While the charity continued to operate in a superficially nonpartisan manner, without distinguishing between orphans from loyalist or opposition families, this very neutrality meant that regime loyalists were put in charge of the children's placement and socialization.

Finally, it needs to be noted how extensively the regime has mediated women's engagement with religious organizations, even beyond the specific example of al-Qubaysiat. This interference is linked to Assad's preferred narrative that the Syrian political opposition is grounded purely in religious fundamentalism. To counter the growth of such perceived religious opposition, the Baathists have reconfigured themselves after the outbreak of the war from being an overtly secularist Party to the newly self-appointed defenders of "true" Islam. Bashar al-Assad, for example, stated in a recent speech that: "Building this trust between the state and religious institutions is a basic thing to challenge those who want to promote conflict."[16] In other words, he has sought to co-opt religious institutions by exchanging state support for political loyalty.[17] Representing his view of Islam as more pro-women than other interpretations has become a central aspect of this legitimization strategy. In January of 2015 the regime launched a "Women's Preaching Department" (*al-da'awa al-nisāiyya*), which sought to promote a role for women in the Islamic clergy. Assad was very clear in his descriptions of the program that it had a nationalist component: "This is not a religious institution in the abstract meaning … it is a national institution. You were representing a religious teaching but now it is also a national teaching … it is not logical to separate religion from the homeland."[18] By intervening in this significant debate about women's role in Islam, the regime sought to co-opt the "progressive" outlook and to merge it with nationalist loyalism.

Similarly, in 2017 Assad announced the formation of the "Youth Religious Group" (*al-farīq al-dīnī al-shabābī*) as part of his project to "modernize" Sunni institutions and to merge them with state authority. He declared that a new arrangement of religious institutions was needed, and that true religious teachers must be patriots. Most significantly, he invited women to join the group, implying that they would be welcome there and treated with greater empowerment compared to other religious organizations.[19] Essentially, this rhetoric served to interfere with feminist movements within Islam and coerce them into patriotic affiliations, seeking to turning women into de facto state agents and propagandists. This strategic instrumentalization of women's concerns by a regime that was otherwise steeped in muscular rhetoric and patriarchal policies (as discussed in Chapter 3 and throughout this book) illuminates how authoritarians are far from shy about adopting the superficial rhetoric of liberation when it suits their needs, as indeed the Baathists have done with various causes and human aspirations throughout their time in power.

The adoption of such liberatory rhetoric as a legitimation strategy, however, comes with the risk that many citizens may come to believe that it is true, breaking down the barriers of silence, repression, and forced performances that ultimately uphold totalitarian regimes. There are some indications that this may be occurring in Syria. Some newly emerging grassroots feminist organizations and social media networks have found the courage to overtly reject the regime's appeal for loyalty, such as the Political Movement for Syrian Feminists and Syria Campaign. Even some of the heavily co-opted organizations such as al-Qubaysiat have experienced rumblings of discontent, as can be seen on social media platforms. In the recently renewed civic demonstrations and calls for resistance, there is an increasing awareness that a new direction for Syria must involve genuine democracy, autonomy, and rights for women and a rejection of Romanticized views of gender roles.

## Challenging patriarchy through new concepts of national belonging and identity

The challenge that faces Syrians of all genders, ethnicities, and orientations is in finding ways to redefine our sense of identity and belonging beyond the Romanticized muscularity that has been reinforced on us throughout our entire lives under Baathist rule. This is a daunting task, but it can be done by introducing new values, attitudes, and practices into both our daily lives and our social institutions. We must be alert to the prospect of what some researchers have termed "authoritarian upgrades," in which oppressive regimes seek to engineer the social terrain in their favor by co-opting and managing superficial, false reforms.[20] The efforts of the Assad regime described in the previous sections—mobilizing women into the military, and interfering with women's movements in civic, charitable, and religious organizations—certainly fall into this category. At the same time, these instrumentalized reforms present opportunities in the sense that they contribute to the destabilization of the long-standing muscular construct in Baathist ideology. If false and superficial reforms can ultimately be translated into truly independent and democratic movements that retire the

Romantic muscular vision, then Syrians may at last be able to create a more free and livable society, grounded in responsible civic virtues.

The Syrian women's movement has gone through several phases under Baathist rule, starting with the creation of the General Women's Union in 1967, in a decree that simultaneously abolished all other previously existing women's organizations and banned efforts to create new ones. After this process of consolidation was complete, the regime began to use the Union as a means of training and indoctrinating women to serve state functions, including as a recruitment ground for women security agents. Finally, when the organization became an unwieldy symbol in the era of increased muscular "crisis," the regime simply dissolved it and assigned its roles to the Ministry of Social Affairs. This trajectory should provoke a sober assessment of the consistency and tenacity with which the Baathists have sought to co-opt and control women's concerns. The regime's newfound commitment to influencing women's roles within religion and enacting symbolic "gender equality" on the battlefield need to be viewed in light of this pervasive top-down instrumentalization of women that has been present from the very start of Baathist rule.

In contrast, since the beginning of the uprising more than a decade ago, Syrian women have visibly and adamantly contributed to the shape of the region's political scene in a more independent fashion. This is not to say that the conflict has liberated Syrian women and put an end to patriarchal injustices; however, it has provided unprecedented opportunities for women to speak out, as can be seen in the surge of recently founded grassroots organizations as well as publications, blogs, and workshops that address the oppressive conditions women have experienced in Syria.[21] The situation of Syrian women has developed so rapidly in the past few years that periodic reviews are needed to update interpretations of the changing cultural scene. It is reasonable to say that independent feminist movements are still in their infancy in Syria, and that even the definition of what constitutes "feminism" (*nisawiyya*) is highly debated.

One of the central issues is the tension between Islamic and secular visions of women's empowerment. The field of women's studies in the Syrian context has, for a long time, been locked into pro-Baathist and anti-Baathist camps, with the former celebrating the secular regime and emphasizing the patriarchal aspects of Islamic law, and the latter mostly contending that the Baathists have abandoned women's rights as a trade-off for tribal leaders' loyalty.[22] The fragmentation of the Baathist hegemony provides an opportunity to reassess these lines of division and seek common ground. While this book has focused primarily on the construction of gender during the period of Baathist hegemony, my emphasis on Romanticized nationalist rhetoric could potentially be extended to some aspects of Islamic nationalism, thus providing additional conceptual insights. One cannot reduce Syrian women to being pawns of either Islamism or Baathism, and I would encourage future researchers and women's advocates to not be constrained in their civic visions by these different forms of nationalist identity.

Another challenge that confronts today's interpreters of women's concerns in Syria is the tendency to focus on ethnic and sectarian divisions, which have become heightened in the country since the onset of the conflict. Looking back prior to the war, in the "Damascus Spring" of 2001 there was a great deal of discussion of women's issues, and most of it focused on legislative concerns that were applicable to all Syrian women. In recent years, however, it has become more common to speak of Kurdish feminism, Yezidi feminism, Shi'i feminism, and so forth, rather than looking for common ground. Emphasizing the interactions between patriarchy, muscularity, and nationalist discourses can help to provide a context for understanding issues that are relevant to all women (and indeed all people) in the region, without negating the specific oppression that various ethnic minorities have experienced.

At the beginning of this book, I recounted a presidential speech given by Bashar al-Assad in July of 2015 that praised the role of the army in defending the "fatherland" and asserted that such military violence was the foundation of Syrian identity. Two years later, speaking to an audience of diplomats in Damascus on August 20, 2017, Assad again praised the role of the army and other loyalist militia fighters for their role in creating what he described as a "homogeneous national community" (*mujtama' mutajānis*):

> We have lost our greatest men and infrastructure that cost us a lot of money and sweat, that is true. Yet we have won a community that is much healthier and much more homogeneous ... this homogeneity is the oneness of ideologies, of cultures, of ideas and visions ... It means that we now have only one color, only one national color, which means national unity.[23]

This vision of unity and homogeneity is profoundly reductionist and frankly terrifying, as it allows no room for differences in outlooks, desires, cultures, or habits of life. I would contrast such enforced homogeneity against a pluralistic civic outlook in which the state acts as a site of democratic compromise among different outlooks within a framework of human rights. One of the central problems with the homogenizing vision is that it effaces actually existing ethnic, cultural, and religious differences, as well as differences in gendered experience, and fails to contend with the marginalization that many such communities face—a mistake that we should not repeat as we pursue the goal of women's liberation. Thus, the question becomes how to identify shared needs and effective policies to promote human rights without overrunning cultural diversity and autonomy. A good starting point in this is to recognize individuals as rights-bearing democratic citizens first and foremost, rather than assigning value that depends on their being members of a unified identity or cause.

## Directions for future research and action

This book was guided by four primary questions. I sought to clarify the specific views of gender that have shaped Baathist thought and practice, the historical origins of these gender constructs, the ways in which they were disbursed and internalized by Party loyalists, and the impact they had on the lives of Syrian women and men. Much of the work here focused on the historical trajectory, showing the profound influence that borrowings from eighteenth- and nineteenth-century Romantic German and French nationalist thought had on the development of Baathist outlooks on nation and gender. These outlooks were central in the education and subsequent writings of the primary Baathist "founding fathers," including Sati al-Husri, Michel Aflaq, and Zaki al-Arsuzi. The later chapters of the book demonstrated how these Romanticized and "muscular" views were implemented through policy and education under the Baathist hegemony, how they were expressed culturally by loyalists through songs and performance, and how they have continued to impact the contours of war and resistance in Syria in the post-2011 period.

Romantic muscular nationalism as it has been practiced in Syria is characterized first and foremost by the normative belief that men must be passionate martial actors, always ready to physically fight and die for the cause in order to demonstrate their value. The Baathist founders linked their nationalist vision intimately to what they regarded as a crisis or sickness in manhood (as I demonstrated in Chapter 2)—which they viewed as being an outcome of dispossession and colonial humiliation that could only be remedied through vigorous action to restore Syrian men's dominion and territorial control. This sense of gendered crisis in the founders' writings has eerie resonances in today's civil war, where protestors have challenged the Romantic muscular construct and loyalists have drawn parallels between the survival of the regime and the survival of masculine identity (as I discussed in Chapter 5). Indeed, one might suggest that the Baathists have been in a continuous state of war, struggle, and masculine crisis throughout the Party's entire existence—that this "being in crisis" is in fact the default and necessary condition of the muscular construct, and that its adherents will always find a way to identify, imagine, or create an enemy. Even during the long decades of Baathist hegemony, the Syrian regime has always imposed a national narrative that Syria was in a state of emergency, in constant need of men's military protection and national defense, as a means of legitimizing the Party's policies and continued authoritarian rule. This "eternal struggle" aspect of toxic masculinity has been noted by previous feminist scholars, and it should be understood as a core aspect of muscular nationalism.[24]

In addition to the violent outcomes and myopic view of men's possibilities that the muscular construct enshrined, it also profoundly complicated women's relationship to citizenship and social belonging, and normalized infringements on women's rights in Syrian legislation and practice (as I discussed in Chapter 3 and throughout the book). By conceptualizing the ideal, heroic Syrian as a fighting man, the muscular vision pushed anyone who did not fit that description into supporting and secondary roles, with associated reductions in rights and privileges. Control of women's bodies and labor was too often represented as an expected reward for men who were willing to participate in the muscular ideal. Recent, cynically performative gestures such as the creation of "women's battalions" in the Syrian army have done little to change this state of affairs, and have even been leveraged by the regime as propaganda for the muscular ideal (conflating it with women's desire to become "human beings," as described at the start of this chapter), and as a means to shame men who don't want to fight. Thus, the concepts of Romantic heroism, defense, and struggle in Syria were directly linked to the perpetuation of a hegemonic, hierarchical, and patriarchal model of national belonging in which women's agency and contributions to society were depreciated.

While a variety of Syrian scholars and activists have been advocating for more civic concepts of nationalism that incorporate just and equal citizenship enshrined through law, I worry that this will not be sufficient if we fail to address the underlying issue of culturally enshrined Romantic "heroism," muscularity, and patriarchy in Syria. The violence of the civil war has rightly been linked to an associated hardening of lines between various sectarian and ethnic communities, but it can be traced even more substantially to the pervasive influence of gendered nationalist ideologies under the Baathists, which have immersed Syrians in the assumption that political belonging and stability is a muscular or manly endeavor. In other words, forward-looking civic nationalism may easily slip back into the realm of primordialist cultural nationalism and dominion in the interest of creating a new social order. The inherent trickiness in considering civic nationalism (*wataniyya*) in the Syrian context is that many pundits, scholars, and analysts believe that a new patriotic vision of a unified Syria has to be forged to substitute for the vision of the Baath regime. Syrian feminists should be cautious about this, and should use our positions to focus strongly on how constructed ideas of masculinity and femininity shape the contours of nation-building projects.

My fear as a scholar in this area is that passionate appeals for muscular national solidarity may continue or reemerge in post-conflict Syria, which will only lead to more state-sanctioned violence, intolerance, and exclusion. The task today that awaits Syrian feminist scholars is to persistently challenge and deconstruct any tendency to return to these Romanticized muscular and patriarchal identifications, as the weary and delightfully heterogeneous Syrian community gradually seeks to rebuild itself.

The political upheavals and reemergence of civil protest over the past few years have given the Syrian experience a fresh relevance, not only to political scientists but also to scholars from an array of other disciplines. Despite this attention, the issue of how gender ideology intersects with nationalism and formal politics is still one of the most ignored topics both in Syria studies and in analyses of the overall Arab region, especially outside of the sequestered area of women's studies. I would suggest that this relevance is profound, and that it ought to be given more attention in general political studies and in interpretations of the region's events, as well as in related topics such as sectarianism, terrorism, and the situation of refugees.[25] There is an abundance of excellent work on women's experiences and political marginalization in Syria and neighboring countries, but this work seldom crosses over into analyses of broader political identities and national trajectories. The current book has shown how central gender was to the Baathist ideal, and how closely it was linked to the Party's overall actions and outcomes. I would challenge other scholars of the region to regard this as an invitation for further research, extending gender studies into other areas of the region's political life and to broader policy considerations.

There is a particular research need in examining how militarism affects women's political participation in current regional contexts, and also in examining how gendered language continues to be applied and revised in new constitutional and legal frameworks. These features of the state are closely tied to the formation of national identity and to the intersection of gender and belonging. Another area that has been profoundly understudied is how national symbolism represents women and how it leverages and influences gendered identities. In Chapters 5 and 6 I discussed Syrian nationalist songs as reflections and reinforcements of the Baathists' muscular culture. This analysis can and should be extended in an ongoing fashion to evaluate many aspects of political symbolism (statues, imagery, performative events, etc.) as it is produced and mobilized to shape identities in the region. I would also suggest that scholars should take an interest in the ongoing evolution of Islamic women's groups and their role in shaping political culture. As indicated in the Introduction, the current book did not include a close examination of religious groups in Syria, primarily due to limitations of space and scope. However, there is much to be considered in that area, and future research might investigate the ways in which Islamist groups such as Qubaysiat and Kuftaru have or have not empowered women.[26]

There is also a continuing need to build bridges between research reported in Arabic and that reported in English. This is a significant problem, as much important research published by the English-language community is inaccessible to Arabic scholars, and vice versa. As noted in Chapter 1, I was surprised to find that so many of the foundational writings of al-Husri, Aflaq, and al-Arsuzi were unavailable in English translation. I also noted that English translations of important speeches by the Assads, and central cultural phenomena such as the national anthem, were either nonexistent or extremely poor in quality. The same situation is true for Arabic-speaking scholars, as very few of the central works on Syria in the English canon have been translated into Arabic.

Finally, it is important to point to nonacademic interest in questions of national identity and politics in Syria, and to consider our responsibility as scholars and writers to make our insights accessible. During the final stages of working on this book, I was invited to take part in a roundtable discussion organized by the British nonprofit Rethink Rebuild Society, which works to improve the lives of Syrians living in the UK and helps them to navigate issues of belonging and identity. Among other questions, this event asked: Are we still Syrians? And what makes us Syrians? The discussion, conducted among participants from many walks of life, was a great opportunity for my research and proved to be timely and relevant. It brought to the forefront the intense need that many Syrians in the diaspora feel to process and understand our experiences in the aftermath of the 2011 uprising. I had the opportunity to share some of my insights about muscularity and gender under the Baathists, and to learn from other participants how they felt about these gendered identities.

I was saddened, but unsurprised, to see how fiercely some of the participants in this roundtable adhered to the view that belonging to Syria was involuntary, natural, emotional, and familial (grounded in shared language, history, and "blood"), and by gendered references that were made especially by some of the men that described Syria as a "mother" and praised the heroic exploits of fathers and grandfathers. Some of the men expressed a desire to go back and fight and die on Syrian soil, which they felt would prove their "dignity" (*karāma*) and "virility" (*rujūla*), and thereby ultimately provide a sense of belonging. All of this is straight out of the Baathist playbook. Despite this, however, the participants were almost universally interested in discussing how Syria should develop in terms of building civic institutions. They were aware of how the Baathists had manipulated our sense of national identity to elicit loyalty and maintain authoritarianism, and they agreed around the need for basic principles of citizenship, democracy, and the rule of law. In my view, these revelations reflected how Syrian nationalism originally emerged from overlapping primordialist and civic concepts of the nation (discussed in Chapter 1), and provided hope that the civic vision may yet win out.

Participating in this event prompted me to reflect on my own positioning in relation to the research, and how much of my knowledge and ability to access and interpret the texts discussed in this book is grounded in my background as a Syrian woman. As this notion of reflexivity and whole-person scholarship is gaining increasing heft in the social sciences, there is a need to recognize that research is deeply grounded in democratic conversations and in the actually existing horizons of political possibility. The current work could not have been produced or discussed under the Baathist regime. Thus, without abandoning the principles of rigor, evidence, and long-term vision that are the hallmarks of scholarly discourse, I would suggest that it is time for scholars to retire the notion of "disinterest" or the "God's-eye view" and recognize that our work is closely tied to our own social positioning and to the public interest.[27] From this perspective, I would encourage future researchers to reflect thoughtfully on their own social positioning as it impacts their outlooks, and to take every available opportunity to engage with the Syrian people who are trying to find their way forward, as well as with the publics of other countries who are seeking to better understand the Middle East.

As these personal and political inquiries persist, there will be questions related to what the future holds for the Syrian people, and how men, women, and non-binary individuals should understand themselves in relationship to their communities and country. Such questions should be given serious considerations during peace negotiations and as part of any future nation-building processes. The possibilities for Syria's future are uncertain, and it may be some time before the country sees the end of despotic regimes, terrorist groups, and ethnic and sectarian conflicts, not to mention the end of patriarchal relationships and institutions. Nonetheless, to the extent that Syria may soon experience opportunities to write new chapters in its political history, a thoughtful awareness of the past trajectories and dynamics of nationalist politics can make a profound difference. Most pertinent to the topic of this book, any novel state or political system in Syria that fails to overtly discourage muscular Romanticism, and that fails to support and encourage gender-inclusive policies, will find it hard to move beyond the legacy of Baathist indoctrination and violence. Scholars should take every opportunity to educate decision-makers and the public about these topics.

In the broader scope, the example of Syria presents an extraordinary opportunity to understand the historical trajectory and global legacy of Romantic nationalism, given the strength of evidence from the Baathist founders' biographies and writings, as well as more recent evidence from loyalist speeches and cultural expressions. Although this book is not, strictly speaking, comparative, its findings and insights coincide with Sikata Banerjee's original analysis of "muscular" nationalism in India and Ireland,[28] and the analysis could likely be extended to other countries in the Middle East and elsewhere in which leaders were influenced by similar intellectual, political, and cultural trends—not to mention to ongoing global developments such as the recent ascendancy of Islamist and Christian nationalisms. The analysis provided here lends support to the conclusion that a specific type of muscular gender ideology has been massively central to these long-term political developments, with the implication that overcoming the troubled legacy of nationalist movements will not be possible without purposefully and decisively addressing their hierarchical gendered dimensions.

## Notes

1 For more, see European Union Agency for Asylum. "Persons Who Evaded or Deserted Military Service." Common Analysis, September 2020. https://2u.pw/VQKxSY. Accessed December 15, 2021.
2 See Azmi Bishara. *Syria 2011–2013: Revolution and Tyranny before the Mayhem*. London: I.B. Tauris, 2021.
3 A video of this speech is currently available on YouTube at: www.youtube.com/watch?v=JM5hXJ5Aaw4&t=623s. Accessed March 27, 2018.
4 I have discussed Bashar's speeches at length in previously published work. See Rahaf Aldoughli. "Departing 'Secularism': Boundary Appropriation and Extension of the Syrian State in the Religious Domain since 2011." *British Journal of Middle Eastern Studies* 49, no. 2 (2020): 360–85; Rahaf Aldoughli. "Securitization as a Tool of Regime Survival: The Deployment of Religious Rhetoric in Bashar al-Asad's Speeches." *The Middle East Journal* 75, no. 1 (2021a): 9–32. https://doi.org/10.3751/75.1.11; and Rahaf Aldoughli. "Romancing the Nation." *Middle East Journal of Culture and Communication* 15, no. 4 (2022): 427–39.
5 Some of these remarks can be seen at www.youtube.com/watch?v=KWqSgaxiwM. Accessed June 19, 2022.
6 A central source for documenting this abuse of prisoners under the Baathist regime is the human rights activist Mazen Darwish, who collected extensive evidence and conducted interviews with former women detainees.
7 *France 24*. "Girls: Syrian Army Commandos on the Front Lines with Opposition Militants." March 27, 2015. https://2u.pw/xvZVDR. Accessed April 15, 2015.
8 Nawar Jaber. "Syrian Army Volunteers: Exposing the Regime without Confusion." *The New Arab*, October 9, 2016. https://2u.pw/5yGihw. Accessed December 15, 2017.

9 Al Jazeera. "'Baath Brigades'. Academics in the Service of the System." *Al Jazeera*, March 13, 2014. https://bit.ly/3WqQcjs. Accessed April 15, 2015.
10 See Lisa Lines. "Female Combatants in the Spanish Civil War: Milicianas on the Front Lines and in the Rearguard." *Journal of International Women's Studies* 10, no. 4 (May 2009): 167–87.
11 Rafaf Aldoughli. "Fighting Together: Emotionality, Fusion and Psychological Kinship in the Syrian Civil War." *Small Wars and Insurgency*. Forthcoming.
12 Nibal Zaitouneh. "The General Women's Union: An Absurd Journey from Foundation to Dissolution." *Coalition of Syrian Women for Democracy*, March 10, 2018. https://2u.pw/Grb9CZ. Accessed July 15, 2019.
13 Lama Rajeh. "My Journey with Al-Qubaysiat Sisterhood." *AlJumhuriya*, January 18, 2017. https://aljumhuriya.net/en/2017/01/18/my-journey-with-al-qubaysiat-sisterhood. Accessed January 20, 2017.
14 An example of a pro-Assad event organized by al-Qubaysiat in 2014 was reported by the television station Orient TV. The footage can currently be viewed on YouTube at: www.youtube.com/watch?v=w2Nv1–0y3r0. Another video clip of Bashar al-Assad celebrating the Prophet's birthday with al-Qubaysiat leaders in 2022 can be found at: www.youtube.com/watch?v=Vry6jJjIvcQ.
15 Karam Mansour. "Syria Trust for Development from the Civilian Face to the Military Uniform." *AlJumhuriya*, August 18, 2017. https://aljumhuriya.net/ar/2017/08/18/38742. Accessed August 20, 2017. See also Ayman Aldassouky and Sinan Hatahet. *The Role of Philanthropy in the Syrian War: Regime-Sponsored NGOs and Armed Group Charities*. Middle East Directions (MED), Wartime and Post-Conflict in Syria, 2020. https://hdl.handle.net/1814/67370. Accessed June 15, 2021.
16 Bashar al-Assad. "President al-Assad's Speech during his Participation in the Regular Meeting of the Ministry of Awqaf." YouTube video, posted by "Syrian Presidency," December 8, 2020. www.youtube.com/watch?v=_G8wzFCDPU8.
17 This phenomenon of interference in religion is not entirely new for the Baathists, but it has greatly expanded since the outbreak of the conflict in 2011. See Aldoughli 2022.
18 Al-Assad 2020.
19 Al-Assad 2022b.
20 See Erik Vollmann, Miriam Bohn, Roland Sturm, and Thomas Demmelhuber. "Decentralisation as Authoritarian Upgrading? Evidence from Jordan and Morocco." *Journal of North African Studies* 27, no. 2 (July 2, 2020): 362–93. https://doi.org/10.1080/13629387.2020.1787837.
21 See, for example, Mia al-Rahbi. "Al-mushāraka al-siyāsyiya li l-mara'a." *Al-Hiwar al-Mutamaddin*, no. 1131 (March 2005). www.ahewar.org/debat/show.art.asp?aid=33062. Accessed July 3, 2015, and posts on the blogging platform www.aljumhuriya.net/en.
22 See Dawn Chatty. *Displacement and Dispossession in the Modern Middle East*. New York: Cambridge University Press, 2010; and Katharina Lange. "Producing (Tribal) History: Gendered Representations of Genealogy and Warfare in Northern Syria." *Nomadic Peoples* 18, no. 2 (2014): 34–52.

23 Bashar al-Assad 2017. www.youtube.com/watch?v=tfritBKrmtM. Accessed August 20, 2017. My translation.
24 See Eric Hobsbawm. *Nations and Nationalism since 1780: Programme, Myth, Reality*. Cambridge: Cambridge University Press, 1990, p. 10. Similar analyses of perpetual masculine "crisis" have been made in other contexts, e.g., Sikata Banerjee. *Gender, Nation and Popular Film in India: Globalizing Muscular Nationalism*. New York: Routledge, 2016.
25 Rahaf Aldoughli. "Missing Gender: Conceptual Limitations in the Debate on 'Sectarianism' in the Middle East." *Middle East Critique* 33, no. 1 (2023): 143–62.
26 A good discussion about the rise of these two Islamist groups in Syria is provided by Omar Imady. "Organisationally Secular: Damascene Islamist Movements and the Syrian Uprising." *Syria Studies* 8, no. 1 (2016): 66–91. There is, however, much room for ongoing scholarship about their recent evolution and impacts.
27 See Yasir Suleiman. "Constructing Languages, Constructing National Identities." In *The Sociolinguistics of Identity*, edited by Topi Omoniyi and Goodith White, pp. 50–71, pp. 51–52. London: Continuum, 2006; Gayle Letherby, *Objectivity and Subjectivity in Social Sciences*. London: SAGE, 2012; and Donna Haraway. "Situated Knowledges: The Science Question in Feminism and the Privilege of Partial Perspective." *Feminist Studies* 14, no. 3 (1988): 575–99, pp. 582–84. https://doi.org/10.2307/3178066.
28 See Banerjee 2016.

# Bibliography

## Primary sources

### General

Damascus Center for Research. www.dcrs.sy. Accessed June 21, 2020.
"The Baath Constitution." 1947. *Shabaket al-busrah*. www.albasrah.net/ar_articles_2007/0307/dstor-b3th_070307.htm. Accessed January 12, 2013.
Syrian Commission for Family Affairs. "First National Primary Policy Report on the State of Population in Syria." 2008. http://engagingmen.com/files/resources/2010/dalia_mohamed/lmlkhS_lssty_nklyzy.pdf. Accessed June 5, 2015.
"Syrian Nationality Act 1969." www.cdf-sy.org/low/mrsom%20276.htm. Accessed December 2, 2014.
"Syrian Penal Code 1949." www.wipo.int/wipolex/en/text.jsp?file_id=243237. Accessed January 5, 2014.
"Syrian Social Insurance Law 1959." http://parliament.gov.sy/laws/Law/1959/work_05.htm. Accessed March 4, 2014.

### Nationalist songs

ʿAbu Bassel Qāʾidnā. www.youtube.com/watch?v=JgtagVYjLzk. Accessed March 7, 2015.
ʿAbu r-rijāl. www.youtube.com/watch?v=b1bNVbMUnww. Accessed June 4, 2015.
ʿAna Sūrī ah yā Niyyālī. www.youtube.com/watch?v=NZ4HTwEmIB. Accessed July 5, 2014.
ʿAna Sūrī wa ʿArdī ʿArabiyya. www.youtube.com/watch?v=VpKP1KNyYas. Accessed July 2, 2014.
Biktub Ismek ya Blādī. www.youtube.com/watch?v=Oj3vXIAzT-s. Accessed June 8, 2014.
Hamāka Allahu ya Assadu. www.youtube.com/watch?v=058eGyHgQqA. Accessed June 7, 2014.
Humāt d-Diyār. www.youtube.com/watch?v=-swst1P2SEc. Accessed October 8, 2014.
Minhibbak. www.youtube.com/watch?v=KzmjdLhMeNU. Accessed September 8, 2015.
Rāyātik bil-ʾĀlī ya Sūriyya. www.youtube.com/watch?v=iUNELQdn1w4. Accessed June 6, 2013.

*Saff l-'Askar.* www.youtube.com/watch?v=yFQw0aR41O4. Accessed July 7, 2014.
*Shaddet l-Hijin.* www.youtube.com/watch?v=LBM414cghQY. Accessed August 6, 2014.
*Sūriyya ya Habībatī.* www.youtube.com/watch?v=yKli72vTPmE. Accessed June 8, 2014.
*Teslam l sh-Sha'b.* www.youtube.com/watch?v=KkTKXhK8Rzw. Accessed August 6, 2014.

## Works of Michel Aflaq

(All accessed in February 2014)
*Fī Sabīl al-Ba'ath.* http://albaath.online.fr/.
"*'Ahd al-būtūla.*" 1935. http://albaath.online.fr/Volume%20I-Chapters/Fi%20Sabil%20al%20Baath-Vol%201-Ch01.htm.
"*Tharwat al-hayāt.*" 1936. http://albaath.online.fr/Volume%20I-Chapters/Fi%20Sabil%20al%20Baath-Vol%201-Ch02.htm.
"*Al-Qawmiyya hub qabla kul shay'.*" 1940a. http://albaath.online.fr/Volume%20I-Chapters/Fi%20Sabil%20al%20Baath-Vol%201-Ch30.htm.
"*Al-qawmiyyah qadar muhabbab.*" 1940b. http://albaath.online.fr/Volume%20I-Chapters/Fi%20Sabil%20al%20Baath-Vol%201-Ch31.htm.
"*Fī thikrā al-rasūl.*" 1943a. http://albaath.online.fr/Volume%20I-Chapters/Fi%20Sabil%20al%20Baath-Vol%201-Ch33.htm.
"*Wājib al-'amal al-qawmī.*" 1943b. http://albaath.online.fr/Volume%20I-Chapters/Fi%20Sabil%20al%20Baath-Vol%201-Ch35.htm.
"*Al-tafkīr al-mujarad.*" 1943c. http://albaath.online.fr/Volume%20I-Chapters/Fi%20Sabil%20al%20Baath-Vol%201-Ch34.htm.
"*'Imān.*" 1943d. http://albaath.online.fr/Volume%20I-Chapters/Baath-Volume%20ICh03.pdf.
"*Al-jīl al-'arabi al-jadīd.*" 1944. http://albaath.online.fr/Volume%20I-Chapters/Fi%20Sabil%20al%20Baath-Vol%201-Ch36.htm.
"*Hawla al-risāla al-'arabiyya.*" 1946. http://albaath.online.fr/Volume%20I-Chapters/Fi%20Sabil%20al%20Baath-Vol%201-Ch25.htm.
"The Party of Radical Change." 1949. http://albaath.online.fr/English/Aflaq-04-on%20heritage.htm.
"*Ma'nā al-risāla al-khālida.*" 1950a. http://albaath.online.fr/Volume%20I-Chapters/Fi%20Sabil%20al%20Baath-Vol%201-Ch26.htm.
"*Al-'alāqa bayn al-'urūba wa al-taghyīr al-jathrī,*" 1950b. http://albaath.online.fr/English/Aflaq-04-on%20heritage.htm.
"*Al-Baath al-'arabī huwa al-'inqilāb.*" 1950c. http://albaath.online.fr/Volume%20I-Chapters/Fi%20Sabil%20al%20Baath-Vol%201-Ch18.htm.
"*Al-Baaath al-'arabī 'irādat al-hayāt.*" 1950d. http://albaath.online.fr/Volume%20I-Chapters/Fi%20Sabil%20al%20Baath-Vol%201-Ch13.htm.
"*Al-'ummāl wa al-ishtirākiyyah.*" 1950e. http://albaath.online.fr/Volume%20I-Chapters/Fi%20Sabil%20al%20Baath-Vol%201-Ch55.htm.
"*Al-ma'raka bayn al-wujūd al-sathi wa al-wujūd al-asīl.*" 1955a. http://albaath.online.fr/Volume%20II-Chapters/Fi%20Sabil%20al%20Baath-Vol%202-Ch38.htm.
"*Khibrat al-shuyūkh wa indifā' al-shabāb.*" 1955b. http://albaath.online.fr/Volume%20I-Chapters/Fi%20Sabil%20al%20Baath-Vol%201-Ch08.htm.

"Al-'urūba wa al-'alam." 1956a. http://albaath.online.fr/Volume%20II-Chapters/Fi%20Sabil%20al%20Baath-Vol%202-Ch22.htm.
"Al-masīr al-'athīm wa al-a'māl al-yawmiyyah." 1956b. http://albaath.online.fr/Volume%20IV-Chapters/Fi%20Sabil%20al%20Baath-Vol%204-Ch23.htm.
"Nidāl al-wahda huwa nidāl al-jamāhīr." 1957a. http://albaath.online.fr/Volume%20II-Chapters/Fi%20Sabil%20al%20Baath-Vol%202-Ch45.htm.
"Li l-wahda tarīq wāhid." 1957b. http://albaath.online.fr/Volume%20II-Chapters/Fi%20Sabil%20al%20Baath-Vol%202-Ch46.htm.
"A Speech to the Branches of the Syrian Region." 1966. http://albaath.online.fr/English/Aflaq-04-on%20heritage.htm.
"Nafham al-turāth b al-fikr al-thawrī w al-mu'ānāh al-nidāliyya." 1967. http://albaath.online.fr/Volume%20III-Chapters/Fi%20Sabil%20al%20Baath-Vol%203-Ch04.htm.
"Hizb al-thawrah al-'arabiyyah." 1970. http://albaath.online.fr/VolumeV-Chapters/Fi%20Sabil%20al%20Baath-Vol%205-Ch08.htm.
"Al-jaish huwa juz' min al-jamāhīr al-munadila." 1974a. http://albaath.online.fr/Volume%20III-Chapters/Fi%20Sabil%20al%20Baath-Vol%203-Ch16.htm.
"Qadaruna 'an nuhārib ma'an." 1974b. http://albaath.online.fr/VolumeV-Chapters/Fi%20Sabil%20al%20Baath-Vol%205-Ch21.htm.
"Al-Baathi huwa al-sūra al-haqīqiyyah li l-'umma." 1975. http://albaath.online.fr/Volume%20III-Chapters/Fi%20Sabil%20al%20Baath-Vol%203-Ch02.htm.
"Al-Baaath wa tahaddiyat al-mustaqbal." 1977. http://albaath.online.fr/Volume%20III-Chapters/Fi%20Sabil%20al%20Baath-Vol%203-Ch11.htm.
"Wilādat marhala jadīda min al-'umma." 1982. http://albaath.online.fr/Volume%20III-Chapters/Baath-Volume%20III-Ch16.pdf.
"Al-Baath ramz li mu'ānāt al-'umma." 1983. http://albaath.online.fr/Volume%20III-Chapters/Baath-Volume%20III-Ch17.pdf.

### Works of Sati al-Husri

"'Awāmil al-qawmiyya" (1928). *Free Arab Voice*, January 19, 2010. http://freearabvoice.org/?page_id=104. Accessed June 17, 2014.
*'Āra' wa 'ahādīth fi 'l-tarbīya wa l-ta'līm*. Cairo: Mataba'at al-Risāla, 1944.
*Safahāt min al-maḍī al-qarīb*. Beirut: Dar al-'ilm li l-malāyīn, 1948.
*Muhadarāt fi nushu' al-fikrah al-qawmiyya*. Cairo: Mataba'at al-Risāla, 1951.
*Mā hiya al-qawmiyya? Abhāth wa Dirāsāt 'ala dhaw' al-ahdāth wa al-nazariyyāt*. Beirut: Dar al-'ilm li l-malāyīn, 1959.
*'Abhāth mukhtāra fi al-qawmiyyah al-'arabiyya*. Volume 1. Cairo: Dar al-ma'ārif, 1964a.
*'Āra' wa 'ahādīth fi l-qawmiyya l-'arabiyya*. Fourth edition. Beirut, 1964b.
*'Ahādīth fi l-tarbiya wa l-ijtimā'*. Beirut: Markaz Dirāsāt al-Wahda al-Arabiyya, 1984.
*'Abhāth mukhtarah fi al-qawmiyyah al-'arabiyya*. Volume 1. Beirut: Markaz Dirāsāt al-Wahda al-Arabiyya, 1985a.
*Hawl al-qawmiyya al-'arabiyya*. Beirut: Markaz Dirāsāt al-Wahda al-Arabiyya 1985b.
*'Ārā' wa 'ahādīth fī l-tārīkh wa l-ijtimā'*. Beirut: Markaz Dirāsāt al-Wahda al-Arabiyya, 1985c.
*Difā'an 'an al-'urūba*. Beirut: Markaz Dirāsāt al-Wahda al-Arabiyya, 1985d.
*Fi l-lugha wa l-'ādāb w 'alāqatuhumā bi l-qawmiyya*. Beirut: Markaz Dirāsāt al-Wahda al-Arabiyya, 1985e.

'Ā'rā' wa dirāsāt fī l-fikr l-qawmī. Edited by Muhmad al-Rumihi. Second edition. Majallat al-'Arabī, 1985f.

## Works of Zaki al-Arsuzi

Baath al-'umma al-'arabiyya wa-risalatuha ila l-'ālam: Al-madaniyya wa-l-thaqāfa. Damascus: Dar al-Yaqaza al-'Arabiyya, 1954.
Mashākiluna al-qawmiyyah w mawqif al-'ahzāb minha. Damascus: Dar al-Yaqaza al-'Arabiyya, 1958.
Al-Jumhūriyya al-muthlā. Damascus: Dar al-Yaqaza al-'Arabiyya, 1965.
Al-Mu'allafāt al-Kāmilah. Volume II. Damascus: Matābi' al-'Idāra al-Siyāsiyya, 1973.
Al-Mu'allafāt al-Kāmilah. Volume IV. Damascus: Matābi' al-'Idāra al-Siyāsiyya, 1974.
"Mafhūm al-'insāniyyia fī 'alāqatihā bi-mafhūmay al-'umma wa-l-qawmiyya." In Al-Mu'allafāt. Volume VI. Damascus: Matābi' al-'Idāra al-Siyāsiyya, 1975.

## Secondary sources

Abdo, Geneive. *The New Sectarianism: The Arab Uprisings and the Rebirth of the Shi'a-Sunni Divide*. Oxford: Oxford University Press, 2017.
Abboud, S. N. *Syria: Hot Spots in Global Politics*. Chichester: John Wiley and Sons, 2018.
Abu-Lughod, Lila. *Remaking Women: Feminism and Modernity in the Middle East*. Princeton, NJ: Princeton University Press, 1998.
Adamson, Robert. *Fichte 1852–1902*. Edinburgh: Blackwood, 1881.
Ahlbäck, Anders. *Manhood and the Making of the Military: Conscription, Military Service and Masculinity in Finland 1917–39*. Abingdon: Routledge, 2016.
Ajami, Fouad. *The Arab Predicament: Arab Political Thought and Practice since 1967*. Cambridge: Cambridge University Press, 1982.
Akhras, Muhammad Safuh. *Tarkīb al-'ā'ila al-'arabiyya wa wazā'ifuhā*. Damascus: Ministry of Culture Press, 1976.
Al Jazeera. "'Baath Brigades'. Academics in the Service of the System." *Al Jazeera*, March 13, 2014. https://bit.ly/3WqQcjs. Accessed April 15, 2015.
Al-Assad, Asma. "Mrs. Asma al-Assad's Meeting with Syrian Lionesses Fighting on the Ghouta Fronts." YouTube video, posted by "golan times," March 22, 2018. www.youtube.com/watch?v=JM5hXJ5Aaw4. Accessed April 22, 2018.
Al-Assad, Bashar. "Al-Assad's Speech on the Occasion of His Winning in the Presidential Elections." YouTube video, posted by "Syrian Presidency." www.youtube.com/watch?v=AYuOolis8iM. Accessed May 28, 2021.
———. "Bashar al-Assad Celebrates the Mawlid Al-Nabi with the Qubaysiat and Addresses Them." YouTube video, posted by "Naher Media." www.youtube.com/watch?v=Vry6jJjIvcQ. Accessed October 9, 2022.
———. "From President Al-Assad's Speech after the End of the Religious Celebration of the Prophet's Birthday in the Umayyad Mosque in Damascus." YouTube video, posted by "Syrian Presidency." www.youtube.com/watch?v=t4qCYLEkJSM. Accessed October 9, 2022.
———. "President al-Assad's Speech during His Participation in the Regular Meeting of the Ministry of Awqaf." YouTube video, posted by "Syrian Presidency." www.youtube.com/watch?v=_G8wzFCDPU8. Accessed December 8, 2020.

———. "President Bashar al-Assad Inaugural Address." *Peoples Assembly*. www.mideastweb.org/bashar_assad_inauguration_2007.htm. Accessed July 18, 2007.

———. "President Bashar al-Assad's Speech at the People's Assembly after Taking the Oath as President of the Republic 07/17/2000." YouTube video, posted by "Syria RTV." www.youtube.com/watch?v=ATC54C4eiPo. Accessed July 10, 2013.

———. "President Bashar al-Assad's Speech during His Meeting with Members of Trade Unions, and Chambers of Industry, Commerce, Agriculture, and Tourism in Damascus." Syrian Arab News Agency (SANA). www.sana.sy/?p=245771. Accessed July 26, 2015.

———. "Syrian President Bashar al-Assad in Aleppo to Inspect the Earthquake Victims." YouTube video, posted by "Al Mashhad." www.youtube.com/watch?v=KWqSgax-iwM. Accessed February 10, 2023.

———. "The Constitutional Oath Ceremony and the Speech of President Bashar al-Assad." YouTube video, posted by "Syrian Presidency." www.youtube.com/watch?v=ATC54C4eiPo. Accessed July 17, 2021.

Al-Assad, Hafez. "The Immortal Leader Hafez al-Assad (I am First and Foremost a Farmer, the Son of a Farmer) a Humane Speech." YouTube video, posted by "ALI HASAN." www.youtube.com/watch?v=tduY8lxBXFc. Accessed March 8, 2015.

———. *The Issue of Women in the Thought of the Leader Hafez al-Assad*. Damascus: Women's General Union, 1994.

———. "Speech by Syrian President Hafez al-Assad during the October 1973 War." YouTube video, posted by "Ba7ebbek Ya Masr." www.youtube.com/watch?v=iGSiQvV_B4U. Accessed October 19, 2016.

Aldassouky, Ayman, and Sinan Hatahet. *The Role of Philanthropy in the Syrian War: Regime-Sponsored NGOs and Armed Group Charities*. Middle East Directions (MED), Wartime and Post-Conflict in Syria, 2020. https://hdl.handle.net/1814/67370. Accessed June 15, 2021.

Aldoughli, Rahaf. "Departing 'Secularism': Boundary Appropriation and Extension of the Syrian State in the Religious Domain since 2011." *British Journal of Middle Eastern Studies* 49, no. 2 (2020): 360–85.

———. "Fighting Together: Emotionality, Fusion and Psychological Kinship in the Syrian Civil War." *Small Wars and Insurgency*. Forthcoming.

———. "Interrogating the Construction of Gendered Identity in the Syrian Nationalist Narrative: Al-Husri, Aflaq, and al-Arsuzi." *Syria Studies* 9, no. 1 (2017): 65–120.

———. "Interrogating the Construction of Masculinist Protection and Militarism in the Syrian Constitution of 1973." *Journal of Middle East Women Studies* 15, no. 1 (2019a): 48–74.

———. "Missing Gender: Conceptual Limitations in the Debate on 'Sectarianism' in the Middle East." *Middle East Critique* 33, no. 1 (2023): 143–62.

———. "Revisiting the Ideological Borrowings in the Syrian Nationalist Narratives: Sati 'al-Husri, Michel Aflaq, and Zaki al-Arsuzi." *Syria Studies* 8, no. 1 (2016): 7–38.

———. "Romancing the Nation." *Middle East Journal of Culture and Communication* 15, no. 4 (2022): 427–39.

———. "Securitization as a Tool of Regime Survival: The Deployment of Religious Rhetoric in Bashar al-Asad's Speeches." *Middle East Journal* 75, no. 1 (2021a): 9–32. https://doi.org/10.3751/75.1.11.

———. "The Symbolic Construction of National Identity and Belonging in Syrian Nationalist Songs (from 1970 to 2007)." *Contemporary Levant* 4, no. 2 (2019b): 141–54.

———. "What Is Syrian Nationalism? Primordialism and Romanticism in Official Baath Discourse." *Nations and Nationalism* 28, no. 1 (2021b): 125–40. https://doi.org/10.1111/nana.12786.

Al-Haj Saleh, Yassin. *Impossible Revolution: Making Sense of the Syrian Tragedy.* London: Hurst, 2017.

Altoma, Salih J. "The Emancipation of Women in Contemporary Syrian Literature." In *Syria: Society, Culture and Polity*, edited by Richard T. Antoun and Donald Quanterat, 71–95. Albany, NY: State University of New York Press, 1991.

Al-Rahbi, Mia. "Al-mushāraka al-siyāsyiya li l-mara'a." *Al-Hiwar al-Mutamaddin*, no. 1131 (March 2005). www.ahewar.org/debat/show.art.asp?aid=33062. Accessed July 3, 2015.

———. *Feminism: Concepts and Issues.* Damascus: Al Rahba Publishing House, 2014.

Anderson, Benedict. *Imagined Communities: Reflections on the Origin and Spread of Nationalism.* London: Verso, 2006.

APSA-MENA newsletter. n.d. Volume 3, pp. 3–6.

Aroudky, Badr al-Dein. "The Syrian National Identity between Problematic and Ambiguous." Harmoon Centre for Contemporary Studies, November 2, 2020. https://2u.pw/5ZVy84. Accessed December 20, 2021.

Arsuzi-Elamir, Dalal. "Nation, State, and Democracy in the Writings of Zaki al-Arsuzi." In *Nationalism and Liberal Thought in the Arab East: Ideology and Practice*, edited by Christoph Schumann, pp. 66–91. Abingdon: Routledge, 2010.

Ayubi, Nazih. *Over-Stating the Arab State: Politics and Society in the Middle East.* London: I.B. Tauris, 2009.

Badran, Margot. *Feminism, Islam, and Nation: Gender and the Making of Modern Egypt.* Princeton, NJ: Princeton University Press, 1995.

Banerjee, Sikata. *Gender, Nation and Popular Film in India: Globalizing Muscular Nationalism.* Abingdon: Routledge, 2016.

Barnard, Frederick M. *Herder's Social and Political Thought.* Oxford: Clarendon Press, 1965.

Baron, Beth. *Egypt as a Woman: Nationalism, Gender, and Politics.* Berkeley, CA: University of California Press, 2005.

Bederman, Gail. *Manliness and Civilization: A Cultural History of Gender and Race in the United States, 1880–1917.* Chicago, IL: University of Chicago Press, 1995.

Beissinger, Mark R., and Stephen Kotkin. *Historical Legacies of Communism in Russia and Eastern Europe.* New York: Cambridge University Press, 2014.

Beshara, Adel (ed.). *The Origins of Syrian Nationhood: Histories, Pioneers and Identity.* Abingdon: Routledge, 2011.

Bishara, Azmi. *Syria 2011–2013: Revolution and Tyranny before the Mayhem.* London: I.B. Tauris, 2021.

Bhabha, Homi K. (ed.). *Nation and Narration.* London: Routledge, 1990.

Billig, Michael. *Banal Nationalism.* London: SAGE, 1995.

Birdsall, Carolyn. *Nazi Soundscapes: Sound, Technology and Urban Space in Germany, 1933–1954.* Amsterdam: Amsterdam University Press, 2012.

Blom, Ida, Karen Hagemann, and Catherine Hall (eds). *Gendered Nations: Nationalism and Gender Order in the Long Nineteenth Century.* Oxford: Oxford International Publishers, 2000.

Bohlman, Philip V. *The Music of European Nationalism: Cultural Identity and Modern History*. California: ABC-CLIO, 2004.
Bracewell, Wendy. "Rape in Kosovo: Masculinity and Serbian Nationalism." *Nations and Nationalism* 6, no. 4 (2000): 563–90.
Breuilly, John. *Nationalism and the State*. Manchester: Manchester University Press, 1993.
Brewer, Marilynn B. "The Many Faces of Socialidentity: Implications for Political Psychology." *Political Psychology* 22, no. 1 (2001): 115–26. https://doi.org/10.1111/0162-895x.00229.
Brincker, Benedikte. "Introduction to Themed Section on Classical Music and Nationalism: Studies into the Political Function of Art." *Nations and Nationalism* 20, no. 4 (2014): 603–05.
Bryman, Alan. *Social Research Methods*. Fifth edition. Oxford: Oxford University Press, 2016.
Buch, Esteban, Igor Contreras Zubillaga, and Manuel Denis Silva (eds). *Composing for the State: Music in Twentieth-Century Dictatorships*. Abingdon: Routledge, 2016.
Butler, Judith. *Bodies That Matter: On the Discursive Limits of "Sex."* New York: Routledge, 1993.
———. *Gender Trouble: Feminism and the Subversion of Identity*. New York: Routledge, 1999.
Butz, David A. "National Symbols as Agents of Psychological and Social Change." *Political Psychology* 30, no. 5 (2009): 779–804. https://doi.org/10.1111/j.1467-9221.2009.00725.x.
Calhoun, Craig. *Nationalism: Concepts in the Social Sciences*. Buckingham: Open University Press, 1997.
Carnegie Middle East Center. "The Syrian Constitution 1973–2012." December 5, 2012. http://carnegie-mec.org/diwan/50255?lang=en. Accessed May 6, 2013.
Carver, Terrell, and Samuel A. Chambers (eds). *Carole Pateman: Democracy, Feminism, Welfare*. Abingdon: Routledge, 2011.
Chatterjee, Partha. *Nationalist Thought and the Colonial World: A Derivative Discourse*. Tokyo: Zed Books, 1986.
Chatty, Dawn. *Displacement and Dispossession in the Modern Middle East*. New York: Cambridge University Press, 2010.
Cleveland, William L. *The Making of an Arab Nationalist: Ottomanism and Arabism in the Life and Thought of Sati' al-Husri*. Princeton, NJ: Princeton University Press, 1971.
Cohen, A. *The Symbolic Construction of Community*. London: Routledge, 1995.
Collelo, Thomas (ed.). *Syria: A Country Study*. Washington, DC: Library of Congress, 1987.
Connell, R. W. *Masculinities*. Berkeley, CA: University of California Press, 1995.
Converse, Philip E. "Information Flow and the Stability of Partisan Attitudes." *Public Opinion Quarterly* 26, no. 4 (1962): 578–99. https://doi.org/10.1086/267129.
Cooke, Miriam. *Dancing in Damascus: Creativity, Resilience, and the Syrian Revolution*. Abingdon: Routledge, 2017.
Crawford, Beverly, and Arend Lijphart. *Liberalization and Leninist Legacies: Comparative Perspectives on Democratic Transitions*. Berkeley, CA: University of California Press, 1997.
Cross, William E. *Shades of Black: Diversity in African-American Identity*. Philadelphia, PA: Temple University Press, 1991.
Curtis, Benjamin. *Music Makes the Nation: Nationalist Composers and Nation Building in Nineteenth-Century Europe*. Amherst, NY: Cambria Press, 2008.

Curtis, Michael (ed.). *People and Politics in the Middle East: The Arab–Israeli Conflict: Its Background and the Prognosis for Peace*. New Jersey: Transaction Publishers, 1977.

Dawisha, Adeed. *Arab Nationalism in the Twentieth Century: From Triumph to Despair*. Princeton, NJ: Princeton University Press, 2003.

———. "Nation and Nationalism: Historical Antecedents to Contemporary Debates." *International Studies Review* 4, no. 1 (2002): 3–22.

Dawn, Ernest. "The Rise of Arabism in Syria." *Middle East Journal* 16, no. 2 (1962): 145–68.

De Grazia, Victoria. *How Fascism Ruled Women: Italy, 1922–1945*. Berkeley, CA: University of California Press, 1992.

Donahue, Amy K., and Rohan Kalyan. "Introduction: On the Imperative, Challenges, and Prospects of Decolonizing Comparative Methodologies." *Comparative and Continental Philosophy* 7, no. 2 (2015): 128. https://doi.org/10.1179/1757063815z.00000000058.

Dreyer, Edward C. "Media Use and Electoral Choices: Some Political Consequences of Information Exposure." *Public Opinion Quarterly* 35, no. 4 (1971): 544–53. https://doi.org/10.1086/267950.

Dwyer, Leslie K. "Spectacular Sexuality: Nationalism, Development and the Policies of Family Planning in Indonesia." In *Gender Ironies of Nationalism: Sexing the Nation*, edited by Tamar Mayer, pp. 25–64. London: Routledge, 2000.

El-Attrache, Mohammed. *The Political Philosophy of Michel Aflaq and the Ba'th Party in Syria*. Michigan: Xerox University Microfilms, 1976.

Elshtain, Jean Bethke. *Public Man, Private Women: Women in Social and Political Thought*. Princeton, NJ: Princeton University Press, 1981.

———. "Reflections on War and Political Discourse." *Political Theory* 13, no. 1 (1985): 39–57.

Enab Baladi. "Women in the Era of Assad between the Women's Union and the First Lady. Intellectual Domestication in the Crucible of Baath." September 25, 2016. https://2u.pw/Q5JiW1. Accessed October 15, 2016.

Enloe, Cynthia. *Bananas, Beaches, and Bases: Making Feminist Sense of International Politics*. Berkeley, CA: University of California Press, 1990.

———. *Manoeuvres: The International Politics of Militarizing Women's Lives*. Berkeley, CA: University of California Press, 2000.

Euro-Mediterranean Women's Foundation. "National Situation Analysis Report: Women's Human Rights and Gender Equality in Syria." July 2010. https://docs.euromedwomen.foundation/files/ermwfdocuments/5668_2.139.nationalsituationanalysis-syria.pdf. Accessed March 6, 2015.

European Union Agency for Asylum. "Persons Who Evaded or Deserted Military Service." Common Analysis, September 2020. https://2u.pw/VQKxSY. Accessed December 15, 2021.

Fiala, Andrew. *The Philosopher's Voice: Philosophy, Politics, and Language in the Nineteenth Century*. Albany, NY: State University of New York Press, 2002.

Fichte, Johann Gottlieb. *Addresses to the German Nation*, edited by G. A. Kelly. New York: Harper and Row, 1968.

———. *Addresses to the German Nation*. Translated and edited by Gregory Moore. Cambridge: Cambridge University Press, 2008.

———. *Reden an die deutsche Nation*. Berlin: Zentral und Landesbibliothek Berlin, 1808.

Fisher, Max. "Here's North Korea's New Official Song, with Creepy Music Video." *The Washington Post*, May 7, 2013. www.washingtonpost.com/news/worldviews/wp/2013/05/07/heres-north-koreas-new-official-song-with-creepy-music-video/?utm_term=.6f241673e136. Accessed January 20, 2014.

France 24. "Girls: Syrian Army Commandos on the Front Lines with Opposition Militants." March 27, 2015. https://2u.pw/xvZVDR. Accessed April 15, 2015.

Frolova-Walker, Marina. *Russian Music and Nationalism: From Glinka to Stalin*. New Haven, CT: Yale University Press, 2007.

Galvani, John. "The October War: Egypt, Syria, Israel." *MERIP Reports* 25 (1974): 10–20.

Geisler, Michael E. (ed.). *National Symbols, Fractured Identities: Contesting the National Narrative*. Hanover, NH: University Press of New England, 2005.

Gellner, Ernest. *Conditions of Liberty: Civil Society and Its Rivals*. London: Hamish Hamilton, 1994.

———. *Language and Solitude: Wittgenstein, Malinowski and the Habsburg Dilemma*. Cambridge: Cambridge University Press, 1998.

Gelvin, James L. "The Social Origins of Popular Nationalism in Syria: Evidence for a New Framework." *International Journal of Middle East Studies* 26, no. 4 (1994): 645–61.

Gilbert, Victoria. "Syria for the Syrians: The Rise of Syrian Nationalism, 1970–2013." Master's thesis, Northeastern University, 2013. www.academia.edu/3432163/Syria_for_the_Syrians_The_Rise_of_Syrian_Nationalism_1970–2013. Accessed June 10, 2016.

Gill, Graeme, and Luis F. Angosto-Ferrandez. "Introduction: Symbolism and Politics." *Politics, Religion & Ideology* 19, no. 4 (2018): 429–33. https://doi.org/10.1080/21567689.2018.1539436.

Gocek, Fatema Muge (ed.). *Social Constructions of Nationalism in the Middle East*. Albany, NY: State University of New York Press, 2002.

Goode, James F. *Negotiating for the Past: Archaeology, Nationalism, and Diplomacy in the Middle East, 1919–1941*. Austin, TX: University of Texas Press, 2007.

Haddad, Fanar. "Sectarian Relations in Arab Iraq: Contextualising the Civil War of 2006–2007." *British Journal of Middle Eastern Studies* 40, no. 2 (2013): 115–38. https://doi.org/10.1080/13530194.2013.790289.

———. *Understanding 'Sectarianism': Sunni-Shi'a Relations in the Modern Arab World*. London: Hurst, 2020.

Haraway, Donna. "Situated Knowledges: The Science Question in Feminism and the Privilege of Partial Perspective." *Feminist Studies* 14, no. 3 (1988): 575–99. https://doi.org/10.2307/3178066.

Harvey, Lee. "The Methodological Problems of Ideology Critique." Birmingham Polytechnic Research Unit Discussion Paper 19, no. 5 (1983).

Hashemi, Nader, and Danny Postel. *Sectarianization: Mapping the New Politics of the Middle East*. Oxford: Oxford University Press, 2017.

Hausmann, Ricardo, Laura D. Tyson and Saadia Zahidi. *The Global Gender Gap Report 2011*. Geneva: World Economic Forum, 2011. www3.weforum.org/docs/WEF_GenderGap_Report_2011.pdf. Accessed April 13, 2015.

Hayes, Carlton J. H. *Historical Evolution of Modern Nationalism*. New York: Macmillan, 1949.

Herder, Johann G. *Herder: Philosophical Writings*. Translated and edited by Michael N. Forster. Cambridge: Cambridge University Press, 2002.

Heuer, Jennifer. "Gender and Nationalism." In *Nations and Nationalism: A Global Historical Overview 1770–1880*, pp. 43–58. California: ABC-CLIO, 2008.

Hill, Fiona. "Syrian Women and Feminist Agenda." In Paul J. White and William S. Logan (eds), *Remaking the Middle East*, pp. 129–51. Oxford: Berg Publishers, 1997.

Hinnebusch, Raymond A. "Identity and State Formation in Multi-Sectarian Societies: Between Nationalism and Sectarianism in Syria." *Nations and Nationalism* 26, no. 1 (2020): 138–54. https://doi.org/10.1111/nana.12582.

———. "Modern Syrian Politics." *History Compass* 6, no. 1 (January 2008): 263–85.

———. *Peasant and Bureaucracy in Ba'thist Syria: The Political Economy of Rural Development*. Boulder, CO: Westview Press, 1989.

———. *Syria: Revolution from Above*. London: Routledge, 2001.

Hippler, Thomas. *Citizens, Soldiers and National Armies*. London and New York: Routledge, 2006.

Hobsbawm, Eric. *Nations and Nationalism since 1780: Programme, Myth, Reality*. Cambridge: Cambridge University Press, 1990.

Hobsbawm, Eric, and Terence Ranger. *The Invention of Traditions*. Cambridge: Cambridge University Press, 1983.

Hooper, Charlotte. *Manly States: Masculinities, International Relations, and Gender Politics*. New York: Columbia University Press, 2001.

Hopkins, Peter E. "Women, Men, Positionalities and Emotion: Doing Feminist Geographies of Religion." *ACME: An International Journal for Critical Geographies* 8, no. 1 (2009): 1–17. https://doi.org/10.1080/13530194.2020.1805299.

Hung, Chang-Tai. "The Politics of Songs: Myths and Symbols in the Chinese Communist War Music, 1937–1949." *Modern Asian Studies* 30, no. 4 (1996): 901–29.

Hutchinson, John. "Cultural Nationalism and Moral Regeneration." In John Hutchinson and Anthony D. Smith (eds), *Nationalism*, pp. 122–31. Oxford: Oxford University Press, 1994.

———. *Dynamics of Cultural Nationalism: The Gaelic Revival and the Creation of the Irish Nation-State*. London: Allen and Unwin, 1989.

Imady, Omar. "Organisationally Secular: Damascene Islamist Movements and the Syrian Uprising." *Syria Studies* 8, no. 1 (2016): 66–91.

Irving, Helen. *Gender and the Constitution: Equity and Agency in Comparative Constitutional Design*. Cambridge: Cambridge University Press, 2008.

Jaber, Nawar. "Syrian Army Volunteers: Exposing the Regime without Confusion." *The New Arab*, October 9, 2016. https://2u.pw/5yGihw. Accessed December 15, 2017.

Jayawardena, Visakha Kumari. *Feminism and Nationalism in the Third World*. London: Zed Books, 1986.

Joseph, Suad. "Working-Class Women's Networks in a Sectarian State: A Political Paradox." *American Ethnologist* 10, no. 1 (1983): 1–22. https://doi.org/10.1525/ae.1983.10.1.02a00010.

Kandiyoti, Deniz. "Bargaining with Patriarchy." *Gender & Society* 2, no. 3 (1998): 273–73. https://doi.org/10.4324/9781315680675-24.

———. "Women, Islam and the State." *Middle East Report*, no. 173 (1991): 9–14. https://doi.org/10.2307/3012623.

Katz, Sheila H. *Women and Gender in Early Jewish and Palestinian Nationalism*. Gainesville, FL: University Press of Florida, 2003.

Kedourie, Elie. *Nationalism*. Edited by W. A. Robson. Second edition. London: Hutchinson, 1961.
Kelly, Sanja, and Julia Breslin. "Syria." In Sanja Kelly and Julia Breslin (eds), *Women's Rights in the Middle East and North Africa: Progress amid Resistance*, pp. 459–86. New York: Freedom House: 2010.
Key, V. O. *Public Opinion and American Democracy*. New York: Knopf, 1961.
Khaizaran, Lora, "Al-Assad Issues a Decree to Repeal a Provision of the Penal Code Relating to Honor Crimes." *Syria News*, July 1, 2009. http://syria-news.com/readnews.php?sy_seq=97733. Accessed June 15, 2015.
Kienle, Eberhard. "Arab Unity Schemes Revisited: Interest, Identity, and Policy in Syria and Egypt." *International Journal of Middle East Studies* 27, no. 1 (February 1995): 53–71.
Kitschelt, Herbert, Zdenka Mansfeldova, Radoslaw Markowski, and Gabor Toka. *Post-Communist Party Systems: Competition, Representation, and Inter-Party Cooperation*. Cambridge: Cambridge University Press, 1999.
Koonz, Claudia. *Mothers in the Fatherland*. London: Methuen, 1988.
Korostelina, Karina V. "Readiness to Fight in Crimea: How It Interrelates with National and Ethnic Identities." *Identity Matters: Ethnic and Sectarian Conflict*, January 1, 2007, pp. 49–72. https://doi.org/10.1515/9780857456892-007.
Kraidy, Marwan M. *Reality Television and Arab Politics: Contention in Public Life*. Cambridge: Cambridge University Press, 2010.
Krämer, Gudrun. "Religion, Culture, and the Secular." Working paper series of the HCAS "Multiple Secularities – Beyond the West, Beyond Modernities," 2021. https://doi.org/10.36730/2020.1.msbwbm.23.
Lange, Katharina. "Producing (Tribal) History: Gendered Representations of Genealogy and Warfare in Northern Syria." *Nomadic Peoples* 18, no. 2 (2014): 34–52.
Letherby, Gayle. *Objectivity and Subjectivity in Social Sciences*. London: SAGE, 2012.
Letherby, Gayle, John Scott, and Malcolm Williams. *Objectivity and Subjectivity in Social Research*. London: SAGE, 2013.
Levant, Ronald F. "The masculinity crisis." *Journal of Men's Studies* 5, no. 3 (February 1997): 221–31.
Liddell, Colin. "The Uses and Abuses of Arab Nationalism: White Nationalist Lessons from Brown Nationalist Failure." *Alternative Right*, February 8, 2015. http://alternative-right.blogspot.com/2015/02/the-uses-and-abuses-of-arab-nationalism.html. Accessed July 10, 2016.
Lines, Lisa. "Female Combatants in the Spanish Civil War: Milicianas on the Front Lines and in the Rearguard." *Journal of International Women's Studies* 10, no. 4 (May 2009): 167–87.
Mabon, Simon. "Saudi Arabia and Iran: Islam and Foreign Policy in the Middle East." In *Routledge Handbook of International Relations in the Middle East*, edited by Shahram Akbarzadeh, pp. 138–52. Abingdon: Routledge, 2019.
MacKinnon, Catharine A. *Are Women Human? And Other International Dialogues*. Harvard, MA: Harvard University Press, 2006.
Makiya, Kanan. *Republic of Fear: The Politics of Modern Iraq*. Berkeley, CA: University of California Press, 1998.
Maktabi, Rania. "Gender, Family Law and Citizenship in Syria." *Citizenship Studies* 14, no. 5 (2010): 557–72.

Malterud, Kirsti. "Qualitative Research: Standards, Challenges, and Guidelines." *The Lancet* 358, no. 9280 (2001): 483–88. https://doi.org/10.1016/s0140-6736(01)05627-6.

Manea, Elham. *The Arab State and Women's Rights: The Trap of Authoritarian Governance*. London and New York: Routledge, 2011.

Mann, Joseph. "The Syrian Neo-Ba'th Regime and the Kingdom of Saudi Arabia, 1966–70." *Middle Eastern Studies* 42, no. 5 (2006): 769–90.

Mansour, Karam. "Syria Trust for Development from the Civilian Face to the Military Uniform." *AlJumhuriya*, August 18, 2017. https://aljumhuriya.net/ar/2017/08/18/38742. Accessed August 20, 2017.

Mayer, Tamar. "Gender Ironies of Nationalism: Setting the Stage." In *Gender Ironies of Nationalism: Sexing the Nation*, edited by Tamar Mayer, pp. 1–22. London and New York: Routledge, 2000.

———. *Women and the Israeli Occupation: The Politics of Change*. London and New York: Routledge, 1994.

McClintock, Anne. "Family Feuds: Gender, Nationalism and the Family." *Feminist Review* 44 (Summer 1993): 61–80.

———. "'No Longer in a Future Heaven': Women and Nationalism in South Africa." *Transition* 51 (1991): 104–23.

Meinecke, Friedrich. *Cosmopolitanism and the National State*. Translated by Robert B. Kimber. Princeton, NJ: Princeton University Press, 1970.

Mikdashi, Maya. "Sex and Sectarianism: The Legal Architecture." *Comparative Studies of South Asia, Africa and the Middle East* 34, no. 2 (2014): 279–93.

Milton-Edwards, Beverley. *Contemporary Politics in the Middle East*. Cambridge: Polity Press, 2006.

Mohanty, Chandra T. "Cartographies of Struggle: Third World Women and the Politics of Feminism." In *Third World Women and the Politics of Feminism*, edited by Chandra T. Mohanty, Ann Russo, and Lourdes Torres, pp. 1–47. Bloomington, IN: Indiana University Press, 1991.

Moi, Toril. *Sexual/Textual Politics*. London and New York: Routledge, 2002.

Montagana, Nicola, Erin Sanders McDonagh, and Jon Mulholland. *Gendering Nationalism Intersections of Nation, Gender and Sexuality*. London: Palgrave Macmillan, 2018.

Mosse, George. *Confronting the Nation: Jewish and Western Nationalism*. Hanover, NH: University Press of New England, 1993.

———. *The Nationalisation of the Masses: Political Symbolism and Mass Movements in Germany from Napoleonic Wars through the Third Reich*. Ithaca, NY: Cornell University Press, 1975.

Motyl, Alexander J. "Traditional Political Theory and Nationalism." In *Encyclopaedia of Nationalism: Fundamental Themes*, edited by Alexander J. Motyl. Oxford: Elsevier Science and Technology, 2000.

Moubayed, Sami. *Men and Women Who Shaped Syria 1900–2000*. Seattle, WA: Cune Press, 2006.

Mukherjee, Sanjukta. "Troubling Positionality: Politics of 'Studying Up' in Transnational Contexts." *The Professional Geographer* 69, no. 2 (2017): 291–98. https://doi.org/10.1080/00330124.2016.1208509.

Mullings, Beverley. "Insider or Outsider, Both or Neither: Some Dilemmas of Interviewing in a Cross-Cultural Setting." *Geoforum* 30, no. 4 (1999): 337–50. https://doi.org/10.1016/s0016-7185(99)00025-1.

Muslih, Muhammad. "The Rise of Local Nationalism in the Arab East." In *The Origins of Arab Nationalism*, edited by Rashid Khalidi, pp. 167–85. New York: Columbia University Press, 1991.

Nagel, Joane. "Masculinity and Nationalism: Gender and Sexuality in the Making of Nations." *Ethnic and Racial Studies* 21, no. 2 (March 1998): 243–69.

Neumann, Cecilie Basberg, and Iver B. Neumann. *Power, Culture and Situated Research Methodology Autobiography, Field, Text*. Cham: Springer International, 2018.

O'Shaughnessy, Nicholas Jackson. *Politics and Propaganda: Weapons of Mass Seduction*. Manchester: Manchester University Press, 2004.

Oettinger, Rebecca Wagner. *Music as Propaganda in the German Reformation*. London: Routledge, 2001.

Okin, Susan Moller. *Women in Western Political Thought*. London: Virago, 1980.

Orient TV. "Al-Qubaysiyyat Perform a Dance Party inside the Umayyad Mosque in Support of Bashar." YouTube video, posted by "Orient TV," June 8, 2014. www.youtube.com/watch?v=w2Nv1-0y3r0. Accessed June 10, 2014.

Peterson, V. Spike. "Gendered Nationalism: Reproducing 'Us' versus 'Them.'" In *The Women and War Reader*, edited by Lois Ann Lorentzen and Jennifer Turpin, pp. 41–49. New York: New York University Press, 1998.

Peterson, V. Spike, and Anne Sisson Runyan. *Global Gender Issues*. Oxford: Westview, 1993.

Pettman, Jan Jindy. *Worlding Women: A Feminist International Politics*. London: Routledge, 1996.

Phillips, Christopher. *Everyday Arab Identity: The Daily Reproduction of the Arab World*. London: Routledge, 2013.

Phillips, Christopher, and Morten Valbjørn. "'What Is in a Name?': The Role of (Different) Identities in the Multiple Proxy Wars in Syria." *Small Wars & Insurgencies* 29, no. 3 (2018): 414–33. https://doi.org/10.1080/09592318.2018.1455328.

Pidd, Helen. "Austrians Look Forward to New National Anthem." *The Guardian*, October 31, 2011. www.theguardian.com/world/2011/oct/31/austrians-national-anthem-new. Accessed April 21, 2016.

Pierret, Thomas. *Religion and State in Syria: The Sunni Ulema under the Ba'th*. Cambridge: Cambridge University Press, 2013.

Pipes, Daniel. *Greater Syria: The History of an Ambition*. Oxford: Oxford University Press, 1992.

Radhakrishnan, R. "Nationalism, Gender, and the Narrative of Identity." In *Nationalisms and Sexualities*, edited by Andrew Parker, Mary Russo, Doris Sommer, and Patricia Yaeger, pp. 77–95. London: Routledge, 1992.

Rajeh, Lama. "My Journey with Al-Qubaysiat Sisterhood." *AlJumhuriya*, January 18, 2017. https://aljumhuriya.net/en/2017/01/18/my-journey-with-al-qubaysiat-sisterhood. Accessed January 20, 2017.

Reeser, Todd W. *Masculinities in Theory: An Introduction*. Chichester: Wiley-Blackwell, 2009.

Renan, Ernest. "What Is a Nation?" Lecture at Sorbonne University, Paris, March 11, 1882. Translated by Ethan Rundell. http://ucparis.fr/files/9313/6549/9943/What_is_a_Nation.pdf. Accessed June 12, 2013.

Revill, George. "Music and the Politics of Sound: Nationalism, Citizenship and Auditory Space." *Environment and Planning D: Society and Space* 18, no. 5 (2000): 597–613.

Rosenfeld, Michel. "Constitutional Identity." In *The Oxford Handbook of Comparative Constitutional Law*, edited by Michel Rosenfeld and András Sajó. Online edition November 2012. http://dx.doi.org/10.1093/oxfordhb/ 9780199578610.013.0037. Accessed September 14, 2015.
Rowbotham, Sheila. *Hidden from History: 300 Years of Women's Oppression and the Fight Against It*. London: Pluto Press, 1973.
Rowe, Wendy. "Positionality in Action Research." Edited by David Coghlan and Mary Brydon Miller. *The SAGE Encyclopedia of Action Research* 1 (2014): 628. https://doi.org/10.4135/9781446294406.n277.
Rubin, Gayle S. "Thinking Sex: Notes for a Radical Theory of the Politics of Sexuality." In *Culture, Society and Sexuality: A Reader*, edited by Richard Parker and Peter Aggleton, pp. 150–87. London: Routledge, 2007.
Saba', Michel. *S'ādeh wa Aflaq fī l-Fikr al-Siyāsī l-Orthodoxī*. Beirut: Manshūrāt 'Āfāq Jāmi'iyya, 2005.
Sadiki, Larbi, and Rima Majed. "The Theoretical and Methodological Traps in Studying Sectarianism in the Middle East." In *Routledge Handbook of Middle East Politics*, pp. 540–53. New York: Routledge, 2020.
Sadowski, Yahya. "The Evolution of Political Identity in Syria." In *Identity and Foreign Policy in the Middle East*, edited by Shibley Telhami and Michael Barnett, pp. 137–54. Ithaca, NY: Cornell University Press, 2002.
Said, Edward W. *Orientalism*. New York: Vintage, 1979.
Salameh, Frank. "The Enigma of the Syrian Nation." *The National Interest*, March 11, 2013. http://nationalinterest.org/commentary/the-enigma-the-syrian-nation-8204. Accessed February 15, 2015.
———. *Language, Memory, and Identity in the Middle East: The Case for Lebanon*. Plymouth: Lexington Books, 2010.
Salem, Paul. *Bitter Legacy: Ideology and Politics in the Arab World*. Syracuse, NY: Syracuse University Press, 1994.
Salem-Babikian, Norma. "Michel Aflaq: A Biographic Outline." *Arab Studies Quarterly* 2, no. 2 (1980): 162–79.
Saouli, Adham. *The Arab State: Dilemmas of Late Formation*. New York: Routledge, 2012.
Savin-Baden, Maggi, and Claire Howell Major. *Qualitative Research: The Essential Guide to Theory and Practice*. London: Routledge, 2013.
Sayigh, Yezid. "Militaries, Civilians and the Crisis of the Arab State." *The Washington Post*, December 8, 2014. www.washingtonpost.com/news/monkey-cage/wp/2014/12/08/militaries-civilians-and-the-crisis-of-the-arab-state/?utm_term=.912536e221d8. Accessed May 10, 2016.
Shaaban, Bouthaina. *Both Right and Left-Handed: Arab Women Talk about Their Lives*. Bloomington, IN: Indiana University Press, 1991.
———. "The Status of Women in Syria." In *Arab Women: Between Defiance and Restraint*, edited by Suha Sabbagh, pp. 54–61. New York: Olive Branch Press, 2003.
Slyomovics, Susan, and Suad Joseph. *Women and Power in the Middle East*. Philadelphia, PA: University of Pennsylvania Press, 2011.
Smith, Anthony D. *The Concept of Social Change: A Critique of the Functionalist Theory of Social Change*. London: Routledge, 1973.
———. *National Identity*. Reno, NV: University of Nevada Press, 1991.
———. *Nationalism*. Oxford: Oxford University Press, 1994.
———. *Nationalism: Theory, Ideology, History*. Cambridge: Polity, 2001.

———. *Theories of Nationalism*. London: Duckworth, 1983.
Stoetzler, Marcel, and Nira Yuval-Davis. "Standpoint Theory, Situated Knowledge and the Situated Imagination." *Feminist Theory* 3, no. 3 (2002): 315–33. https://doi.org/10.1177/1464700002762492024.
Sulayman, Nabil. *An-Nisawiyya fī'l-Kitāb s-Sūrī l-Madrasī 1967–1976*. Damascus: Ministry of Culture, 1978.
Suleiman, Yasir. *The Arabic Language and National Identity*. Washington, DC: Georgetown University Press, 2003.
———. "Constructing Languages, Constructing National Identities." In *The Sociolinguistics of Identity*, edited by Topi Omoniyi and Goodith White, pp. 50–71. London: Continuum, 2006.
Syria Women Bloc for Democracy. "Was the General Women's Union the Supreme Hand of the Baath to Paralyze the Syrian Women's Movement?" March 11, 2018. https://2u.pw/nOQXlv. Accessed April 10, 2020.
Tarabishi, George. *Al-Mar'a l-'arabiyya s-sūriyya fī 'ahd al-mar'a d-dawlī 1975–1985*. Damascus: Ministry of Culture, 1985.
Tauber, Eliezer. *The Formation of Modern Syria and Iraq*. London: Frank Cass, 1995.
Theweleit, Klaus. *Male Fantasies*. Volume 1. Minneapolis, MN: University of Minnesota Press, 1987.
Tibi, Bassam. *Arab Nationalism: Between Islam and the Nation-State*. London: Macmillan, 1997.
Tibi, Bassam (ed.). *Arab Nationalism: A Critical Enquiry*. Second edition. Translated by Marion Farouk-Sluglett and Peter Sluglett. London: Palgrave Macmillan, 1990.
Tolz, Vera, and Stephenie Booth. *Nation and Gender in Contemporary Europe*. Manchester: Manchester University Press, 2005.
Trentin, Massimiliano. "Modernizing as State Building: The Two Germanies in Syria, 1963–1972." *Diplomatic History* 33, no. 3 (2009): 487–505.
UNESCO. "The National Report about the State of the Adult Education Development in Syrian Arab Republic Presented to Preparing for the Sixth International Conference on Adult Education." Report by Abdulfattah al-Obaid, Director of Adult Education, Syria, for Sixth International Conference on Adult Education, Belem, December 1–4, 2009. www.unesco.org/fileadmin/MULTIMEDIA/INSTITUTES/UIL/confintea/pdf/National_Reports/Arab%20States/Syrian_Arab_Republic__English_.pdf. Accessed June 4, 2015.
Valbjørn, Morten, and Waleed Hazbun. "Scholarly Identities and the Making of Middle East IR." *APSA-MENA Newsletter* 3 (2017): 3–6.
Van Eijk, Esther. *Family Law in Syria: Patriarchy, Pluralism and Personal Status Codes*. London: I.B. Tauris, 2016.
Vollmann, Erik, Miriam Bohn, Roland Sturm, and Thomas Demmelhuber. "Decentralisation as Authoritarian Upgrading? Evidence from Jordan and Morocco." *Journal of North African Studies* 27, no. 2 (July 2, 2020): 362–93. https://doi.org/10.1080/13629387.2020.1787837.
Walby, Sylvia. *Theorising Patriarchy*. Oxford: Blackwell, 1990.
Watenpaugh, Keith D. "'Creating Phantoms': Zaki Al-Arsuzi, the Alexandretta Crisis, and the Formation of Modern Arab Nationalism in Syria." *International Journal of Middle East Studies* 28, no. 3 (1996): 363–89. https://doi.org/10.1017/s0020743800063509.
Watson, Hugh Seton. *Nations and States: An Enquiry into the Origins of Nations and the Politics of Nationalism*. London: Methuen, 1977.

Weber, Charlotte. "Between Nationalism and Feminism: The Eastern Women's Congresses of 1930 and 1932." *Middle East Women's Studies* 4, no. 1 (2008): 83–106. https://doi.org/doi.org/10.2979/mew.2008.4.1.83.

Wedeen, Lisa. *Authoritarian Apprehensions: Ideology, Judgment, and Mourning in Syria*. Chicago, IL: University of Chicago Press, 2019.

———. "Acting 'as If': Symbolic Politics and Social Control in Syria." *Comparative Studies in Society and History* 40, no. 3 (1998): 503–23. https://doi.org/10.1017/s0010417598001388.

———. *Ambiguities of Domination: Politics, Rhetoric, and Symbols in Contemporary Syria*. Chicago, IL: University of Chicago Press, 1999.

West, Ellis M. "A Proposed Neutral Definition of Civil Religion." *Journal of Church and State* 22, no. 1 (1980): 23–40.

Yuval-Davis, Nira. *Gender & Nation*. London: SAGE, 1997.

Yuval-Davis, Nira, and Pnina Werbner (eds). *Women, Citizenship and Difference*. London: Zed Books, 1999.

Zaitouneh, Nibal. "The General Women's Union: An Absurd Journey from Foundation to Dissolution." *Coalition of Syrian Women for Democracy*, March 10, 2018. https://2u.pw/Grb9CZ. Accessed July 15, 2019.

Zakzak, Sawsan, Fayek Hjeieh, and Maya Al Rahabi, "Gendered Constitution Building Process for Syria." Report, SIDA, Sweden, November 2014. www.efi-ife.org/sites/default/files/001%20Gendered%20Constitution%20Building%20Process%20for%20Syria%20Report%20%28November%202014%29.pdf. Accessed June 6, 2015.

Zaller, John R. "Diffusion of Political Attitudes." *Journal of Personality and Social Psychology* 53, no. 5 (1987): 821–33. https://doi.org/10.1037/0022-3514.53.5.821.

Zisser, Eyal. "The 'Struggle for Syria': Return to the Past?" *Mediterranean Politics* 17, no. 1 (2012): 105–10.

———. "Who's Afraid of Syrian Nationalism? National and State Identity in Syria." *Middle Eastern Studies* 42, no. 2 (2006): 179–98.

# Index

adultery 109–10
Aflaq, Michel
  "Age of Heroism, The" 47–8, 69
  "Arabism and Suffering" 49, 73
  "Army Is Part of the Fighting Masses, The" 75–6
  early life and influences 30, 37–8, 46–7, 48
  "Nationalism is Beloved Destiny" 71–2
  theories 1–2, 47–50, 68–77
agency and women
  domestic role 68, 80–4
  lack of 11, 13, 22, 77, 112–14, 179
  passive imagery 127–8, 138–40
  public roles 63–4
al-Arsuzi, "Woman" 80–1
al-Arsuzi, Zaki
  early life and influences 30, 37–8, 50
  theories 1–2, 51–3, 78–83
al-Assad, Asmaal 170, 173–4
al-Assad, Bashar
  fatherland 177
  funding for 169–70
  language 3–4
  loyalty 151, 165
  military violence 177
  muscular nationalism 171
  personality cult 2–3, 154, 162–4
  power 141–2
  religion 174
  veneration of 138
  women's rights 13
al-Assad, Bassel 138–9
al-Assad, Hafez 2, 3–4, 13, 78, 90, 93–4, 152
Alawites 37, 159
al-Husri, Sati
  early life and influences 30, 37–8, 40, 44–5
  "Elements of Nationalism" 41
  "Nationalism is Love Before Anything Else" 48–9, 70–1
  theories 1–2, 39, 40–6, 61–8
Almasalmeh, Samira 117
al-Qubaysiat 174, 175
Anderson, Benedict 11, 43
Arab culture 70
Arab nationalism 35–6, 75
Arabic 22, 23, 30, 61, 62, 181
Arabism 37, 42–3, 45, 49–50, 96, 98, 144–5
  pan 34–5
Arab–Israeli War 48, 129–30
  songs 123, 129–34, 140–1, 163
"Army of the Homeland, The" 159
Attar, Najah 117
authoritarianism 141, 155–7
Ayyash, Salma 173

Baathism 6–8, 17–19, 22–3, 134, 178
Baathist party 36, 48, 51–2, 93–4, 140–1, 151–3, 174
Banerjee, Sikata 15–16, 183
"Bassel's Father, Our Leader" 138–9
blood 1, 3, 134–5, 164
brotherhood/brother
  al-Assad, Hafez 4, 129
  nation 34, 52–3, 60–3, 66–7
  rhetoric and conflict 152–3
  soldiers 133, 164
  solidarity 131
  women 8, 22, 83
Butler, Judith, *Bodies That Matter: On the Discursive Limits of "Sex"* 157

children 5, 8, 67, 129–31
chivalry 75, 81, 133, 158, 165
choice, women 8, 13, 80, 84–5, 91
citizens and participation 23–4, 51, 93–4, 151–2, 155
citizenship
  1973 Constitution 114–15
  gender roles 5, 8
  love of leader and nation 164
  masculinity 21, 23, 95–7, 102–5, 128
  paternal transfer 80, 91, 114–15
  physical strength 100–1
  rights-based 36, 177–9
  women 102–6, 114–15, 179
civic participation 18, 51–3, 79, 83, 100, 115, 141–2, 169
civil war
  exemptions and defections 165, 169–70
  hardening of lines 179
  increase in masculinity 9
  loyalty to regime 156
  masculinity 178
  muscular identity 23, 153
  personality cult 162–3
  protests 1, 152–3
  questioning of identity 18
  symbolism 147
  women's role 171–2
class, social 68
clothing of women 8, 82–3
coercion 8, 65, 156, 165
collective identity 123–4
Commission for Family Affairs 113–14
commonalities
  destiny 33, 43, 45
  language 38–9, 40, 51, 62
  national history 64
conscription 5, 45–6, 100–5, 165, 169–70, 172
Constitution of 1973
  importance 85, 90, 94
  muscular nationalism 23
coups
  1963 78, 93, 98, 129
  1966 78
  1970 3–4
  frequent 90, 94
cultural identity
  development of 34, 43

family 84
forging 39
gender 158
heterogeneity 31–2, 51
reshaping 123–5
women's role 61–2
cultural nationalism 23, 32, 52, 179

Damascus Spring 141, 177
defense of the homeland 102–5
democracy
  1973 Constitution 96, 102, 103, 106
  al-Arsuzi, Zaki 50, 52, 78–9, 82, 83
  al-Husri, Sati 46
  future 18, 165, 175–6, 177–8
diaspora 170, 181
discourses
  Baathist party 39
  gender 10, 11, 17, 73–4
  liberal 12–13
  loyalty 154
  manhood 71–4
  military 102–5
  social 83, 157
  use of Arabism 37
dissemination 129–30, 155, 162
dissent see opposition
diversity
  of movements 12
  of nations 31
  of Syria 39
domestic
  sphere 62, 81–2, 84, 107–8
  violence 108, 109–10

economic rights 111–13
education
  gender constructs 5, 8, 19
  language 63
  militarism in 5, 8, 16, 44–6, 101, 136
  reinforcement of ideology 2, 40, 44–6, 66, 116, 126, 134, 156
  relevance to men 74
  songs 126, 129–31
  universal right 111
emotional appeals
  loyalty to regime 1–3, 21, 47–9, 70–1, 157
  speeches 128–9
  state 42

ethnicity *see* race
European influence
 Baathism 22, 30, 31–3
 gender constructs 6, 12
 muscular nationalism 16, 19, 60
 new ideology 37–9
 rejection of imperialist rule 5
 romantic nationalism 6, 16, 31, 34–5, 37, 38, 169
 theorists 40, 42, 44, 47, 48, 50, 52

Fakoush, Shahinaz 117
familial bond 31, 39, 41, 42, 61, 70–1, 131
family
 1973 Constitution 112
 conventional 83
 inheriting belonging 71–2
 nation 1–2, 39, 79–80, 84, 123–4, 134, 138–40, 142, 164
 nation above 131
 national identity 22, 145
 rhetoric 52
 in song 160
 songs 124, 142
 women 21, 107–8, 109–10, 112–14
father 16, 62, 135, 136, 138–9, 158–9
fatherland 4, 61–2, 64, 66, 70–1, 130, 134–7
femininity 14–15, 91, 127–8, 129–30, 133–4
feminism
 challenges 179–80
 ethnicity 177
 forced patriotism 174–5
 political organizations 116
 scholars 9–10, 12–13, 18, 90, 180
Fertile Crescent region 35–6
Fichte, Johann Gottlieb 31–2, 38–9, 43–4, 48, 49
flag, symbol 130, 134–5, 139, 154
founding fathers 20–1, 22, 30, 37–8, 39, 134, 144
fraternity *see* brotherhood/brother
freedom 102

gender
 constructs 5–6, 8, 20–2, 42, 60, 79–83, 116, 169
 hierarchy 183

identity 11, 23, 39, 42, 153, 158
 of Syria 129–30
General Trust for Development 173–4
General Women's Union (GWU) 116–17, 173, 176
geographic state 33, 90
grandfathers 62, 129, 135
grassroots participation 152, 155, 161, 165, 175

hegemony 18, 164–5
Herder, Johann Gottfried 31–2, 38–9, 41–3
heroism
 1973 Constitution 96–8, 101, 104
 addressing the issue 179
 Aflaq, Michel 47–9, 69, 70–3, 75–7
 ancestral 129
 citizenship 169
 education of 8
 male 15, 66–7, 75–6, 95, 171
 songs 127–8, 133–5, 137–9, 146, 158–62
 women 77, 172, 173
heterogeneity 2, 83, 177, 180
Hezbollah 161
hierarchy
 gender 20, 23, 68–9, 77, 97, 172, 183
 men 68–9, 73–4, 76–7, 103–4, 163
history of Syria
 forgetting the past 33, 39, 43, 45
 gendered 64–5, 72–3, 95, 98
 glorifying 48, 70, 98, 102, 129, 134–5, 137, 146
 impact on women 90
 national anthem 144–5
 shared 40, 43, 64–5, 134–5
honor killing 14, 109–10

"I am Syrian and My Fatherland Is Arab" 134–5
"I am Syrian, Oh How Blessed I am" 135
"I Engrave Your Name, Oh My Country" 130–1
"I Engrave Your Name, Oh Syria" 153
ideology
 adherence to 83
 al-Assad, Hafez 152
 al-Husri, Sati 61–3

Baathism 36–7, 51–2, 69, 74–6
conflict 39
critique 90–1
dissemination through song 124, 126, 146, 147
education 40
gender 10, 17–18, 20–1, 63, 79–82, 179
history 6, 30, 129, 169
masculinity 15, 19, 66–7, 98, 108, 118
military 74–6, 98–9
muscular nationalism 16, 170–1, 179
pan-Syrianism 34–7
performance 123–5
Syrian nationalism 36–7
unified nation 2
intellectual aspect 22, 30, 31–3, 38, 60, 62
intermarriage 12, 13, 51, 61–2, 80
international aid 173–4
Islam 113, 173, 174, 176–7

Kaffiyeh 137
kinship 2, 42, 45, 52, 61

language
  1973 Constitution 94–7
  Arabic 9, 62
  exclusion of women 22, 62, 96–7
  gender neutrality 68, 73, 75, 94–5, 100
  gender roles 79–81
  ideology 61
  masculine 4, 23, 64, 67–8, 75, 100
  national identity 33, 39, 61
  references to men 60, 62–5, 102, 180
  research accessibility 22, 181
  shared 31–3, 38–9, 40–3
  theorists 47, 53, 61–8
leadership, songs of 138–41, 142–3, 146, 162–4
legislation, impact on women 23, 91, 92, 109–12, 113
legitimization of the regime
  creating 156
  through love 164
  through song 123–4, 127

use of women 12, 13, 105, 107–8, 113–14, 172
Levant, greater 34
love of the nation 34, 48–9, 61, 153–4
loyalty to regime
  active participation 23–4, 151–2, 154–5
  civil war 153–5
  education 8, 44–5
  emotional appeals 1–3, 31, 47–9, 128–32, 155–6, 157
  faltering 165
  hardening of 161
  ideology 23
  imagery 162
  manifestation of loyalty 164
  masculinism 15, 19, 21, 162
  pragmatic 156–7
  religious organizations 173–4
  songs of 1, 19, 123, 126, 128, 153–5, 161–5
  women 77, 92, 106–7, 117, 158–9, 171–2

marriage 12, 13, 51, 61–2, 112, 114, 117
masculinity
  1973 Constitution 90, 94–7, 98–9, 102
  Aflaq, Michel 71–4
  concept 14–16
  hierarchical 68–9, 73–4
  identity crisis 170–1, 172, 178–9
  national anthem 144–5
  national identity 4, 15, 60, 84, 135, 146–7, 153, 159, 164–5
  nationalism 12, 64–5, 69–70, 71–2, 161
  political culture 107–8
  protecting the nation 70
  protecting role 13, 16, 91, 102–4, 130, 138–41, 158–9, 178–9
  romantic 19, 141–3
  songs 124, 130–1, 135, 138–43, 153, 158–61, 163–5
  state adoption 3, 18
  struggle 2, 11
  women's support 77, 158–9, 163
  *see also* language; non-conforming men

"May God Protect You, Oh
    Assad" 140–1
"May God Save Our Army" 158
men
    as the default 10, 95, 100, 101, 140
    identity crisis 170–1, 172, 178–9
    male privilege 12, 96, 118, 154,
        161, 170–1
    male struggle 66, 73–4, 95, 123–4
    *see also* heroism; masculinity;
        non-conforming men
men, young
    military training 5, 8, 44–6, 67–8
    nationalism 69, 73
    realizing manhood 66
    songs 135, 137–8
    use of term 65
metaphors
    family 71, 84, 91
    maternal 62, 81, 129–30, 170
    nation 79, 131, 145
    women 127–8
methodology 18–19
Middle East 6, 118, 183
militarism
    1973 Constitution 96, 99, 103
    changes 152, 165
    demonstrating against 152–3
    in education 5, 8, 16, 44–6, 101, 136
    effect on women 99–100, 108,
        115, 118
    embedding 76–7, 84–5, 96, 103, 128
    intellectual aspect 16
    and masculinity 19, 66–7, 91
    songs 124, 130, 132–3, 136–8, 163
military
    citizenship 100–1, 102–5
    defections and exemptions 165,
        169–70, 172
    glorifying through song 128, 130,
        146, 158–9, 161–2
    ideology 5, 8, 138–9
    national anthem, place in 144–6
    political role 3–4, 23, 78, 93–4,
        98, 165
    songs 128, 129–34, 135–8,
        158–9, 164
    women in 158, 170–2, 176, 179
military struggle
    1973 Constitution 97, 98, 99, 101,
        102, 104

individual 73–4
    songs 123–4, 128
"Millions and Millions of
    Syrians" 160–1
Milton-Edwards, Beverly,
    *Contemporary Politics in the
    Middle East* 17
modernization
    1973 Constitution 90
    men and military service 170–1
    regime 5
    state institutions 93–4
    women 6–7, 10, 12–14, 105–6,
        107–8
motherland 128
mothers 12, 13, 112, 160
multivocality 154
muscular nationalism
    1973 Constitution 92
    breakdown of 175–6, 178–9
    concept 4, 15–16, 19, 39
    hierarchies 21, 68, 159–61
    national anthem 144–5
    return to 141–3
muscularity 60, 137–8, 152, 161,
    171, 175–6
myth building 126–7, 134–5, 144–5,
    161–2

nation, building 6, 11, 39, 40, 79,
    93–4, 136–7
national anthem 144–5
national identity
    1973 Constitution 98–9, 102, 103
    change in thinking 172, 175
    collective will 51
    consent 39, 46, 82
    creating 33–7, 43
    diaspora 181
    emotional appeals 1–3, 38, 42, 151
    framework 147
    heterogeneity 34–5, 39, 51
    masculine experience 75–6
    military 3–5, 100–1, 118, 135
    national character, creation of
        41, 45
    primordial view 11, 40–2, 48,
        52, 71–2
    shared experience 33, 129
    songs 124, 126, 128, 145–7, 153–5
    threat to 154–5

women, exclusion of 14–15, 62–5, 67, 73, 75, 94–7, 118
  *see also* muscular nationalism
national love 65–6, 70–1, 128–32
national struggle 13, 65, 73–4, 133, 135
nationalism
  Baathist 17–18
  civic perspective 179, 182
  concept 36–7, 152
  gender 5–6, 12, 14–15, 70, 127–8, 138–9, 159
  involuntary 31, 38–8, 39, 41, 46, 48–9, 51, 71–2, 164, 181
  masculine 64–5, 71–2
  pan-Syrianism 34–7
  songs 5, 8, 21, 123–7, 138–9
  voluntary 33, 39, 40
  Western construct 31–3
  *see also* education; European influence; muscular nationalism; romantic nationalism
non-conforming men 15–16, 22, 70–4, 77, 124, 179

"Oh Bashar, Who Is Like You?" 163
"Oh, My Beloved Syria" 131–3
"Oh, My Mother, My Syria" 160
opposition
  Assad regime 36–7, 165
  internal enemy 161–2
  militant belonging 152–3
  muscular nationalism 159–60
  patriarchal norms 16–17
  protests 1, 2–3
  social media 175
organic nation 38–9, 40
organizations 173–5
other 97, 153, 162
Ottoman Empire 6, 34, 40, 60

Palestine 133–4
pan-Syrianism 33–7
participation of women
  1973 Constitution 95, 101–2
  agency 11, 13, 80
  Baathist thinking 22
  domestic and family sphere 63, 68, 71, 84, 112
  economic 112–13
  effect of language 60, 62, 138–40
  national service 101–2, 104–5
  state controlled 77, 78–9, 116–17, 173, 176
  supporting role 21
  women in politics 6–7, 77, 82, 105–8, 115, 117, 118
  women in religion 17, 174–5
patriarchy 17–18, 112–13
  adoration of Assad 1
  Baathism 7, 16, 91
  embracing of 5
  family structures 13–14
  future away from 171
  inevitability 12
  language 61
  legal entrenchment 110
  military 75–6
  national community 60
  national love 71
  public sphere 84
patriotism 65–6, 96, 123–4, 131, 151, 155, 174
performative displays 146, 151, 157–8, 171, 179
Personal Status Law 113
personality cult 34, 146, 152, 162–3
philology 79
physical strength 23, 100–1, 130, 135, 164–5
political culture 107, 147, 155–6, 157
Political Movement for Syrian Feminists 175
political state 32, 39, 40
postcolonialism 5–6, 12–13, 17, 90–1, 102
primordial view
  versus civic nationalism 179, 181–2
  nationalist loyalty 164
  return to 141–2
  romanticized 2, 158
  in song 129, 153–4
  theories 11, 32, 39–46, 48–50, 51–2, 71–2, 78–9
private sphere 63–4, 138–9
pronouns 100, 133, 143, 160
propaganda 23, 36–7, 141, 152, 162, 172–3, 179
public roles 60, 63, 81, 83, 104–8
public sphere 62, 63, 138–9

race
  creating military solidarity 67–8
  heterogeneity 2, 38–9
  homogeneity 177
  irrelevance of 61
  nation building 31–5, 51–2
  purity 48, 80
  unifying 6, 41–2
"Raise Your Arms Higher" 162
rape 14, 108, 110
recycling of songs 151–2
religion
  1973 Constitution 113
  dress codes as resistance 8, 82–3
  heterogeneity 2, 42
  limit of influence 8, 13, 17–18
  organisations 173
  rise of Islam 174
  secularism 8, 13, 174, 176–7
  songs 137
Renan, Ernest 33, 39, 43, 45, 46, 50–1
reproduction 12, 13, 14, 91, 112–14, 118
research 7–8, 9–10, 147, 180
Rethink Rebuild Society 181
romantic masculinity 19, 152, 175–6
romantic nationalism
  Assad, Bashar al- 4, 141–2
  breakdown of 175–6, 178
  conceptual images 16
  primordial view 2
  primordial or voluntary 39
  songs 128–33, 142, 154, 160, 163–4
  theories 19, 42, 47, 48–9, 50, 66
  view of belonging 1–2, 22, 155–6

Sa'adeh, Antun 35–6
sacrifice
  1973 Constitution 96, 97, 99, 102
  absence of 52
  effect on women 118
  love 61, 71
  masculinity 15, 16, 19
  regime rhetoric 1–2, 4, 157, 171
  songs 123–4, 128, 130–3, 140, 144–6, 160
  theories 43–5, 46, 49, 64–6, 73
Sadowski, Yahya, "The Evolution of Political Identity in Syria" 35, 37
sanctions, international 169–70, 173–4

scope of study 20–2
sectarian loyalty 6
secularism
  1973 Constitution 113
  Baath Party 6, 8–9, 108
  clothing 8, 82–3, 116
  forced decline 174
  founders 37–8
  gender hierarchy 23
  women 13, 17, 90, 108
sexual conduct and obligations 80–4, 172
shared experience 33
Sharia law 113
social media 162
Socialist Arab Baath Party 96, 98, 116
society, concept of 78–80
songs
  devotion 131, 162–4
  history 126, 134–4, 146
  importance of 126, 147
  subversion of 152–3
Sons, veneration of 160
"Speeches and Reflections upon Arab Nationalism" 44
State, development of 32, 33, 39, 93–4
State of Emergency 115, 178–9
Sunni Islam 174
symbolism
  animal 126, 137, 140
  lack of research 147
  loyalty to regime 154, 162
  objects 126, 130, 139
  performance and display 21, 123–5, 126, 127, 157–8
  political 124
  songs 135, 137, 139, 140, 154
  Sun 135, 143
Syria
  future 182–3
  national identity 6, 11
  State of Emergency 178–9
"Syria, Oh My Love" 153
Syria Campaign 175
Syrian Commission for Family Affairs 116–17
Syrian National Organization for Childhood 5
Syrian Nationality Act 1969 115
Syrian Penal Code 108, 109–11, 113

Syrian Revolutionary Youth Union 5
Syrian Social Nationalist Party 35–6

Tamayoz Orphan Care Project 174
teenage marriage 114, 117
*Toward the Resurrection* 68–9

UNESCO 173–4
United States 169–70
uprisings *see* civil war

violence 107–8, 109–11, 159–60, 164, 165
volunteerism 45, 46, 51

warrior figure of Syria 16, 90–1, 101, 170
"We Challenge" 161
"We Love You" 142, 153
"We Want to Preserve" 163
West, influence on Baathism 31–3
widowed women 112
will and determination 45, 46, 51, 98–9, 104
women
　1973 Constitution 94–6, 99, 101–2, 105–7
　absence of discourse 10

academic contributions 62
disempowerment 12, 15, 17–18, 83, 118
exclusion 20, 71, 101–2, 104–5
exclusion in language 4, 22, 53, 60, 62–4, 73, 75, 138–40, 158, 160
marginalization 65–6, 70–1, 73–4, 95, 105–6, 115, 118, 135–6, 146
role in nation forming 12, 23, 53, 63–4, 68, 70–1, 101–5, 179–80
songs 127–8, 158–9, 160
submission 2
subordination 13, 77, 84, 91, 108, 112, 124, 169
supporting role 5, 21, 77, 163
symbols of progress 12
*see also* agency and women; education; participation of women
women's organizations 12, 14, 18, 116, 173, 175, 176
Women's Preaching Department 174

"Your Flags Are Forever High, Oh Syria" 130